GABRIEL FAURÉ

Complete Songs

Volume 2: 1884–1919

medium voice / voix moyennes / mittlere Stimme

33 songs for voice and piano
33 mélodies pour chant et piano
33 Lieder für Singstimme und Klavier

Critical edition by / Édition critique de / Kritische Ausgabe von
Roy Howat & Emily Kilpatrick

Urtext

ALLE RECHTE VORBEHALTEN · ALL RIGHTS RESERVED

EDITION PETERS

PUBLISHED BY FABER MUSIC

Leipzig · London · New York

Cover Painting:

Rue Halévy – seen from a balcony (1877). Oil on canvas. Gustave Caillebotte (1848–1894)

Every effort has been made to trace and acknowledge copyright owners of texts.
If any credits have been omitted, the publishers offer their apologies and will rectify this in subsequent editions following notification.

Tous les efforts ont été faits pour retrouver et citer les ayants droit des textes.
Au cas où des mentions auraient été omises, l'éditeur présente ses excuses et y remédiera dans les éditions suivantes après notification.

Bei der Ermittlung der Rechteinhaber an den Liedtexten wurde größtmögliche Sorgfalt angewandt.
Sollten dennoch einzelne urheber- oder nutzungsrechtliche Hinweise fehlen, bedauern wir dies und werden nachgereichte Angaben in nachfolgenden Auflagen ergänzen.

© 2017 by Peters Edition Ltd, London
Alle Rechte vorbehalten · All rights reserved
Vervielfältigungen jeglicher Art sind gesetzlich verboten.
Any unauthorized reproduction is prohibited by law.
ISMN 979-0-014-11792-4

CONTENTS

General Preface VIII
Preface to Volume 2 IX

Préface générale XVI
Préface au volume 2 XVII

Allgemeines Vorwort XXIV
Vorwort zu Band 2 XXVI

Index of Songs / Table des mélodies / Liederverzeichnis XXXIV

Poetic texts / Textes poétiques des mélodies / Liedtexte XXXVI

Select Bibliography / Bibliographie sélective / Auswahlbibliographie XLIX

SONGS / MÉLODIES / LIEDER 2

Chronology and dedicatees / Tableau chronologique / Chronologie und Widmungsträger 134

Critical Commentary 136

Appendix / Appendice / Anhang 159

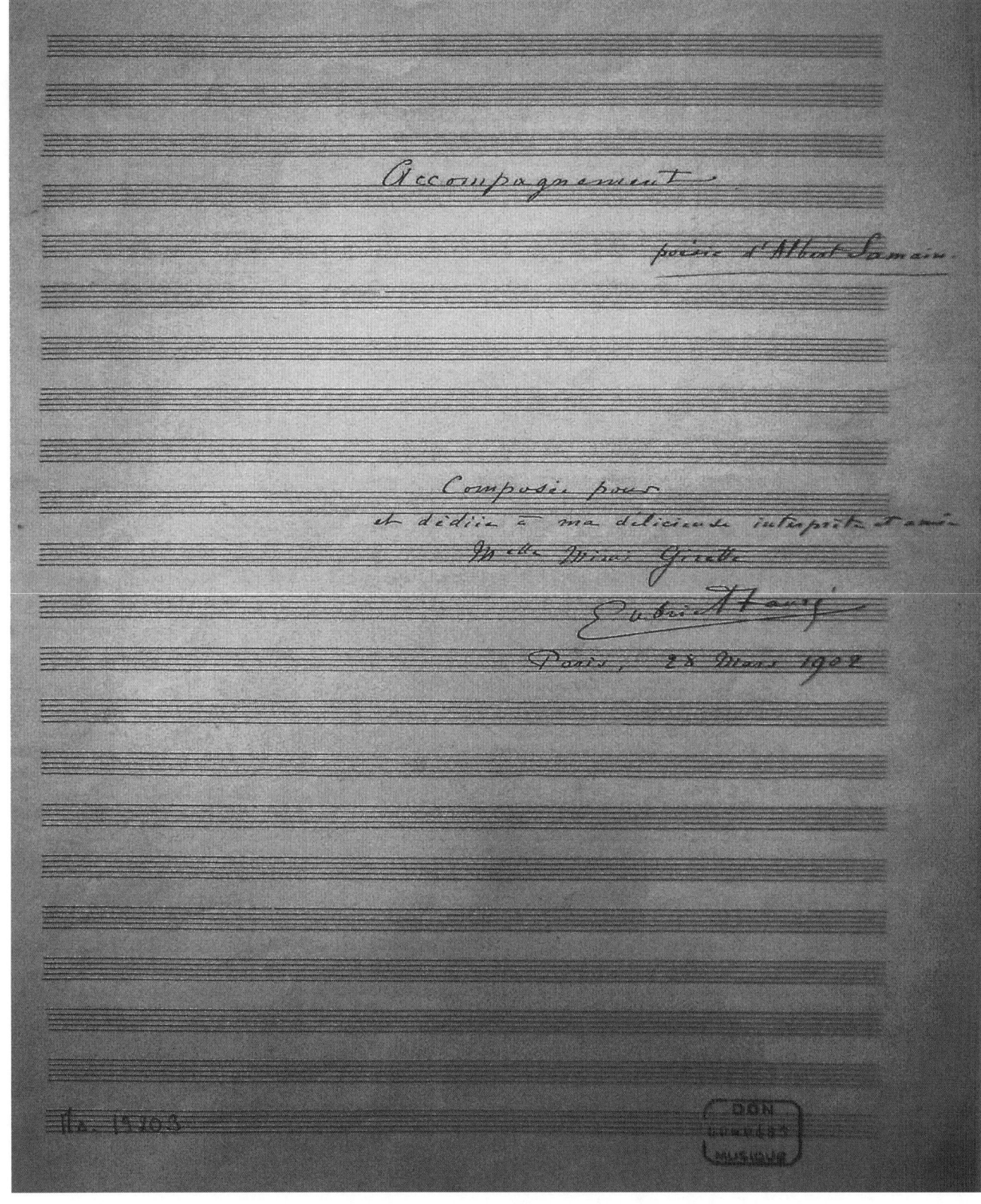

Accompagnement (1902), **A2**: autograph title page with Fauré's signed and dated dedication
"Composed for and dedicated to my delightful interpreter and friend / Mlle Mimi Girette"

Accompagnement (1902), **A2** : page de titre autographe
dateé avec dédicace à Mimi Girette

Accompagnement (1902), **A2**: Titelseite des Autographs mit datierter Widmung
„Komponiert für und gewidmet meiner reizenden Künstlerin und Freundin / Mlle Mimi Girette"

Reproduced by kind permission of the Bibliothèque nationale de France.

Sérénade (*Le Bourgeois Gentilhomme*), **A1**: early autograph manuscript
(27 February 1893), notated in $\frac{3}{4}$ metre

Sérénade (*Le Bourgeois Gentilhomme*), **A1**: premier manuscrit autographe
(27 février 1893), métrique en $\frac{3}{4}$

Sérénade (*Le Bourgeois Gentilhomme*), **A1**: erstes Autograph
(27. Februar 1893), im $\frac{3}{4}$-Takt notiert

Reproduced by kind permission of the Bibliothèque nationale de France.

Soir, **A**: autograph manuscript, first version of the ending, dated 17 December 1894

Soir, **A**: manuscrit autographe, version primitive de la fin, datée du 17 décembre 1894

Soir, **A**: Autograph, erste Fassung der Schlusstakte, datiert 17. Dezember 1894

Reproduced by kind permission of the Fondation Royaumont – Bibliothèque musicale François Lang.

Soir: revised ending on following page of autograph manuscript

Soir: version remaniée de la fin, page suivante du manuscrit autographe

Soir: revidierte Fassung der Schlusstakte auf der folgenden Seite des Autographs

Reproduced by kind permission of the Fondation Royaumont – Bibliothèque musicale François Lang.

General Preface

It is truly in his songs that Fauré reveals the flower of his genius.
— Maurice Ravel[1]

No composer made a more substantial and varied contribution to the French song repertoire than Gabriel Fauré. *Mélodies* span his career, from the delightful *Le Papillon et la fleur* of 1861 to the masterly cycle *L'Horizon chimérique*, composed sixty years and more than a hundred songs later. The importance of this contribution has long been compromised by its erratic publication history: dispersed across different publishers and collections, many of the songs have been marred by serious misprints and conflicting readings across different printed versions. This first complete critical edition presents a text both authoritative and flexible, bringing together the familiar compendium of sixty songs (as established by the publisher Hamelle in 1908) with other songs and cycles issued separately, including three songs unpublished during Fauré's lifetime as well as four songs for more than one voice. The associated volume of Fauré's collected *Vocalises* (EP 11385) includes his wordless *Vocalise-Étude* first published in 1907, alongside forty-four others published for the first time.

With its focus both practical and scholarly, the present edition aims to encourage creative, confident and well-informed performance. Founded on study of hundreds of manuscript and printed sources, it has been tested internationally in masterclasses, workshops, seminars, concerts and recordings, with the participation of professional singers, students, teachers, coaches and specialists. In this it takes a lead from the composer, who prepared his own editions on the basis of performing experience. The edition also assimilates interpretative insights from musicians who worked with Fauré, as well as from his documented performing preferences.

Sources and editorial approach

Fauré's principal song publishers were Choudens (1869–1879), Hamelle (1880–1904), Heugel (1905–1910) and Durand (1915–1921); various of his songs were also issued at different times by Hartmann, Durand & Schœnewerk, Fromont, and the London firm Metzler (plus some secondary American editions derived from French originals). Most of his songs were published singly before being brought together in collections, the first of these in 1879 (Choudens), the second in 1897 (Hamelle), and the third in 1908 (Hamelle).[2] These collections, like most of the single prints, were issued in high- and medium-voice keys; some songs were published separately in additional transpositions. Against this wealth of printed sources, manuscripts are more sparsely preserved. Of those now traced, many – particularly for the earlier songs – are early drafts, presentation copies or intermediate versions.

Editorial treatment of such varied sources demands care. Manuscripts, for all the valuable corrections, verifications and variants they offer, have to be treated with caution, particularly when they were not directly in the source chain leading to publication. Meanwhile, even from the plethora of printed sources it is often impossible to adhere to one source as representing a "final" or definitive composer's text, for every source mixes essential information with problems and corruptions (again, most notably in the earlier songs). In order to present a text as faithful as possible to Fauré's corrections over many years, the present edition has had to combine the best of various sources within bounds of logical source priority and musical sense, always respecting coherence across single songs, groupings, cycles and collections, and taking into account all that is known about Fauré's composing, revising and performing habits, along with any circumstantial evidence. *Ossia* versions are given wherever more than one reading is clearly viable. These include some early readings that clarify aspects of compositional intent, elements that were sometimes masked by later revisions aimed at "fireproofing" the music against inept performance. The **Critical Commentary** provides full explanations.

Keys

There is no evidence whatever that Fauré was opposed to transposition of his songs, in principle or practice.[3] Several of his songs exist in more than one autograph key (including some post-publication transpositions), others first appeared in a key (or keys) different from surviving manuscripts, while for songs whose manuscripts are lost it is sometimes impossible to identify an original key from the printed sources, let alone any authorially preferred one. (Even in the established Hamelle collections, "Original key" labels are not always reliable.)[4] As a lifelong practical musician, accompanist and skilled choirmaster, Fauré was used to working with a large range of voices. Surviving concert programmes show that he regularly performed his songs with different voice-types, often in circumstances that clearly involved transpositions (including a few important premieres). Like any composer, for a few songs Fauré did have intrinsic preferences of tessitura or key colour; any such evidence is quoted here and taken into editorial account.

In those respects the present edition honours Fauré's own pragmatic approach, in making his songs accessible to as many singers as possible within appropriate bounds of taste and scholarship. The high- and medium-voice keys of the three long-established collections are mostly maintained, except when a source offers a more compelling option or suggests this was Fauré's preference, and occasionally to offer a more realistic distinction between high and medium voices. Practicality at the keyboard is also a consideration. In a very few cases the present edition adopts a new transposed key, prompted by musical sense and tessitura along with consideration of sources. For those few songs published in only one key or unpublished in Fauré's lifetime, a second key has been determined editorially. In a few select cases, where sources present additional useful keys, a third key is available online through www.fabermusic.com/editionpetersresources. For each song the present edition lists original known key (or keys); where no manuscript is traced or original printed keys differ, the latter are shown in parentheses, using bold print for keys indicated as original in the Hamelle collections.

Performance

Witness accounts of Fauré's playing and interpretative preferences all indicate his assumption of forward motion, with a strong aversion to any gratuitous slowing, rubato or sentimental affectation.[5] His sense of tempo relates to the natural pace of the spoken poem; his close colleague, the distinguished mezzo-soprano Claire Croiza, emphasised the importance he attached to the poem and its articulation in song. Croiza further recalled:

> Fauré was a metronome incarnate ... Above all, slowing him down distorts him ... For Fauré more than anyone else the expression has to be found within a framework of keeping in time ... I once heard *Après un rêve* sung by a singer who [almost] literally ground to a halt. Dining with Fauré that evening, I asked him, "What tempo do you really want in *Après un rêve*, maître?" And he said, "*Sans ralentir, sans ralentir.*"[6]

While emphasising the intensity of tragic moments (*Chanson du pêcheur* or *Prison*), Croiza repeatedly warns against treating Fauré's more melancholy songs in a dolorous manner, the essence of refinement and understatement in this idiom lying in not exaggerating or caricaturing what the composer has already balanced finely.[7] Among Fauré's early songs in particular, an overtly melancholy poem like *Tristesse* can entail a degree of parody or self-mockery,[8] to which Fauré responds with a light touch that relates to numerous accounts, via his family and colleagues, of his lively sense of humour and inherent gaiety right through to his final years.[9]

EDITORIAL PRESENTATION

Ossia readings are transposed as necessary from their source keys. Any debatable musical readings are footnoted. Editorial ties and slurs (and slur completions) are printed in broken lines; other editorial additions are placed in square brackets. Cautionary accidentals in parentheses appear thus in sources. Parentheses are also added around non-essential breath marks that appear only in some sources, and around useful dynamics and other indications that come from secondary sources, as detailed in the **Critical Commentary**.

London and Paris, 2017   *Roy Howat & Emily Kilpatrick*

---

[1] Maurice Ravel, 'Les Mélodies de Gabriel Fauré', *La Revue musicale* 3 (October 1922), in Arbie Orenstein (ed.), *Maurice Ravel: Lettres, écrits, entretiens* (Paris: Flammarion, 1990), p. 325.

[2] The 1908 publication of the Third Collection coincided with Hamelle's reissue of the First and Second Collections (he bought out the First Collection from Choudens in 1887 and issued a high-voice edition of it in 1890), and involved some redistribution of contents; see **Critical Commentary**.

[3] For detailed discussion of this and other editorial issues vital to the present edition, see the present editors' articles "Editorial Challenges in the Early Songs of Gabriel Fauré" and "Gabriel Fauré's Middle-Period Songs".

[4] These are indicated only in the Hamelle Second and Third Collections, from op. 18 onwards. Nor was pitch then standard through Europe – across borders it could vary by a semitone or more – although over Fauré's professional life it was regulated in France (by parliamentary decree of 1859) at $a' = 435$ Hz, slightly lower than today's norms of 440 or slightly above.

[5] Several of these witness accounts, from his family and musical colleagues, are quoted in Roy Howat, *The Art of French Piano Music* (London and New Haven: Yale UP, 2009), p. 247 and generally through Chapters 17, 18 and 21.

[6] Quoted in Abraham (ed.), *Un Art de l'interprétation*, pp. 199 and 212–13, and partly in Bannerman (ed.), *The Singer as Interpreter*, pp. 80–82; the latter adds a specific reference that prompts the present edition's "(*sans ralentir*)" at bar 46. Fauré's violinist colleague Hélène Jourdan-Morhange corroborates this trait, adding an anecdote about a (nameless) singer given to pausing and languishing over phrase-ends: accompanied by Fauré once at an afternoon concert, "she was horrified to find herself being propelled by the piano along an undulation-free road... the motorway of the future!" (Jourdan-Morhange, *Mes amis musiciens*, pp. 22–23).

[7] See Bannerman (ed.), *The Singer as Interpreter*, pp. 84–88, and Abraham, *Un Art de l'interprétation*, pp. 31, 40 and 212.

[8] Vladimir Jankélévitch (*Gabriel Fauré et ses mélodies*, p. 49) similarly observes, "Again we shouldn't regard any of this tragically. Fauré was immune to the wave of neuraesthenia which, with Duparc and Chausson, starts to descend on France ... and the melancholy of *Tristesse* isn't too serious."

[9] The composer's daughter-in-law remembered him thus: "Fauré était un méridional, très gai et enclin à la plaisanterie [Fauré was a southerner, very merry by nature and inclined to jocularity]" ("Brève rencontre avec Blanche Fauré-Fremiet", *Journal de Vichy*, 28 June 1958). Hélène Jourdan-Morhange referred to him as having never lost something of the "street urchin [*l'esprit gavroche*]"(*Mes amis musiciens*, p. 24). Some memoirs that Fauré penned in his late seventies recount, with undisguised glee, adolescent pranks he and his classmates used to perpetrate on their teachers at the École Niedermeyer ("Souvenirs", *La Revue musicale* 4/11, special Fauré number, 1 November 1922, pp. 3–9).

Preface to Volume 2

This volume comprises Gabriel Fauré's songs from 1884 onwards.[1] From the attractive settings of Armand Silvestre with which the volume opens to the rich chromaticism of the 1890s and the near-aphoristic brevity of some of his last songs, the collection affords a fascinating voyage through Fauré's creative maturity.

In May 1884 Fauré returned to song composition after a hiatus of almost two years – the first such gap in his œuvre, songs having dominated his output between 1862 and 1882. In the space of three weeks, he completed the four songs comprising op. 39. The first three were settings of Armand Silvestre, whose poetry had provided Fauré with most of his preceding three song groups (opp. 18, 23 and 27, of 1878–82; see *Complete Songs* vol. 1). *Aurore* provides an entrancingly limpid opening, before the fury of *Fleur jetée*. *Le Pays de Rêves* restores calm, its deceptively simple surface masking a series of daring harmonic excursions that anticipate numerous songs of the next three decades. Silvestre's text there explores one of the era's artistic tropes, the voyage to an idyllic foreign land, a fantasy inspired by Antoine Watteau's famous painting *Embarkation for Cythera* of 1717 and reawakened in Baudelaire's poem "L'Invitation au voyage", which Fauré's friends Duparc and Chabrier both set to music in 1870.

For the final song of the op. 39 group, Fauré made one of his periodic returns to Leconte de Lisle, whose penchant for exoticism always inspired a vein of concentrated beauty and harmonic richness (perhaps explaining why Fauré only ever set his poems singly).

In 1886 Fauré made the acquaintance of Comte Robert de Montesquiou, one of the famous æsthetes of the era. The inspiration for Des Esseintes in Huysmans' 1884 novel *À rebours* and later for Proust's Baron Charlus, Montesquiou was a fervent Wagnerian and deeply involved in the Symbolist world. An equally enthusiastic admirer of Fauré's music, he organized an all-Fauré concert in spring 1887 and seems to have appointed himself the composer's informal literary advisor, introducing him to the darker, more complex poetry of Villiers de L'Isle-Adam and Paul Verlaine.[2] Fauré's two Villiers settings, *Nocturne* and *Les Présents* (op. 43 no. 2 and op. 46 no. 1), are drawn from the seven poems in Villiers' 1883 collection *Contes cruels* (which otherwise comprises prose writings). Although seemingly conceived as companion songs – matching post-publication manuscripts of both survive, copied out within days of each other in 1892 – they appeared in different opus groups, probably because of their shared introspective mood.

If *Nocturne* instead shares its opus, incongruously and arbitrarily, with *Noël* (a *cantique*, discussed below), *Les Présents* – dedicated to Montesquiou – makes a fitting opus pair with *Clair de lune*, the first of Fauré's Verlaine settings. *Clair de lune* was composed in autumn 1887, within weeks of the op. 50 *Pavane*: the two pieces received their orchestral *premières* together in April 1888 (both were encored).[3] The "Menuet" subheading to *Clair de lune* – the only dance title on any of Fauré's songs – underlines its affinity with the *Pavane*: both pieces feature extended instrumental introductions, followed by what Graham Johnson aptly calls "a vocal obbligato" over essentially autonomous music, voice and accompaniment coalescing at focal moments "as if by chance".[4]

That orchestral première of *Clair de lune* was given with the tenor Maurice Bagès de Trigny, one of the leading song performers in the Parisian salons and at the Société Nationale from the mid-1880s until his untimely death in 1908. In 1946 the composer Pierre de Breville, for many years Bagès's companion, recalled how Fauré first heard Bagès sing *Nell* and *Après un rêve* at one of Henri Duparc's *soirées*:

> The expressive timbre of his voice, his incomparable diction, his musicality, all enchanted Fauré. "Do you sing any other of my songs?" he asked him. "I love them all and sing them all", replied Maurice Bagès, and from that day Fauré adopted him as his best interpreter, booked him to give the premières of *Clair de lune* and *Au cimetière* at the Société nationale, and asked him to accompany him to London on his first trip to England, to make his works known there.[5]

That close collaboration can be glimpsed in a letter from Marcel Proust to Paul Lavallée of 30 September 1894: "Incidentally Bagès left all his Fauré with me. But half of it was in manuscripts by Fauré, the rest printed but with dedications inside, and I was so afraid of damaging them that I sent the whole lot back."[6]

In November 1888 Fauré wrote to the Comtesse Greffulhe:

> I have composed three new songs, all very cheerful!!! The titles are:
> 1. *Au cimetière*! (Richepin)
> 2. *Larmes*! ditto
> 3. *Spleen*! (Verlaine)
>
> One of them [*Au cimetière*] I tried to give a very easy accompaniment for right hand only, but after ten bars the assistance of the left hand became necessary, and from bar 20 the difficulties begin to pile up for both hands! Another paving-stone on the road to Hell![7]

The vocal abilities of Maurice Bagès undoubtedly echo in the two Jean Richepin settings *Larmes* and *Au cimetière*, whose unusually operatic character may reflect Fauré's pilgrimage that summer to Bayreuth. Graham Johnson plausibly suggests that Fauré's interest in this unusual poet may have been sparked by the latter's collaborations with Emmanuel Chabrier, for whom he wrote the libretto of *La Sulamite* and ghosted that of *Le Roi malgré lui*.[8] *Au cimetière* was first published in the very high key of E minor; later editions for high voice amended this to D minor, doubtless in acknowledgement of its challengingly high tessitura with the sustained *forte* of the *declamato* middle section. If Bagès was able to bring that off with aplomb, the efforts of lesser singers may have been what prompted the normally admiring Proust to consider this song "vraiment affreux" ("truly awful").[9]

Spleen is drawn from Verlaine's 1874 collection *Romances sans paroles* (in which it appears untitled; Fauré imported the title from another poem in the collection[10]). Far from the moonlit, sardonic charm of Verlaine's *Fêtes galantes*, it eschews the metric fluidity of *Clair de lune* for short lines and a largely monosyllabic delivery evoking the remorseless ostinato of drumming rain, as echoed in Fauré's setting.

La Rose dates from 1890, two years after its opus companions. The subtitle 'Ode anacréontique' nods to the Greek poet Anacreon, whose poetry celebrated love and wine (though the poem does not employ the seven-syllable metre characteristic of Anacreontic verse). Another one-off Leconte de Lisle setting, *La Rose* appears to have been thrown in with op. 51 because of Hamelle's slowness in publishing the first three songs.[11] An element of continuity through the set comes from the dedication of *La Rose* to Bagès, for whose voice it was clearly designed: this is particularly evident on the last page, where the vocal challenges seemingly exceeded the capacities of other early performers. The revised Third Collection of 1908 amends the last page to make a less vocally challenging ending – one that in turn engenders some new problems, not least a moment of odd harmonic discontinuity around bar 48, as well as the occasional disparity across high- and medium-voice editions.[12] The present edition shows both the 1890 and 1908 endings. Nor was the 1890 ending Fauré's first version, as he explained in a letter to Bagès that autumn:

> My dear friend, you were very right to give me your opinion, but I believe that had we looked at the new ending together then perhaps I could have helped you to understand it differently. Firstly (perhaps there is also a copying error) the words "avec la beauté" must be sung to a diminuendo.

> Then the accompaniment must have a <u>rich</u> but <u>gentle</u> sonority; pedal is necessary in order to sustain the bass arpeggio properly and only accent this: both times.
>
> The first ending did not satisfy me: had I arrived at Cuy two days later I would not have brought with me the song as you saw it there. That version seemed to me overly abrupt and you must remember that I had [already] lengthened the phrase *salua la Fleur* by a bar. But that did not satisfy me! It kept niggling me until I had made the complete modification.
>
> I think that after a little while, once you have forgotten the first version, you will agree with me. I must add that S[aint-]Saëns knows only the second version, and didn't seem shocked: that makes me think that had you not begun by singing the first ending, the second wouldn't have surprised you.
>
> All that doesn't mean that I am not mistaken too: but what reassures me is that this niggling only left me once I had changed my peroration.[13]

It was undoubtedly to Maurice Bagès that Fauré had alluded in a letter to the poet Edmond Haraucourt a year earlier (27 September 1889): "Would you like to come to lunch at Bougival on Sunday week, 6 October, with a young friend of mine who will sing you the two *Shylock* songs? I have had them copied and sent to him so that he can work on them."[14]

Although Fauré was to complete just one opera (*Pénélope*, 1913), like most French composers he was continually drawn to the theatre, and the decade 1888–1898 saw him compose incidental music for several plays: *Caligula* (1888), *Shylock* (1889), *La Passion* (1890),[15] *Le Bourgeois Gentilhomme* (1893) and *Pelléas et Mélisande* (1898). *Shylock*, an adaptation by Haraucourt of *The Merchant of Venice*, was first staged at the Théâtre de l'Odéon in December 1889; a concert version of Fauré's incidental music was premiered the following May. The two songs it includes, "Chanson" and "Madrigal", have no equivalent in Shakespeare's play: both are serenades, the first sung by an offstage singer to Jessica, the second by the Prince of Aragon under Portia's window in Act 2. ("Chanson" as published carries its opening voice dynamic over from the theatre score; concert performance may necessitate discreet adjustment.) The present edition includes, as an option, an extended introduction to "Chanson" omitted from the Hamelle Collections; **Appendix 1** presents a voice-piano reduction of a hitherto unpublished encore version of "Chanson" from the orchestral manuscript material, setting a punning (and gently risqué) third verse.

A third "Sérénade" in this volume comes from Fauré's incidental music to Molière's *Le Bourgeois Gentilhomme*, a commission palmed off by Saint-Saëns (then busy with the opera *Phyrné*) to his former pupil and friend. "I like the idea, but can I manage it?? It won't be easy", Fauré replied in September 1892.[16] In the event, the theatre (Eden-Théâtre) went bankrupt in March 1893, but the abandoned project left us not only this song but also one of Fauré's best-known short pieces, a *Sicilienne* that he later reworked for cello and piano, and also incorporated in his incidental music for a 1898 London season of Maurice Maeterlinck's *Pelléas et Mélisande*. This production, given in English translation by Jack Mackail, featured designs by the pre-Raphaelite artist Edward Burne-Jones, and the formidable actress Mrs Patrick Campbell [*née* Beatrice Stella Tanner] in the role of Mélisande. The commission came from Mrs Campbell herself, after an initial approach to Debussy – who was known to have completed his opera on Maeterlinck's play – was met with an unambiguous refusal.[17] Fauré himself conducted the opening performance at the Prince of Wales Theatre on 21 June 1898, four days after Burne-Jones's death. "Mélisande's Song", the only vocal number, derives from the "tower" scene in Act 3.[18] Fauré set it only in English, of which his grasp was rudimentary (the manuscript shows him initially setting "hope" as two syllables). The present edition accordingly suggests remedies at two moments of unidiomatic underlay. Maeterlinck's original French text has such different syllabification, including line repetitions not in the English version, as to be incompatible with the song's vocal line. In 1906, however, Fauré was to rework this song to a different French text, as "Crépuscule", opening part of his cycle *La Chanson d'Ève*, to poetry by Maeterlinck's compatriot and friend Charles van Lerberghe.

Prison and *Soir* are Fauré's final compositions of 1894, an extraordinary year that had seen him complete *La Bonne Chanson* and three major piano works (the Fourth Valse-Caprice, Sixth Nocturne and Fifth Barcarolle), along with a clutch of sacred choral music. The present edition restores the songs' correct opus number, which later editions by Hamelle changed several times, for extraneous reasons explained in the **Critical commentary** (**Publication history**). *Prison*, Fauré's final return to the poetry of Paul Verlaine, is one of the most emotionally explosive settings in all French *mélodie*, the tolling piano accompaniment as unyielding as prison bars while it literally ticks away the seconds (according to Fauré's metronome indication) through the devastating final "Qu'as-tu fait de ta jeunesse?"

Soir – Fauré's first setting of Albert Samain – forms a pendant to the composer's Verlaine years. Its musical content suggests overflow from two recent works, the cello *Romance* op. 69 (an earlier piece that Fauré had reworked for publication in autumn 1894), and the Sixth Nocturne op. 63 (in the same key of D♭, with a closely related ending). Like *La Bonne Chanson*, *Soir* is closely associated with the singer Emma Bardac, with whom Fauré pursued a passionate affair in the early 1890s. (Mme Bardac was later to marry Claude Debussy.) Earlier in 1894 Fauré had presented her with a recently published volume of Samain's poetry, *Au jardin de l'Infante*, with the inscription "I beg you will accept this book and choose the poems you would like to sing".[19] Among the poems in the volume to show Mme Bardac's pencil annotations are "Élégie" – from which Fauré derived the three strophes that he set as *Soir* – and "Arpège". On hearing her perform *Soir* early in 1896, Samain wrote to his sister:

> I found the said Mme Bardac at Fauré's, a young woman of about thirty. She's a pretty, elegant woman of the world; her husband's a banker. […] After dinner she sang [*Soir*]. Fauré said to me "You'll never hear it sung better". And in fact she has a most unusual feeling for nuance and above all a purity of expression.[20]

Fauré did not attempt his second solo setting of Samain for almost three years (though in the interim he composed the duet *Pleurs d'or*). *Arpège* and its companion, the Leconte de Lisle setting *Le Parfum impérissable*, date from late summer 1897. The flute-like melody and lilting compound rhythms of *Arpège* recall the aforementioned *Sicilienne*, but with more modal adventurousness, while the measured tread of *Le Parfum impérissable* compresses a harmonic boldness akin to that of *Prison*, though its character is quietly intense rather than overtly dramatic.

This op. 76 pair marked only a brief return to the realm of *mélodie*: apart from "Mélisande's Song" Fauré did not attempt another song for almost five years, the longest such gap in his career. He was now occupied with new duties as professor of composition at the Paris Conservatoire, and with the composition of the "tragédie lyrique" *Prométhée* (1900, almost but not quite an opera). He eventually returned to the genre with *Accompagnement* (March 1902), composed for and dedicated to Mimi [Émilie] Girette Risler, a gifted amateur singer who was one of Fauré's favourite interpreters during the first decade of the century. The diary of Mlle Girette (as she then was) excitedly documents the progress of "her" song – together with many other musical encounters – and provides a surprisingly intimate view of Fauré's working life and compositional process:

> 7 January 1902
>
> Cortot said [to Fauré] that he should compose something for piano and orchestra; he [Fauré] said to me "I will do nothing until I've written a song for you", to which I replied that that would be one of the greatest joys of my life. "Only I haven't found the *poetry*, for I know just what you would like", he said, and I replied that I didn't care about the words, but only about the music. But for him words and music are one, and it is words that inspire him. That's obvious in his music, where everything is considered, meticulous and finely-hewn.[21]

> 8 March 1902
>
> He has begun "my song", though he doesn't want to tell me which poem he has finally chosen! Musically, it will be in the same vein as *Soir*, I'd told him how much I love those sorts of songs – he is thinking of me, of my voice, as he is writing it[.] He told me that he composes in his head, first, *on the words*, it is the poetry that inspires him, the melody grows inside him little by little, almost unconsciously, and the work of getting it down on paper comes last of all – though that's by no means the easiest part.[22]

> 29 March 1902
>
> What an unforgettable date this is for me!! I have received "my song" from Fauré! He sang it to me once, then I sang it.[23]

> 2 April
>
> Nobody in the world except him and myself knows *Accompagnement*. […] He told me that to him it felt like a little piece of myself, and he incorporated that in its entirety.[24]

It was surely Mimi's intelligent musicality that Fauré had in mind when he wrote to the Comtesse Greffulhe in November 1902: "I'm sure there are many of my songs, out of those of recent years, that you do not know as yet! I dream of performing them for you with perfect interpreters, but I know of none among the professionals. It is amateurs who understand and express me best."[25]

Although composed first, *Accompagnement* was to become the third of Fauré's op. 85 set: *Dans la forêt de septembre* and *La Fleur qui va sur l'eau*, both on texts by Catulle Mendès, joined it in September 1902. Dual autographs survive of both *Dans la forêt de septembre* and *Accompagnement*, both pairs seemingly worked on in tandem: each manuscript shows revised readings in different places. Another song sketched for this group, *Dans le ciel clair*, would have been Fauré's last Leconte de Lisle setting: Fauré worked on it that same autumn before abandoning it. The surviving fragments are transcribed in the present **Appendix 2**.

Mimi Girette was to inspire one more offering, *Le plus doux chemin* (op. 87 no. 1), marking her marriage to the pianist Édouard Risler. Like its eventual opus companion *Le Ramier*, *Le plus doux chemin* is far from the richly chromatic, extended canvases of the op. 85 songs, the simpler textures showing Fauré's modal fluidity at its most focussed. The two songs mark Fauré's final return to the poetry of Armand Silvestre, each maintaining Silvestre's generic subtitle "Madrigal". In that respect they echo an earlier wedding offering, for Fauré's composer friend André Messager: the *Madrigal* op. 35 (1883) for four solo voices and piano, whose text is drawn from the same Silvestre collection. Fauré subsequently orchestrated *Madrigal*, but Jean-Michel Nectoux observes that his intention remained for four solo voices, despite Hamelle labelling it as also performable with SATB choir (during Fauré's lifetime it was sometimes performed by eight singers, two to a part).[26] It may have been for Messager's private amusement that Fauré took the opening theme of *Madrigal* from Bach's cantata *Aus tiefer Not schrei' ich zu dir* (a shade of mischievous irony, perhaps), a theme Bach also used in the first D♯ minor fugue of his "48".[27]

By 1906 Fauré had acrimoniously terminated his contract with Hamelle and signed a new one with Henri Heugel, before finally moving to the publisher Jacques Durand in 1910. His last three single songs, never incorporated in the traditional Hamelle Collections, remain little-known. *Le Don silencieux* (op. 92) was the fruit of a few concentrated days at the end of Fauré's happy summer stay in Vitznau, near Lucerne, in 1906. To his wife he wrote:

> As it doesn't at all resemble any of my other songs, or anything else I know, I'm very happy. For one thing, there's not even a principal theme. It develops with a freedom which would upset Théodore Dubois considerably. It follows the words, as they come, it begins, continues and finishes, no more than that; yet at the same time it's a *whole*. But now I'm getting pedantic.[28]

In the published collection *L'Anémone des mers* the poem is untitled. Fauré initially titled his setting *Offrande*, writing to Octave Maus:

> If Jean Dominique doesn't like the title, which I've had to think up because of my publisher's insistence, then tell him that the thirteen-foot lines with which he has decorated his poetry, nice though they are, have given me more than enough to get my teeth into! Still, I hope that my music has allowed them to retain their suppleness: I've done my best, at least.[29]

(Fauré appears to have been still unaware that Jean Dominique was a nom-de-plume for the Belgian poet Marie Closset.)

Chanson (1906) returns to the more open textures of the late Silvestre "madrigals". This was Fauré's last single song for Heugel (for whom he was just embarking on the cycle *La Chanson d'Ève*), and almost his last of all. In 1919, he was obliged – most reluctantly – to set the winning poem in a competition run by *Le Figaro* in celebration of the end of the First World War, extolling the bravery of the French soldiers (*poilus*). To his wife Fauré described the text as "a horrible little poem"; two days later he added that he had changed the "frightful word" (*poilus*) to *soldats* – "If the poetess doesn't like it, too bad! I'm doing her enough of a favour as it is!"[30] For all his best musical will and efforts (he omitted half the poem), the tawdry text of *C'est la Paix* makes an anticlimactic end to Fauré's output of individual songs.[31] We can only regret the excess of modesty that prompted the composer, in 1924, to tear up his setting of Pierre de Ronsard's "Ronsard à son âme" on hearing that his former pupil Maurice Ravel had set the same poem (each of them having chosen it as his contribution to a special issue of *La Revue musicale* in honour of the poet's 400th birthday).[32]

The present volume includes Fauré's two *cantiques*, to religious poems in French by two of the composer's contemporaries, Stéphan Bordèse (*En prière*) and the musical writer Victor Wilder (*Noël*). *En prière* was first published by Durand in *Les Contes mystiques*, an 1890 collection of settings of religious poetry by Bordèse (a Durand employee), before being incorporated in Hamelle's 25-song Second Collection of Fauré's songs in 1897.[33] *Noël*, composed in 1885, was taken into the Hamelle collections only in 1908, as a makeweight in the much earlier First Collection (from which Hamelle had arbitrarily removed the earlier song *Barcarolle*, all in a complicated attempt to make up three 20-song volumes of Fauré's songs: see **Critical commentary** under **Publication history**). In a long letter of August 1907, Fauré vigorously protested against Hamelle's redistributions, demanding "What difference does it make, what can it possibly matter whether this 3rd volume comprises fourteen or fifteen songs?"[34] *Noël* he would rather have excluded, partly because of its "hybrid character" and partly because its style lagged "very much behind everything that will be in the 3rd volume", which Fauré had intended to comprise only op. 57 onwards. (Hamelle's eventual insertion of *Noël* in the First Collection was perhaps his attempt to deal with this.) A passing suggestion by Hamelle to replace Wilder's "paltry" lines for *Noël* with a new text by Charles Grandmougin (the poet of Fauré's earlier *Poème d'un jour*) was vetoed by the composer:

> Whether good or mediocre, this is *Christmas* music. Its innocent, expressionless character, its accompaniment conveying a *continuous* ringing of bells [...] does not go with Grandmougin's *tender, sentimental* little poem at all. So let's keep Wilder's lines because after all they inspired the *character* of the music, its *physiognomy*, its *looks*.[35]

In the same letter Fauré stressed that the song's harmonium accompaniment, marked *ad libitum* in the separate edition, was "truly necessary" (perhaps in an attempt to make Hamelle either include the part or drop the song altogether); omitted from the Hamelle Collection, the harmonium part is restored in the present edition.

Completing the present volume are Fauré's secular songs for more than one solo voice. The duets *Puisqu'ici bas toute âme* and *Tarentelle* were premiered in 1875 by Claudie Chamerot and Marianne Viardot, the daughters of the great mezzo-soprano Pauline Viardot and accomplished performers themselves, as the virtuosic vocal writing of *Tarentelle* makes plain (the text is by Marc Monnier, a poet from the Viardot social circle).[36] Although it has been posited that the Victor Hugo setting *Puisqu'ici bas* was adapted for the Viardot sisters from an earlier solo setting, its present vocal writing and structure are intrinsic to a duet conception.[37] The much later *Pleurs d'or* shows the same fluid chromaticism as its fellow Samain setting *Arpège*. It was composed for a London concert in May 1896, of which reports noted the inclusion of a violin obbligato; no trace of this now remains.[38] The two different opus numbers attached to the song result from confusion between its two original publishers (see **Critical commentary**, **Publication history**).

Musical sources

For the majority of the songs in the present volume, our prime editorial sources are the Third and revised First and Second Collections of Fauré's songs, as issued by Hamelle in 1908, though other sources contribute important details. The songs deriving from theatrical ventures take additional account of surviving orchestral sources, as do some that were orchestrated by Fauré for other purposes. For the songs external to the Hamelle Collections, our prime source is the first edition, except for the two songs unpublished in Fauré's lifetime.

Successive engravings and amended reprints of various songs resulted in numerous discrepancies across high- and medium-voice editions of the Hamelle Collections, primarily concerning dynamics and articulation, to the extent that neither of them can be taken as a coherently definitive version. For the present edition, therefore, source priority for each song varies between high- and medium-voice versions, according to which one suggests the more coherent preparation or revision. Whichever is taken as the default is supplemented by corrections and revisions from other sources.

Autographs are traced for just over half the songs in the present volume. Of these, sixteen served either for engraving or as probable sources for scribal engraving copy. Other autograph sources include sketches (*Clair de lune*), orchestral manuscripts, annotated scribal copies and corrected proofs. Although most of these are essentially superseded by the published versions, they often resolve misprints and clarify details of voicing and layout.

Throughout the present volume, viable variants are shown as *ossia* staves or footnotes; other variants of interest are shown in **Appendix 2** or the **Critical Commentary**. Essential corrections are taken into the musical text from any relevant source; less essential but useful performing indications from secondary sources (including orchestral versions) are incorporated in parentheses.

Keys

All Fauré's solo songs published by Hamelle up to op. 87, plus the duet *Pleurs d'or*, appeared in medium- and high-voice editions. The present edition retains these keys as defined in the 1908 version of the Hamelle Collections. The op. 35 *Madrigal* calls for no transposition; *Tarentelle* effectively permits none, its high tessitura essential to its nature while its second voice part lies more within mezzo or baritone range.[39] For the remaining songs published in just one key, and the two unpublished in Fauré's lifetime, a second key has been selected editorially.

Many of Fauré's songs appeared from Hamelle singly in additional transpositions: *Les Roses d'Ispahan*, for example, in B and D♭ as well as the D and E of Hamelle's Second Collection. The intriguing case of *Nocturne* throws exceptional light on Fauré's proactive approach to the practice of transposition. The song was first published in E♭ (in 1886), its cover unusually stipulating "pour / Contralto ou Basse". A later autograph dated 1892 gives it in F♯; although this manuscript bears Hamelle's house stamp, the song was never printed in that key.[40] Instead, *Nocturne* was incorporated into the 1897 Second Collection in A♭ for medium voice and C for high voice – the vocal line respectively a fourth and a sixth up from the original, a degree of transposition approached nowhere else in Fauré's output. These transpositions, clearly planned with care, introduce new elements such as pedalling and a metronome marking, along with vocal phrasing and other variants of dynamics and texture including some added bass grace notes for piano. Most radically – and again uniquely in Fauré's song output – they transpose the piano part not upwards with the voice but downwards to meet it an octave below.

In 1902 Mimi Girette wrote in her diary that "nobody ever sings *Nocturne* to [Fauré], and he likes it; I will work on it with him but he will try to have me do it in the original key, which is very low, because he likes it in the contralto register".[41] Accordingly, perhaps, the 1908 reissue of the Second Collection restored the original E♭ key in its medium-voice edition. These many versions of *Nocturne* bear witness to serious compositional engagement with the practice (or art) of song transposition, entailing a considered exploration of tessitura, timbre and balance. With all those issues in mind, along with the present edition's practical remit, the present medium-voice edition presents the song in both its original E♭ contralto key and the F♯ of Fauré's 1892 manuscript, while the high-voice edition presents it in the standard high-voice key of C as well as the A♭ of the 1897 medium-voice collection.

Notes on performance

The songs in the present volume tellingly reflect Fauré's creative and professional interactions with performers such as Maurice Bagès, Emma Bardac and Mimi Girette Risler, who all influenced his selection of poems, choices of form and vocal writing. Mimi Risler's annotated scores in particular corroborate the testimony of other colleagues of Fauré, revealing a dynamic compositional process of creative and practical exchange, a practice that underpins the philosophy of the present edition.

Besides the comments in the **General Preface** above, knowledge of Fauré's habits and performing preferences can illuminate some notational and editorial quirks peculiar to his songs. His use of *Allegretto* is typically near *Allegro*, but with more lightness of texture and character (most evident in the *Shylock* songs, *Sérénade* and op. 35 *Madrigal*). His frequent use of *Andante* – often qualified by *quasi allegretto* or even *quasi adagio* – suggests moderate, flowing tempi that embody the literal sense of *andante* as "moving" and of *adagio* as "at ease".

Particularly in the later songs, slow-to-moderate tempo headings entail a taut harmonic rhythm and often necessitate deceptively rapid vocal delivery. The dense poetry of songs such as *Le Parfum impérissable*, *Accompagnement* and *Le Don silencieux* demands focussed, vigorous enunciation, notwithstanding their intimate, almost murmuring character. In a 1919 letter to Robert Lortat, Fauré wrote that *Le Don silencieux* was "to be declaimed, above all [*surtout à dire*], with its marvellous art of word-colouring."[42] Inherent in that is the necessity to "play out the drama" (*jouer le drame*) that Fauré's son Philippe insisted was central to his father's music.[43] If the *drame* is overt in *Fleur jetée*, *Au cimetière* or *La Fleur qui va sur l'eau*, the quiet, word-driven intensity of *Les Présents* and *Le Don silencieux* is no less striking.

Fauré's concern for dramatic structure is evident in substantial revisions to dynamic shaping that he made to a few songs at a late stage (occasionally even post-publication). An early feuilleton publication of *Aurore*, apparently engraved from a proof or early manuscript, shows an intriguingly different conception of the song's dynamic shape, the final melodic descent from bar 42 marking the *forte* apex of a crescendo rather than the unexpected *piano* of later sources. *Larmes* shows similar reworking, notably at bar 31 where the reprise of the opening, marked *forte* in the first edition, is amended to *piano* in the 1897 Second Collection. Fauré's intended revisions here, corrupted by engraving errors, are clarified in the present edition.

Piano parts in some later songs (from *Dans la forêt de septembre*) show angled brackets covering wide left-hand spreads: Fauré appears to have started using them post-1900 in place of his earlier arpeggiando signs, probably to signify as crisp an arpeggiando as possible, without lingering.

Within the bounds of his firm rhythmic sense (see **General Preface**), Fauré expected a degree of rhythmic suppleness at key moments such as cadence points, typically returning to tempo at – or just before – the cadential resolution. Recordings of singers who worked with him attest to this, for example the remarkable 1928 recording by Jane Bathori of *Clair de lune* (in which she accompanies herself), around bars 54–55.[44] In general, however, Fauré demanded unfaltering forward motion (Claire Croiza called it an *"allant"*) with strict attention to rhythmic detail. The pianist Vlado Perlemuter, who worked with the composer in his last years, called him "the terror of singers", as "he wanted the *mélodie* to be played quite in measure, no rubato", to the discomfiture of singers "who like to be at ease with the rhythm".[45]

On 12 January 1902 Mimi Girette recorded in her diary:

> When [Fauré] is accompanying me we are one person, he follows me and yet I sense everything that he wishes. He even allows me to make tiny rallentandos and accelerations – hardly anything! – because he knows I would never exaggerate, I wouldn't distort the sense of his music.[46]

In the early years of the century Fauré gave to Mlle Girette not just an autograph of *Accompagnement* (of which she then made her own copy to annotate for performance) but also his corrected proofs of its opus companions and of *Chanson*. These scores show her performing indications (see **Appendix 3**), almost certainly made as she worked with the composer. Tellingly, not one of these indicates any fluctuation of tempo.

Texts and poets

Spanning almost forty years, the present volume encompasses poets from the luminaries Verlaine and Leconte de Lisle to Jean Richepin (remembered mostly for his prose), the popular Armand Silvestre and the esoteric Villiers de L'Isle-Adam, along with bright poetic stars of the new century in Henri de Régnier and Marie Closset (Jean Dominique). Most of Fauré's poets he knew personally; with Verlaine and Albert Samain he also contemplated theatrical collaborations in the early 1890s. The catalogue of Fauré's songs thus continues the narrative of *Complete Songs* vol. 1 by echoing his interaction with poets and literary movements.

The careful consideration Fauré gave to the process of transforming poetry into sung text is evident in his textual modifications. Occasional word substitutions and amendments to word order are typically directed at rendering the lines more singable: *Dans la forêt de septembre* shows him replacing the poet's "vivace" with "alerte" in the line "Je viens d'un pas vivace encore", avoiding ungainly repetition of a stressed [a] vowel; analogously, in Henri de Régnier's *Chanson* the repeated sibilant "Sur le sable" becomes "Dans le sable".[47]

More subtly again, Fauré often made small adjustments to punctuation: exclamation marks and full stops could be exchanged, as could commas, semi-colons and ellipses. Such adjustments often have a musical purpose relative to phrase and paragraph structure, serving as useful performance indications. Exclamation marks can reinforce dynamic intensity, particularly through a sustained note (the end of *Larmes*, for example, where the composer's exclamation mark replaces the poet's full stop), while commas may indicate a breath or non-elision (as in the opening bars of *Au cimetière*) or serve to echo a musical gesture.[48] The present edition respects these amendments provided they are consistent in musical sources, convey a discernible purpose, and engender no syntactic or musical problems.

Acknowledgements

The editors' grateful thanks are extended to those who kindly made sources available for study or helped in practical ways, notably the music staff at the Bibliothèque nationale de France, Paris, Bibliothèque François Lang, Royaumont (Valérie De Wispelaere and Thomas Vernet), Médiathèque musicale Mahler, Paris, Bibliothèque municipale de la ville de Genève, Bibliotheca Bodmeriana, Cologny (Nicolas Ducimetière), the Morgan Library and Museum, New York (J. Rigbie Turner and Frances Barulich), the Memorial Library of Music, Stanford University, the Beinecke and Irving S. Gilmore Libraries, Yale University, the McLennan Library, McGill University, Montreal, and the Library of Congress, Washington; the libraries of the Conservatoire Royal de Bruxelles, Conservatoire de Genève (Jacques Tchamkerten), Royal College of Music and Royal Academy of Music, London, along with Thierry and Pierrette Bodin, Carlo Caballero, James David Christie, Mary Dibbern, Ulrich Drüner, Judith Gordon, Denis Herlin, Nigel Hughes, Peter Jost, Sylvia Kahan, Robin Lehman, John and Judith Lubrano, Dr Simon Maguire (Sothebys), Roger Nichols, Robert Orledge, Herbert Schneider and Robin Tait. Performing and teaching colleagues and students have provided supportive enthusiasm, expertise and invaluable musical feedback through workshops and concerts; the editors thank in particular Tony Boutté, Mary Dibbern, Guy Flechter, François Le Roux, Rosalind Martin, Jared Schwartz and Christopher Underwood. The project's base at the Royal Academy of Music, London, has been supported by a Project Grant from the Arts and Humanities Research Council (UK); special thanks go to Nicole Tibbels for an immeasurable degree of enthusiastic cooperation and insights in practical and linguistic matters, to Richard Stokes for kindly authorizing reproduction of his English translations of song texts, and to the Academy's postgraduate singing students, along with David Gorton, Neil Heyde and Timothy Jones.

London and Paris, 2017   *Roy Howat and Emily Kilpatrick*

---

[1] The five "Venetian" songs op. 58 and *La Bonne Chanson* can be found in *Complete Songs* vol. 3, the four late cycles in vol. 4.

[2] Nectoux (ed.), *Gabriel Fauré: His Life through his Letters*, pp. 199–201.

[3] Montesquiou provided the text for the *ad libitum* chorus to the *Pavane*, which was dedicated to the Comtesse Greffulhe. His words spoof Verlaine's *Fêtes galantes*, particularly "Clair de lune" and "Mandoline". An editorial reconstruction of the *Pavane* for two voices, flute and piano (as sometimes performed impromptu by the composer) is available as Peters Edition EP 7526.

[4] Johnson and Stokes, *A French Song Companion*, p. 165. A review of the première (*Ménestrel*, 6 May 1888) refers to *Clair de lune* simply as "Menuet".

[5] Pierre de Bréville, "Quelques souvenirs", *La Revue musicale* 201 (September 1946), p. 229. On 2 February 1889, Bagès gave the first performances of two of Debussy's *Ariettes* (later *Ariettes oubliées*) and Fauré's *Au cimetière*, as well as Chausson's *Sérénade*. Bagès would also give the first salon and Société Nationale performances of Fauré's op. 58 "Venetian" songs, the first salon performance of *La Bonne Chanson* in April 1894, and the première of Fauré's transcription of that cycle with string quintet and piano (in London) on 1 April 1898. (Breville's surname was habitually printed "Bréville", though he consistently signed it without the accent.)

[6] Philip Kolb (ed.), *Correspondance de Marcel Proust* (Paris, 1970), i:338; cited in Nectoux (ed.) *Gabriel Fauré: His Life through his Letters*, p. 210. Some of the scores in question are listed in the **Critical commentaries** to the present volume and *Complete Songs* vol. 3.

[7] Nectoux (ed.), *Gabriel Fauré: His Life Through His Letters*, p. 142.

[8] Johnson, *Gabriel Fauré*, p. 170.

[9] Nectoux (ed.), *Gabriel Fauré: His Life Through His Letters*, p. 215.

[10] Debussy included the same poem, titled by its first line ("Il pleure dans mon cœur"), along with its companion "Spleen", in his *Ariettes* (later retitled *Ariettes oubliées*), first published in the same year as Fauré's *Spleen*.

[11] A drafted letter of the mid-1890s (possibly not sent) shows Fauré furiously addressing Hamelle: "The proofs of the songs haven't arrived, though there can be no possible reason to delay them. It is three years since I gave you the transposed copy for the songs in question. *Three years*. And I have been asking you ceaselessly to get on with them. It is absolutely impossible to put up with your lack of concern for getting my works published." (Nectoux (ed.), *Gabriel Fauré : Correspondance*, letter 189. The unnamed songs in question could be *Nocturne* and *Les Présents*; see **Critical commentary**.)

[12] See Howat and Kilpatrick, "Gabriel Fauré's Middle-Period Songs", pp. 330–4.

[13] Nectoux (ed.), *Gabriel Fauré : Correspondance*, letter 120. No trace remains of that original ending.

[14] Nectoux (ed.), *Gabriel Fauré: His Life Through His Letters*, p. 145.

[15] Also a collaboration with Haraucourt; Fauré completed only a Prologue for chorus and orchestra. See Nectoux, *Gabriel Fauré: A Musical Life*, p. 146.

[16] Ibid., p. 147.

[17] Ibid., pp. 149–50. See also Orledge, "Fauré's *Pelléas et Mélisande*", *Music and Letters* 56/2 (April 1975), pp. 170–79.

[18] Maeterlinck offered this text as an alternative to the song originally published in Act 3 scene 2 of the play, "Mes longs cheveux descendent", which opens Act 3 of Debussy's opera. For the London performances, "Mélisande's Song" was moved to the end of Act 3 scene 1, as Mélisande sits spinning; see Nectoux, *Gabriel Fauré: A Musical Life*, p. 156.

[19] Bibliothèque nationale de France, music department, VMD-3211.

[20] Nectoux, *Gabriel Fauré: A Musical Life*, pp. 172 and 189 (the quote appears on both pages, translated differently; see Nectoux, *Gabriel Fauré : les voix du clair-obscur*, p. 260).

[21] Nectoux, "Deux interprètes de Fauré : Émilie et Édouard Risler", *Études fauréennes* 18 (1981), p. 10.

[22] Ibid., p. 12.

[23] Ibid., p. 12.

[24] Ibid., p. 13.

[25] Nectoux (ed.), *Gabriel Fauré: His Life Through His Letters*, p. 252.

[26] Nectoux, *Gabriel Fauré : les voix du clair-obscur*, pp. 161–2.

[27] The Bachian reference was first noted by Charles Koechlin, as amplified in Nectoux, *Gabriel Fauré: A Musical Life*, p. 108.

[28] Nectoux (ed.), *Gabriel Fauré: His Life Through His Letters*, p. 252.

[29] Nectoux, *Gabriel Fauré: A Musical Life*, p. 304.

[30] Ibid., p. 404.

[31] He was still to set the cycle *L'Horizon chimérique* in 1921; see *Complete Songs* vol. 4. Five other songs from the early 1900s occasionally attributed to Fauré are known not to be by him: *Le Courlis dans les roseaux* and *Cette fille, elle est morte* are by Émile Riadis (see "Carlton Lake: An Inventory of Music in his Collection at the Harry Ransom Humanities Research Center", The University of Texas at Austin, www.hrc.utexas.edu); and three songs printed around 1910 by the firm Rouart-Lerolle as by "G. FAURE" (the only known exemplar of each held in the Irving Gilmore Music Library, Yale University), to texts by Sully Prudhomme (*Les Yeux*), Theuriet (*Pleurs d'avril*) and "G. FAURE" himself (*Souffles de printemps*). This last attribution, plus their simplistic musical language, points their authorship to the writer Gabriel Faure (a keen amateur musician and friend of Fauré); possibly private vanity prints, they nonetheless show plate numbers, prices and even the shop stamp of the publisher Eschig.

[32] Nectoux, *Gabriel Fauré: A Musical Life*, pp. 459–60. Ravel, in turn, was horrified by Fauré's chivalrous gesture and offered to withdraw his own setting; see Gustave Samazeuilh, *Musiciens de mon temps* (Paris: Daubin, 1945), p. 430.

[33] The collection's plate numbers, S.B. 2–4, suggest that it may have been a vanity publication. In his letter to Bagès of September or October 1890, quoted above (see note 13), Fauré wrote "I've written a little song on an idiotic text by a Durand employee".

[34] Nectoux (ed.), *Gabriel Fauré: His Life Through His Letters*, p. 274.

[35] Ibid., p. 275.

[36] In 1877 Fauré proposed to Marianne Viardot, but she ended the engagement after some months.

[37] See Orledge, *Gabriel Fauré*, p. 52 and Nectoux, *Gabriel Fauré, a musical life*, pp. 11 and 28; *Puisqu'ici-bas* figures on a list of Hugo settings that Fauré had reportedly made by early 1864 (see *Complete Songs*, Preface to volume 1). No surviving source material (see **Critical commentary**) leaves any trace of an earlier solo setting.

[38] See Orledge, *Gabriel Fauré*, p. 87.

[39] See **Critical commentary** regarding keys for *Pusiqu'ici bas toute âme*.

[40] After Fauré's death Hamelle issued an offprint in the enharmonically equivalent G♭. See **Critical commentary** regarding further advertised keys for *Nocturne* (and for "Chanson" from *Shylock*) that were apparently never issued.

[41] Nectoux, "Deux interprètes de Fauré", p. 11. See Howat and Kilpatrick, "Fauré's Middle-Period Songs", pp 319–25.

[42] Nectoux (ed.), Gabriel Fauré, *Correspondance*, letter 452.

[43] Fauré-Fremiet, *Gabriel Fauré*, pp. 158–62.

[44] *Jane Bathori: The Complete Solo Recordings*, CD, Marston MR 51009 (1999).

[45] Roger Nichols, transcript of conversation with Vlado Perlemuter (1970s), reported in an email communication to Roy Howat, 12 February 2013.

[46] Nectoux, "Deux interprètes de Fauré", p. 11.

[47] See also Nectoux, *Gabriel Fauré: A Musical Life*, pp. 351–3.

[48] For a detailed discussion of this issue in Fauré's early songs in particular, see Kilpatrick, "Moot point"

Préface générale

C'est vraiment dans ses mélodies que Fauré nous livre la fleur de son génie.
— Maurice Ravel [1]

Nul compositeur n'a fait de contribution plus substantielle et plus variée au répertoire de la mélodie française que Gabriel Fauré. La mélodie couvre toute sa carrière, du charmant *Papillon et la fleur* de 1861 au magistral cycle *L'Horizon chimérique*, composé soixante ans et plus de cent mélodies plus tard. L'importance de cette contribution a longtemps été compromise par l'histoire erratique de la publication des mélodies : dispersées dans différents recueils et chez divers éditeurs, bon nombre d'entre elles ont eu à pâtir de graves fautes d'impression et de leçons contradictoires dans les différentes versions imprimées. Cette première édition critique complète présente un texte qui fait autorité mais reste flexible, rassemblant la collection connue de soixante mélodies (telle qu'établie en 1908 par les éditions Hamelle), d'autres mélodies et cycles publiés séparément, dont trois mélodies restées inédites du vivant de Fauré, ainsi que trois mélodies à deux voix et un quatuor vocal. Le volume associé des *Vocalises* complètes de Fauré (EP 11385) comprend sa *Vocalise-Étude* sans paroles publiée pour la première fois en 1907, ainsi que quarante-quatre autres vocalises restées inédites jusque-là.

Avec son caractère à la fois pratique et scientifique, la présente édition vise à encourager les interprétations créatives, assurées et bien informées. Fondée sur l'étude de centaines de manuscrits et sources imprimées, elle a été éprouvée au plan international dans des master-classes, ateliers, séminaires, concerts et enregistrements, avec la participation de chanteurs professionnels, étudiants, professeurs, répétiteurs et spécialistes. En cela elle s'inspire du compositeur, qui préparait ses propres éditions sur la base de l'expérience interprétative. L'édition intègre aussi les idées d'interprètes qui ont travaillé avec Fauré, ainsi que ses propres préférences attestées dans ce domaine.

Sources et principes d'édition

Les principaux éditeurs des mélodies de Fauré étaient Choudens (1869–1879), Hamelle (1880–1904), Heugel (1905–1910) et Durand (1915–1921) ; diverses mélodies de lui furent également publiées à différents moments par Hartmann, Durand & Schœnewerk, Fromont, et la firme londonienne Metzler (outre certaines éditions américaines secondaires tirées d'originaux français). La plupart de ses mélodies furent imprimées séparément avant d'être réunies en recueils : le premier d'entre eux parut en 1879 (Choudens), le deuxième en 1897 (Hamelle), et le troisième en 1908 (Hamelle) [2]. Ces recueils, comme la plupart des éditions séparées, parurent dans des tonalités destinées aux voix élevées et aux voix moyennes ; et certaines mélodies furent publiées séparément dans des transpositions supplémentaires. À l'opposé de cette abondance de sources impri-mées, les manuscrits conservés sont moins nombreux. Parmi ceux qui ont maintenant été retrouvés, beaucoup — en particulier pour les premières mélodies — sont des ébauches, des manuscrits de présentation ou des versions intermédiaires.

Des sources aussi variées demandent à être traitées avec attention par l'éditeur. Les manuscrits, malgré les précieuses corrections, vérifications et variantes qu'ils offrent, réclament une certaine prudence, surtout lorsqu'ils n'étaient pas directement dans la chaîne de sources conduisant à la publication. Dans le même temps, même parmi la pléthore de sources imprimées, il est souvent impossible de s'en tenir à une source unique qui représenterait le texte « final » ou définitif du compositeur, car chacune des sources mêle des informations essentielles à des problèmes et des corruptions (là encore, le plus apparents dans les premières mélodies). Pour présenter un texte aussi fidèle que possible aux corrections faites par Fauré au fil des ans, la présente édition a dû recourir aux meilleures parmi les sources variées tout en restant dans les limites de la priorité logique des sources et du bon sens musical, en respectant toujours la cohérence au sein des mélodies uniques, groupes, cycles et recueils, et en prenant en compte tout ce qu'on sait des habitudes de Fauré en matière de composition, révision et interprétation, ainsi que toute indication circonstancielle. Des *ossia* sont donnés partout où plusieurs leçons sont manifestement viables. Il s'agit entre autres de quelques leçons anciennes qui clarifient certains aspects des intentions du compositeur – éléments qui furent parfois masqués par des révisions ultérieures visant à « protéger » la musique des interprétations ineptes. Le **commentaire critique** donne à ce sujet des explications complètes.

Tonalités

Absolument rien ne dit que Fauré s'opposait à la transposition de ses mélodies, en principe ou en pratique [3]. Plusieurs de ses mélodies existent dans différentes tonalités autographes (dont des transpositions faites après publication), d'autres ont d'abord paru dans une ou plusieurs tonalités qui diffèrent des manuscrits qui subsistent, tandis que pour les mélodies dont le manuscrit est perdu il est parfois impossible d'identifier à partir des sources imprimées la tonalité originale, et à plus forte la tonalité préférée de l'auteur. (Même dans les recueils d'Hamelle, on ne peut se fier toujours aux indications « ton original » [4].) Fauré, qui fut toute sa vie un musicien pratique, un accompagnateur et un habile chef de chœur, avait l'habitude de travailler avec une large palette de voix. Les programmes de concert qui subsistent montrent qu'il interprétait régulièrement ses mélodies avec différents types de voix, souvent dans des circonstances qui supposaient manifestement une transposition, notamment plusieurs créations importantes. Comme tout compositeur, Fauré avait ses propres préférences de tessiture ou de couleur tonale pour quelques mélodies ; toute indication de ce genre est citée ici et prise en compte.

À cet égard, la présente édition respecte la démarche pragmatique de Fauré lui-même, en rendant ses mélodies accessibles à autant de chanteurs que possible dans les limites appropriées du goût et de la rigueur. Les tonalités pour voix élevées et voix moyennes des trois recueils traditionnels sont pour la plupart maintenues, sauf lorsqu'une source offre une option plus convaincante ou laisse à penser que c'était la préférence de Fauré, et parfois pour faire une distinction plus réaliste entre voix élevées et moyennes. L'aspect pratique au clavier est également pris en considération. Dans quelques rares cas, la présente édition adopte une nouvelle tonalité transposée, pour des raisons de logique musicale et de tessiture, en tenant compte des sources. Pour les quelques mélodies publiées dans une seule tonalité du vivant de Fauré, une deuxième tonalité a été déterminée par l'éditeur. Dans certains cas, lorsque les sources présentent d'utiles tonalités supplémentaires, une troisième tonalité est disponible en ligne à www.fabermusic.com/editionpetersresources. Pour chaque mélodie, la présente édition indique la ou les tonalités originales connues ; lorsque le manuscrit est perdu ou que la tonalité originale imprimée diffère, cette dernière est indiquée entre parenthèses, en gras pour les tonalités données comme originales dans les recueils Hamelle.

Interprétation

Les témoignages sur le jeu et les préférences interprétatives de Fauré indiquent tous qu'il tenait à ce que la musique avance, avec une forte aversion pour tout ralentissement, rubato ou affectation sentimentale gratuits[5]. Son sens du tempo était lié au rythme naturel du poème parlé, et sa collègue Claire Croiza, mezzo-soprano distinguée, soulignait l'importance qu'il attachait au poème et à son articulation dans la mélodie. Croiza rapporte en outre :

> Fauré était un vivant métronome. [...] Par-dessus tout, c'est en le ralentissant qu'on le déforme. [...] Pour Fauré plus que pour quiconque il faut trouver l'expression dans le cadre de la mesure. [...] J'ai entendu une fois chanter *Après un rêve* par un chanteur qui mourait littéralement. Le soir même, dînant avec Fauré, je lui dis : « Enfin, Maître, dans quel mouvement voulez-vous *Après un rêve* ? » Et lui : « Sans ralentir, sans ralentir ! »[6]

Tout en soulignant l'intensité des moments tragiques (*Chanson du pêcheur* ou *Prison*), Croiza met en garde à plusieurs reprises contre une interprétation douloureuse des mélodies plus mélancoliques de Fauré, l'essence du raffinement et de la retenue de ce langage étant de ne pas exagérer ni caricaturer ce que le compositeur a déjà subtilement équilibré[7]. Parmi les premières mélodies de Fauré, en particulier, un poème ouvertement mélancolique comme *Tristesse* peut receler un certain degré de parodie ou d'autodérision[8], à quoi Fauré répond avec une touche légère qui rappelle de nombreux témoignages de ses amis et collègues sur son humour vivace et sa gaieté innée jusque dans ses dernières années[9].

Présentation

Les *ossia* sont transposés, suivant les besoins, à partir de leur tonalité source. Toute leçon musicale sujette à discussion fait l'objet d'une note de bas de page. Les liaisons ajoutées (ou complétées) par l'éditeur sont en pointillés ; les autres ajouts de l'éditeur sont entre crochets. Les altérations de précaution entre parenthèses apparaissent telles quelles dans les sources. Des parenthèses sont également ajoutées autour des respirations non essentielles qui apparaissent uniquement dans certaines sources, et autour de nuances et d'autres indications utiles provenant de sources secondaires, comme le détaille le **commentaire critique**.

Londres et Paris, 2017 *Roy Howat et Emily Kilpatrick*
(Traduction: Dennis Collins)

---

[1] Maurice Ravel, « Les mélodies de Gabriel Fauré », *La Revue musicale* 3, octobre 1922, dans Arbie Orenstein (éd.), *Maurice Ravel : Lettres, écrits, entretiens*, Paris, Flammarion, 1990, p. 325.

[2] La publication du troisième recueil en 1908 coïncidait avec la réédition par Hamelle des deuxième et troisième recueils (il racheta le premier recueil à Choudens en 1887 et en publia une édition pour voix élevée en 1890), avec quelques modifications dans la répartition du contenu ; voir **commentaire critique**.

[3] Pour une discussion détaillée de cette question éditoriale et d'autres, essentielles pour la présente édition, voir nos articles « Editorial Challenges in the Early Songs of Gabriel Fauré » et « Gabriel Fauré's Middle-Period Songs ».

[4] Celles-ci ne figurent que dans les deuxième et troisième recueils Hamelle, à partir de l'op. 18. Le diapason n'était alors pas standardisé en Europe – il pouvait varier d'un demi-ton de l'autre côté de la frontière –, même si, pendant la carrière de Fauré, il était fixé en France (par décret parlementaire de 1859) à la^3 = 435 Hz, un peu plus bas que la norme actuelle, de 440 Hz ou un peu plus.

[5] Plusieurs de ces témoignages, provenant de sa famille et de ses collègues musiciens, sont cités dans Roy Howat, *The Art of French Piano Music*, Londres et New Haven, Yale UP, 2009, p. 247, et de façon générale dans les chapitres 17, 18 et 21.

[6] Cité dans Abraham (éd.), *Un art de l'interprétation*, p. 199 et 212–13, et en partie dans Bannerman (éd.), *The Singer as Interpreter*, p. 80–82 ; ce dernier ouvrage ajoute une référence spécifique qui explique le « (sans ralentir) » de la présente édition à la mesure 46. La collègue violoniste de Fauré, Hélène Jourdan-Morhange, confirme ce trait, livrant une anecdote sur une chanteuse (anonyme) qui avait l'habitude de marquer des pauses et de traîner sur les fins de phrase : accompagnée par Fauré un jour pour un concert dans l'après-midi, « elle fut horrifiée d'être entraînée par le piano dans une route sans vallonnements... l'autostrade future ! » (Jourdan-Morhange, *Mes amis musiciens*, p. 22–23).

[7] Voir Bannerman (éd.), *The Singer as Interpreter*, p. 84–88, et Abraham (éd.), *Un art de l'interprétation*, p. 31, 40 et 212.

[8] Vladimir Jankélévitch (*Gabriel Fauré et ses mélodies*, p. 49) note de même : « Toujours ne prenons rien au tragique. Fauré reste en dehors de la vague de neurasthénie qui, avec Duparc et Chausson, commence à s'abattre sur la France [...] et la mélancolie de *Tristesse* n'est pas trop sérieuse. »

[9] La belle-fille du compositeur se souvenait ainsi de lui : « Fauré était un méridional, très gai et enclin à la plaisanterie » (« Brève rencontre avec Blanche Fauré-Fremiet », *Journal de Vichy*, 28 juin 1958). Hélène Jourdan-Morhange disait qu'il n'avait jamais perdu son « esprit gavroche » (*Mes amis musiciens*, p. 24). Certains souvenirs que Fauré nota vers la fin de sa vie évoquent, avec une jubilation non déguisée, les farces d'adolescent que lui et ses condisciples faisaient subir à leurs professeurs à l'École Niedermeyer (« Souvenirs », *La Revue musicale* 4/11, numéro spécial Fauré, 1er novembre 1922, p. 3–9).

Préface au volume 2

Ce volume comprend les mélodies de Gabriel Fauré composées à partir de 1884[1]. Des belles mises en musique d'Armand Silvestre, sur lesquelles s'ouvre le volume, au chromatisme des années 1890 et à la brièveté quasi-aphoristique de certaines de ses dernières mélodies, il offre un fascinant voyage à travers la maturité créatrice de Fauré.

En mai 1884, Fauré se remit à composer des mélodies après une coupure de près de deux ans – la première de ce genre dans son œuvre, dominée par la mélodie entre 1862 et 1882. En l'espace de trois semaines, il acheva les quatre mélodies formant l'op. 39. Les trois premières sont écrites sur des poèmes d'Armand Silvestre, dont Fauré avait utilisé la poésie pour la plupart des mélodies de ses trois précédents recueils (op. 18, 23 et 27, de 1878-1882 ; voir *Complete Songs* vol. 1). *Aurore* forme une ouverture d'une envoûtante limpidité, avant la fureur exceptionnelle de *Fleur jetée*. *Le Pays de Rêves* rétablit le calme, son apparence d'une simplicité trompeuse masquant une série d'audacieuses excursions harmoniques qui préfigurent les nombreuses mélodies des trois décennies suivantes. Le texte de Silvestre explore l'un des grands thèmes artistiques de l'époque, le voyage vers une terre étrangère idyllique – fantasme inspiré par le célèbre tableau d'Antoine Watteau, l'*Embarquement pour Cythère* (1717), et réveillé par le poème « L'Invitation au voyage » de Baudelaire, que deux amis de Fauré, Duparc et Chabrier, avaient mis en musique en 1870. Pour la dernière mélodie du recueil op. 39, Fauré fit l'un de ses retours périodiques à Leconte de Lisle, dont le penchant pour l'exotisme inspira toujours une veine de beauté concentrée et de richesse harmonique (ce qui explique peut-être pourquoi Fauré ne mit jamais ses poèmes en musique qu'isolément).

En 1886, Fauré fit la connaissance du comte Robert de Montesquiou, l'un des célèbres esthètes de l'époque. Montesquiou, qui fut l'inspiration pour Des Esseintes dans le roman *À rebours* d'Huysmans (1884) et ensuite pour le baron Charlus de Proust, était un fervent wagnérien, profondément engagé dans le monde symboliste. Admirateur non moins enthousiaste de la musique de Fauré, il organisa un concert entièrement consacré au compositeur au printemps de 1887 et semble s'être nommé son conseiller littéraire informel, lui faisant découvrir la poésie plus sombre et plus complexe de Villiers de L'Isle-Adam et de Paul Verlaine [2]. Les deux mélodies de Fauré d'après Villiers, *Nocturne* et *Les Présents* (op. 43 n° 2 et op. 46 n° 1), sont tirées des sept poèmes du recueil de Villiers de 1883, *Contes cruels* (qui contient par ailleurs des écrits en prose). Bien qu'apparemment conçues comme une paire – il subsiste des manuscrits similaires des deux postérieurs à la publication, copiés à quelques jours d'intervalle l'un de l'autre en 1892 –, elles parurent dans différents opus, sans doute en raison de leur climat introspectif commun.

Tandis que *Nocturne* partage plutôt son opus, de manière incongrue et arbitraire, avec *Noël* (un cantique, commenté ci-dessous), *Les Présents* – dédié à Montesquiou – forme une paire appropriée avec *Clair de lune*, la première des mélodies de Fauré sur un poème de Verlaine. *Clair de lune* fut composé à l'automne de 1887, à quelques semaines de la *Pavane* op. 50 : les deux œuvres furent données pour la première fois ensemble avec orchestre en avril 1888 (et toutes deux furent bissées) [3]. Le sous-titre « Menuet » de *Clair de lune* – le seul titre de danse dans les mélodies de Fauré – souligne son affinité avec la *Pavane* : les deux pièces comportent une longue introduction instrumentale, suivie par ce que Graham Johnson appelle très justement « un obbligato vocal » sur une musique essentiellement autonome, voix et accompagnement fusionnant à des moments cruciaux « comme par hasard [4] ».

Cette création orchestrale de *Clair de lune* fut donnée avec le ténor Maurice Bagès de Trigny, l'un des grands interprètes de mélodies dans les salons parisiens et à la Société nationale, du milieu des années 1880 jusqu'à sa mort prématurée en 1908. En 1946, le compositeur Pierre de Breville, qui fut pendant de nombreuses années le compagnon de Bagès, raconta comment Fauré entendit pour la première fois Bagès chanter *Nell* et *Après un rêve* lors d'une des soirées d'Henri Duparc :

> Le timbre expressif de sa voix, son incomparable diction, sa musicalité l'enchantèrent. « Chantez-vous d'autres mélodies de moi ? lui demanda-t-il. Je les aime et chante toutes » lui répondit Maurice Bagès, et de ce jour Fauré l'adopta comme son meilleur interprète, lui confia à la Société nationale la création de *Clair de lune* et *Au cimetière*, et lui demanda de l'accompagner à Londres lors de son premier voyage en Angleterre pour y faire connaître ses œuvres [5].

Cette collaboration étroite se devine dans une lettre de Marcel Proust à Paul Lavallée du 30 septembre 1894 : « Bagès m'avait laissé tout son Fauré. Mais la moitié est en manuscrits de Fauré, le reste imprimé, mais porte des dédicaces, et j'ai eu si peur de les abîmer que j'ai tout renvoyé [6]. »

En novembre 1888, Fauré écrivit à la comtesse Greffulhe :

> J'ai composé trois nouvelles Mélodies très gaies ! ! ! en voici les titres :
> 1. *Au cimetière* ! (Richepin)
> 2. *Larmes* ! id.
> 3. *Spleen* ! (Verlaine)
>
> Pour l'une d'elles [*Au cimetière*] j'ai tenté de faire un accompagnement très facile et pour la main droite seulement : mais au bout de dix mesures le secours de la main gauche est devenu nécessaire et au bout de vingt mesures les difficultés pour les deux mains s'accumulent ! Encore un pavé pour l'Enfer [7] !

Les facultés vocales de Maurice Bagès se reflètent certainement dans les deux mélodies d'après Jean Richepin, *Larmes* et *Au cimetière*, dont le caractère opératique inhabituel pourrait s'expliquer par le pèlerinage à Bayreuth que fit Fauré cet été-là. Graham Johnson pense, de manière plausible, que l'intérêt de Fauré pour ce poète inhabituel pourrait avoir été suscité par les collaborations de celui-ci avec Emmanuel Chabrier, pour qui il écrivit le livret de *La Sulamite* et (comme nègre) celui du *Roi malgré lui* [8]. *Au cimetière* fut publié pour la première fois dans la tonalité très haute de *mi* mineur ; les éditions ultérieures pour voix élevée la changèrent en *ré* mineur, certainement en raison de sa tessiture redoutablement aiguë dans le *forte* soutenu de la section centrale déclamée. Si Bagès était capable de la chanter avec assurance, les efforts de chanteurs moindres furent peut-être ce qui incita Proust, normalement admiratif, à juger *Au cimetière* « vraiment affreux [9] ».

Spleen est tiré du recueil *Romances sans paroles* (1874) de Verlaine (où le poème apparaît sans titre ; Fauré emprunta le sien à un autre poème du même recueil [10]). Loin du charme sardonique des *Fêtes galantes* de Verlaine, le poème renonce à la fluidité métrique de *Clair de lune* pour des vers brefs et une prosodie dans une large mesure monosyllabique, qui évoque l'implacable ostinato de la pluie battante, dont la mélodie de Fauré se fait l'écho.

La Rose date de 1890, deux ans après les autres mélodies de l'opus. Le sous-titre « Ode anacréontique » est un clin d'œil au poète grec Anacréon, dont la poésie célèbre l'amour et le vin (encore que le poème n'utilise pas le mètre heptasyllabique caractéristique de la poésie anacréontique). Une autre mélodie isolée d'après Leconte de Lisle, *La Rose*, semble avoir été ajoutée à l'op. 51 en raison de la lenteur de Hamelle à publier les trois premières mélodies [11]. Un élément de continuité à travers le recueil vient de la dédicace de *La Rose* à Bagès, pour la voix de qui la mélodie fut manifestement conçue : c'est particulièrement évident dans la dernière page, où les difficultés vocales semblent excéder les capacités des autres premiers interprètes. Sa réédition dans le troisième recueil de 1908 présente une fin révisée et vocalement moins difficile – qui pose à son tour quelques nouveaux problèmes, notamment un moment d'étrange discontinuité harmonique autour de la mesure 48, ainsi que d'occasionnelles divergences entre les éditions pour voix élevée et pour voix moyenne [12]. La présente édition donne les deux fins, de 1890 et de 1908. Celle de 1890 n'était du reste pas la première version de Fauré, comme il l'explique dans une lettre à Bagès cet automne-là :

> Mon cher ami, tu as très bien fait de me donner ton avis : seulement je crois que si nous avions vu ensemble la nouvelle fin je te l'aurais peut-être fait comprendre autrement. D'abord (il y a peut-être aussi une erreur de copie) les mots : « avec la beauté » doivent se chanter en diminuant.

> Puis l'accompagnement est d'une sonorité pleine mais douce ; il faut de la pédale pour bien soutenir l'arpège de la basse et n'accentuer que ceci :

 les deux fois.

> La première fin ne me satisfaisait pas : si j'étais arrivé à Cuy deux jours plus tard je n'aurais pas apporté la mélodie telle que tu l'as vue là bas. Cela me paraissait écourté et tu dois te souvenir que j'avais prolongé d'une mesure la période salua la Fleur. Mais ça ne me suffisait pas ! Je suis resté tracassé jusqu'à ce que j'aie eu fait le changement complet.

Je crois que dans quelque temps, quand tu auras oublié la première version tu seras de mon avis. Je dois dire que S͏ᵗ Saëns ne connaît que la seconde et qu'il n'a pas paru choqué : ce qui en fait supposer que si tu n'avais pas d'abord chanté la première fin la seconde ne t'aurait pas causé de surprise.

Tout ça n'empêche pas que je me trompe peut-être aussi : mais ce qui me rassure c'est ce tracassin qui ne m'a quitté qu'après que j'ai eu changé ma péroraison.[13]

C'est certainement à Maurice Bagès que Fauré faisait allusion dans une lettre au poète Edmond Haraucourt un an auparavant (27 septembre 1889) : « Voudriez-vous déjeuner le dimanche en huit, *6 octobre*, à Bougival avec un des mes jeunes amis qui vous chantera les deux chansons de *Shylock* ? Je les lui ai fait copier et remettre pour qu'il les travaille [14]. »

Bien que Fauré n'ait achevé qu'un seul opéra (*Pénélope*, 1913), il était constamment attiré par le théâtre, comme la plupart des compositeurs français, et la décennie 1888-1898 le vit composer la musique de scène pour plusieurs pièces : *Caligula* (1888), *Shylock* (1889), *La Passion* (1890) [15], *Le Bourgeois Gentilhomme* (1893) et *Pelléas et Mélisande* (1898). *Shylock*, adaptation par Haraucourt du *Marchand de Venise*, fut monté pour la première fois au Théâtre de l'Odéon en décembre 1889 ; une version de concert de la musique de scène de Fauré fut créée au mois de mai suivant. Les deux mélodies qu'elle comprend, « Chanson » et « Madrigal », n'ont pas d'équivalent dans la pièce de Shakespeare : toutes deux sont des sérénades, la première chantée par un chanteur en coulisses à Jessica, la deuxième par le prince d'Aragon sous la fenêtre de Portia à l'acte II. (« Chanson », dans la version publiée, reprend sa nuance vocale initiale de la partition théâtrale ; une exécution au concert pourrait nécessiter un discret ajustement.) La présente édition comprend, en guise d'option, une page d'introduction à « Chanson » omise des recueils Hamelle ; et l'**Appendice 1** présente une réduction pour voix et piano d'une version jusqu'ici inédite de « Chanson », tirée du matériel d'orchestre manuscrit, qui met en musique une troisième strophe (discrètement risquée) avec jeux de mots.

Une troisième « Sérénade » de ce volume provient de la musique de scène de Fauré pour *Le Bourgeois Gentilhomme* de Molière, commande transmise par Saint-Saëns (alors occupé par l'opéra *Phyrné*) à son ancien élève et ami. « Moi ça me plaît beaucoup mais saurai-je ? ? cela ne sera pas facile », répondit Fauré en septembre 1892 [16]. En l'occurrence, le théâtre (l'Éden-Théâtre) fit faillite en mars 1893 ; le projet abandonné nous a cependant laissé non seulement cette mélodie, mais aussi l'une des pièces brèves les plus connues de Fauré, une *Sicilienne* qu'il adapta par la suite pour violoncelle et piano, et qu'il intégra aussi à sa musique de scène pour une saison londonienne du *Pelléas et Mélisande* de Maurice Maeterlinck en 1898. Cette production fut donnée dans une traduction anglaise de Jack Mackail, avec des décors et costumes de l'artiste préraphaélite Edward Burne-Jones, et l'imposante actrice Mrs Patrick Campbell [née Beatrice Stella Tanner] en Mélisande. La commande émanait de Mrs Campbell elle-même, qui, après s'être adressée d'abord à Debussy – dont on savait qu'il avait achevé son opéra sur la pièce de Maeterlinck –, avait essuyé un refus catégorique [17]. Fauré dirigea lui-même la première représentation au Prince of Wales Theatre le 21 juin 1898, quatre jours après la mort de Burne-Jones. « Mélisande's Song », le seul numéro vocal, provient de la scène de la tour à l'acte III [18]. Fauré ne la mit en musique qu'en anglais, avec ses connaissances rudimentaires de la langue (le manuscrit montre qu'au départ il traita « hope » comme deux syllabes). La présente édition propose donc des remèdes à deux passages où la mise en musique du texte n'est pas idiomatique. La syllabation du texte français original de Maeterlinck est tellement différente, avec notamment des répétitions de vers qui ne sont pas dans la version anglaise, que celui-ci est incompatible avec la ligne vocale de la mélodie. En 1906, toutefois, Fauré adapta cette mélodie à un autre texte français, sous le titre « Crépuscule », pour son cycle *La Chanson d'Ève*, utilisant un poème de Charles van Lerberghe, compatriote et ami de Maeterlinck.

Prison et *Soir* sont les dernières compositions de Fauré en 1894, année extraordinaire qui le vit achever *La Bonne Chanson* et trois œuvres majeures pour piano (la Quatrième Valse-Caprice, le Sixième Nocturne et la Cinquième Barcarolle), ainsi que plusieurs œuvres chorales sacrées. La présente édition rétablit le numéro d'opus correct des mélodies, que les éditions ultérieures de Hamelle ont changé plusieurs fois, pour des raisons extérieures expliquées dans le **Commentaire critique (Historique de la publication)**. *Prison*, dernier retour de Fauré à la poésie de Paul Verlaine, est l'une des compositions les plus explosives sur le plan de l'émotion de toute la mélodie française ; en égrenant littéralement les secondes (d'après l'indication métronomique de Fauré) jusqu'au vers final dévastateur, « Qu'as-tu fait de ta jeunesse ? », le glas de l'accompagnement de piano apparaît aussi implacable que des barreaux de prison.

Soir – première mélodie de Fauré sur un poème d'Albert Samain – forme un pendant aux années Verlaine du compositeur. Le contenu musical laisse deviner un débordement de deux œuvres récentes, la *Romance* pour violoncelle op. 69 (pièce plus ancienne que Fauré avait retravaillée pour publication à l'automne de 1894), et le Sixième Nocturne op. 63 (dans la même tonalité de ré♭, avec une fin étroitement apparentée). Comme *La Bonne Chanson*, *Soir* est étroitement associé à la cantatrice Emma Bardac, avec qui Fauré eut une liaison passionnée au début des années 1890. (M͏ᵐᵉ Bardac devait épouser Claude Debussy une décennie plus tard.) Un peu plus tôt en 1894, Fauré lui avait offert un volume récemment publié de poésie de Samain, *Au jardin de l'Infante*, avec l'inscription : « Je vous prie d'accepter ce livre et d'y choisir les vers que vous aimeriez chanter [19]. » Parmi les poèmes du volume qui comportent des annotations au crayon de M͏ᵐᵉ Bardac se trouvent « Élégie » – dont Fauré tira les trois strophes qu'il mit en musique sous le titre *Soir* – et « Arpège ». Après l'avoir entendue chanter *Soir* au début de 1896, Samain écrivit à sa sœur :

J'ai trouvé chez Fauré M͏ᵐᵉ Bardac en question, une jeune femme d'une trentaine d'années… type : jolie mondaine élégante ; son mari serait financier. […] Après dîner, elle a chanté. Fauré m'a dit : « Vous ne l'entendrez jamais mieux chanté que par elle. » De fait, elle a un sentiment des nuances et une pureté d'expression surtout, tout à fait rares [20].

Fauré attendit presque trois ans avant de mettre Samain en musique pour voix seule une seconde fois (bien qu'entre-temps il eût composé le duo *Pleurs d'or*). *Arpège* et son pendant, *Le Parfum impérissable*, sur un poème de Leconte de Lisle, datent de la fin de l'été de 1897. La mélodie évoquant la flûte et les rythmes composés bien cadencés d'*Arpège* rappellent la *Sicilienne*, mentionnée plus haut, mais avec plus d'audace tonale, tandis que l'allure mesurée de *Parfum impérissable* recèle une hardiesse harmonique proche de celle de *Prison*, avec cependant un caractère tranquillement intense plutôt qu'ouvertement dramatique.

Cette paire op. 76 ne marqua qu'un bref retour au monde de la mélodie : mis à part « Mélisande's Song », Fauré n'en écrivit pas d'autre avant près de cinq ans – la plus longue interruption de ce genre dans sa carrière. Il était désormais occupé par ses nouveaux devoirs de professeur de composition au Conservatoire de Paris, et par la composition de la « tragédie lyrique » *Prométhée* (1900, presque mais pas tout à fait un opéra). Il revint ensuite au genre avec *Accompagnement* (mars 1902), composé pour Mimi [Émilie] Girette Risler, cantatrice amateur de talent, qui fut l'une des interprètes favorites de Fauré dans la première décennie du siècle, et à qui la mélodie est dédiée. Le journal de Mlle Girette (elle s'appelait encore ainsi) relate avec enthousiasme les progrès de « sa » mélodie – ainsi que beaucoup d'autres rencontres – et offre une vision étonnamment intime du travail de Fauré et du processus compositionnel :

> 7 janvier 1902
>
> Cortot disait [à Fauré] qu'il devrait composer une chose pour piano et orchestre ; il m'a dit « je ne ferai rien avant de vous avoir composé une mélodie » ; à quoi je lui ai répondu que ce serait une des grandes joies de ma vie – « Seulement je ne trouve pas la *poésie* car je sais bien ce que vous aimez » m'a-t-il dit – j'ai encore répondu que les paroles me seraient plus égales, que je tiens surtout à la musique. Mais il trouva que les paroles et musique ne font qu'un et que les paroles l'inspirent. Cela se voit bien dans sa musique où tout est voulu, si fouillé et ciselé [21].

> 8 mars 1902
>
> Il a commencé « ma mélodie », sans vouloir me dire quelle poésie il a enfin trouvée ! Ce sera dans le genre du *Soir* musicalement, je lui avais dit que j'aimais tant ce genre là – Il pense à moi, à ma voix, en l'écrivant – Il me disait qu'il composait dans sa tête d'abord, *par les paroles*, c'est la poésie qui l'inspire – la mélodie se forme peu à peu en lui, même sans y penser cela mûrit inconsciemment et ensuite vient le travail de mise au point qui n'est pas le plus facile, au contraire [22].

> 29 mars 1902
>
> Quelle date inoubliable pour moi ! ! J'ai été recevoir « ma mélodie » chez Fauré ! Il me l'a chantée une fois, puis moi ensuite [23].

> 2 avril
>
> *Accompagnement*, personne au monde que moi et lui ne le connaît. J'en suis heureuse... Il m'a dit qu'il lui semblait que c'était un peu de moi et qu'il s'y était mis *tout entier* [24].

C'est sûrement la musicalité intelligente de Mimi que Fauré avait en tête quand il écrivit à la comtesse Greffulhe en novembre 1902 : « Je suis sûr qu'il est beaucoup de mes mélodies, parmi celles de ces dernières années, que vous ne connaissez pas encore ! Je rêve de vous les faire entendre avec des interprètes parfaits, et je n'en connais pas parmi les professionnels. Ce sont les amateurs qui me comprennent et me traduisent le mieux [25]. »

Bien que composé en premier, *Accompagnement* allait devenir la troisième des mélodies du recueil op. 85 de Fauré : *Dans la forêt de septembre* et *La Fleur qui va sur l'eau*, tous deux sur des textes de Catulle Mendès, la rejoignirent en septembre 1902. Il subsiste des autographes doubles à la fois de *Dans la forêt de septembre* et d'*Accompagnement*, et Fauré semble avoir travaillé en parallèle sur les deux paires : chaque manuscrit révèle des leçons révisées en différents endroits. Une autre mélodie esquissée pour ce groupe, *Dans le ciel clair*, aurait été la dernière de Fauré sur un poème de Leconte de Lisle : Fauré y travailla ce même automne avant de l'abandonner. Les fragments qui subsistent sont transcrits dans l'**Appendice 2**.

Mimi Girette allait lui inspirer une autre mélodie, *Le plus doux chemin* (op. 87 n° 1), écrite pour son mariage avec le pianiste Édouard Risler. Comme son futur pendant, *Le Ramier*, *Le plus doux chemin* est loin des grandes toiles extrêmement chromatiques des mélodies op. 85, les textures plus simples révélant la fluidité modale de Fauré dans ce qu'elle a de plus concentré. Les deux mélodies marquent le dernier retour de Fauré à la poésie d'Armand Silvestre, chacune conservant le sous-titre générique de Silvestre, « Madrigal ». À cet égard, elles font écho à un cadeau de mariage plus ancien, pour André Messager, ami compositeur de Fauré : le *Madrigal* op. 35 (1883) pour quatre voix solistes et piano, dont le texte est tiré du même recueil de Silvestre. Fauré orchestra par la suite *Madrigal*, mais Jean-Michel Nectoux fait remarquer qu'il le destinait toujours à quatre voix solistes, bien que Hamelle indique qu'il soit également possible de l'exécuter avec chœur SATB (du vivant de Fauré, il était parfois chanté par huit chanteurs, deux par partie) [26]. C'est peut-être pour l'amusement privé de Messager que Fauré emprunta le thème initial de *Madrigal* à la cantate *Aus tiefer Not schrei' ich zu dir* de Bach (avec une éventuelle pointe d'ironie malicieuse), thème que Bach utilisa dans la fugue en ré♯ mineur du premier livre de son *Clavier bien tempéré* [27].

En 1906, rempli d'amertume, Fauré avait mis un terme à son contrat avec Hamelle et en avait signé un nouveau avec Henri Heugel, avant de finalement passer chez l'éditeur Jacques Durand en 1910. Ses trois dernières mélodies isolées, jamais intégrées aux recueils Hamelle traditionnels, restent peu connues. *Le Don silencieux* (op. 92) est le fruit de quelques jours concentrés à la fin de son heureux séjour estival à Vitznau, près de Lucerne, en 1906. Il écrivit à son épouse :

> Comme elle ne ressemble nullement à aucune de mes précédentes œuvres, ni à rien que je sache, je suis très content. Et puis, il n'y a pas même un thème principal ; elle est d'une liberté d'allure qui déconcerterait fort Théodore Dubois. Elle traduit les mots, au fur et à mesure qu'ils se produisent, elle commence, se déroule et finit, sans plus, et cependant elle est *une*. Et voilà que je fais le pédant [28].

Dans le recueil publié, *L'Anémone des mers,* le poème est sans titre. Fauré intitula à l'origine sa mélodie *Offrande*, écrivant à Octave Maus :

> Si Jean Dominique *boude* pour le titre que l'insistance de l'éditeur m'a obligé à imaginer, dites-lui que les treizièmes pieds (fort jolis du reste) dont il a émaillé sa poésie m'ont donné du fil à retordre ! J'espère cependant les avoir musiqués avec souplesse ; du moins j'ai fait de mon mieux [29].

(Fauré semble toujours ignorer que Jean Dominique était un nom-de-plume de la poétesse belge Marie Closset.)

Chanson (1906) revient aux textures plus ouvertes des « madrigaux » d'après Silvestre. C'est la dernière mélodie isolée de Fauré pour Heugel (pour qui il venait de commencer le cycle *La Chanson d'Ève*), et presque sa dernière de toutes. En 1919, il fut contraint de mettre en musique – à contrecœur – le poème gagnant d'un concours organisé par *Le Figaro* pour célébrer la fin de la Première Guerre mondiale, louant la bravoure des poilus. Fauré décrivit le texte dans une lettre à sa femme comme « une horrible petite poésie » ; deux jours plus tard, il ajouta qu'il avait changé « cet affreux mot » (« poilus ») en « soldats » – « Tant pis pour la poétesse si elle n'est pas contente. Je lui fais assez d'honneur comme ça [30] ! » Malgré sa bonne volonté musicale et ses efforts (il omit la moitié du poème), le piètre texte de *C'est la Paix* met un terme décevant à l'œuvre de Fauré pour ce qui est de la mélodie individuelle [31]. On ne peut que regretter l'excès de modestie qui poussa le compositeur, en 1924, à déchirer sa composition sur « Ronsard à son âme » de Pierre de Ronsard en apprenant que son ancien élève Maurice Ravel avait mis en musique le même poème (tous deux l'avaient choisi pour leur contribution à un numéro spécial de *La Revue musicale* en l'honneur du quatrième centenaire de la naissance du poète) [32].

Le présent volume comprend les deux « cantiques » de Fauré, sur des poèmes religieux en français de deux contemporains du compositeur, Stéphan Bordèse (*En prière*) et le musicographe Victor Wilder (*Noël*). *En prière* fut publié pour la première fois par Durand en 1890 dans *Les Contes mystiques,* recueil de poésie religieuse de Bordèse (employé de Durand), avant d'être intégré au deuxième recueil de vingt-cinq mélodies de Fauré publié par Hamelle en 1897 [33]. *Noël*, composé en 1885, ne fut incorporé aux recueils Hamelle qu'en 1908, pour donner plus de poids au premier recueil, beaucoup plus ancien (dont Hamelle avait arbitrairement supprimé la mélodie plus ancienne *Barcarolle*, tout cela dans une tentative compliquée pour réunir trois volumes de vingt mélodies de Fauré : voir **Commentaire critique, Historique de la publication**). Dans une longue lettre d'août 1907, Fauré proteste vigoureusement contre les nouvelles répartitions de Hamelle, demandant : « Qu'est-ce que cela fait, quelle importance cela peut-il avoir que ce 3ᵉ volume soit formé de quatorze ou de quinze mélodies [34] ? » Il aurait préféré voir exclure *Noël*, à la fois en raison de son « caractère hybride » et « à cause de son style très *en retard* sur tout ce que contiendra le 3ᵉ volume », où Fauré n'avait l'intention d'inclure de mélodies qu'à partir de l'op. 57. (C'est peut-être pour régler ce problème que Hamelle inséra ensuite *Noël* dans le premier recueil.) Hamelle suggéra en passant de remplacer les « piètres » vers de Wilder dans *Noël* par un nouveau texte de Charles Grandmougin (auteur du *Poème d'un jour* plus ancien de Fauré), mais le compositeur s'y opposa :

> La poésie de Grandmougin […] ne cadre pas de tout avec la musique. Bonne ou médiocre, cette musique est celle d'un *Noël*. Son caractère naïf, inexpressif, son accompagnement qui traduit une sonorité *continue* de CLOCHES, va avec les vers assez piètres de Wilder puisque, en somme, ils ont inspiré le *caractère* de la Musique, sa *physionomie*, son *aspect* [35].

Dans la même lettre, Fauré soulignait que l'accompagnement d'harmonium de la mélodie, marqué *ad libitum* dans l'édition séparée, était « vraiment nécessaire » (peut-être dans un effort pour amener Hamelle soit à inclure la partie, soit à abandonner complètement la mélodie) ; omise du recueil Hamelle, la partie d'harmonium est rétablie dans la présente édition.

Les mélodies profanes de Fauré pour plus d'une voix soliste complètent le présent volume. Les duos *Puisqu'ici bas toute âme* et *Tarentelle* furent créés en 1875 par Claudie Chamerot et Marianne Viardot, filles de la grande mezzo-soprano Pauline Viardot et elles-mêmes interprètes accomplies, comme le montre clairement l'écriture virtuose de *Tarentelle* (sur un texte de Marc Monnier, poète du cercle mondain de Viardot) [36]. Bien qu'on ait avancé l'idée que *Puisqu'ici bas*, sur un poème de Victor Hugo, avait été adapté pour les sœurs Viardot à partir d'une version à voix seule plus ancienne, l'écriture vocale et la structure sont inhérentes à la conception en duo [37]. *Pleurs d'or*, beaucoup plus tardif, révèle le même chromatisme fluide qu'*Arpège*, également sur un poème de Samain. Ce duo fut composé pour un concert à Londres en mai 1896, dont les comptes rendus rapportent la présence d'une partie de violon obligé ; il n'en reste aucune trace aujourd'hui [38]. Les deux numéros d'opus différents attachés au duo résultent d'une confusion entre ses deux éditeurs d'origine (voir **Commentaire critique, Historique de la publication**).

Sources musicales

Pour la majorité des mélodies du présent volume, nos principales sources sont le troisième recueil et les premier et deuxième recueils révisés des mélodies de Fauré publiés par Hamelle en 1908, encore que d'autres sources fournissent des détails importants. Les mélodies provenant de spectacles théâtraux prennent en outre en compte les sources orchestrales qui subsistent, de même que certaines mélodies orchestrées par Fauré pour d'autres raisons. Pour les mélodies étrangères aux recueils Hamelle, notre source principale est la première édition, sauf pour les deux qui sont restées inédites du vivant de Fauré.

Les gravures successives et les réimpressions corrigées de diverses mélodies ont conduit à de nombreuses divergences entre les éditions pour voix élevée et voix moyenne des recueils Hamelle, concernant avant tout les nuances et l'articulation, au point que ni l'une ni l'autre ne peut être prise comme version définitive cohérente. Pour la présente édition, priorité est donnée tour à tour aux versions pour voix élevée et pour voix moyenne, suivant celle qui semble présenter la préparation ou la révision le plus cohérente. La version prise comme source principale est complétée par les corrections et révisions provenant d'autres sources.

On conserve des autographes pour un peu plus de la moitié des mélodies du présent volume. Parmi eux, seize ont servi soit pour la gravure, soit comme sources probables de copies manuscrites destinées à la gravure. Les autres sources autographes comprennent des esquisses (*Clair de lune*), des manuscrits orchestraux, des copies manuscrites annotées et des épreuves corrigées. Bien que la plupart d'entre elles soient pour l'essentiel supplantées par les versions publiées, elles résolvent souvent des fautes d'impression et clarifient des détails de polyphonie et de disposition.

Tout au long de ce volume, des variantes viables sont présentées sur des portées en *ossia* ou en note de bas de page ; d'autres variantes intéressantes sont citées dans l'**Appendice 2** ou le **Commentaire critique**. Les corrections essentielles sont intégrées au texte musical à partir de toute source pertinente ; les indications d'interprétation moins essentielles mais néanmoins utiles provenant de sources secondaires (y compris les versions orchestrales) sont incorporées entre parenthèses.

Tonalités

Toutes les mélodies à voix seule de Fauré publiées par Hamelle jusqu'à l'op. 87, ainsi que le duo *Pleurs d'or*, ont paru dans des éditions pour voix moyenne et voix élevée. La présente édition conserve ces tonalités telles que définies dans la version de 1908 des recueils Hamelle. Le *Madrigal* op. 35 n'appelle pas de transposition ; *Tarentelle* n'en permet en réalité aucune, sa tessiture élevée étant essentielle à sa nature, tandis que la seconde partie vocale est plutôt dans l'étendue d'une mezzo ou d'un baryton [39]. Pour les autres mélodies publiées dans une seule tonalité, ainsi que celles restées inédites du vivant de Fauré, une deuxième tonalité a été choisie par l'éditeur.

Bon nombre de mélodies de Fauré ont paru isolément dans des transpositions supplémentaires : *Les Roses d'Ispahan*, par exemple, en *si* et *ré*♭, outre les versions en *ré* et *mi* du deuxième recueil Hamelle. Le cas curieux de *Nocturne* jette une lumière exceptionnelle sur l'attitude pragmatique de Fauré en matière de transposition. La mélodie fut d'abord publiée en *mi*♭ (en 1886), la couverture comportant l'indication inhabituelle « pour / Contralto ou Basse ». Un autographe ultérieur daté de 1892 la présente en *fa*♯ ; bien que ce manuscrit porte le tampon maison de Hamelle, elle ne fut jamais publiée dans cette tonalité [40]. Au lieu de quoi *Nocturne* fut incorporé au deuxième recueil de 1897 en *la*♭ pour voix moyenne et en *ut* pour voix élevée – avec une ligne vocale respectivement une quarte et une sixte plus haut que dans l'original, soit un intervalle de transposition dont aucune autre composition de Fauré ne s'approche. Ces transpositions, manifestement conçues avec soin, introduisent de nouveaux éléments tels qu'indications de pédale et une indication métronomique, avec des phrasés vocaux et d'autres variantes de nuances et de texture, y compris quelques ornements dans la basse pour le piano. L'aspect le plus radical – lui aussi unique dans les mélodies de Fauré – est le fait que la partie de piano est transposée non pas vers le haut avec la voix, mais vers le bas, pour la retrouver une octave en dessous.

En 1902, Mimi Girette notait dans son journal, à propos de *Nocturne,* « on ne lui chante jamais et il l'aime, je le travaillerai mais il tâchera de m'avoir le ton original qui est très bas, car il l'aime en contralto [41] ». Par conséquent, peut-être, la réédition de 1908 du deuxième recueil rétablit la tonalité originale de *mi♭* dans son édition pour voix moyenne. Ces nombreuses versions de *Nocturne* témoignent du travail d'écriture sérieux que représentait la pratique (ou l'art) de la transposition des mélodies, supposant une exploration réfléchie de la tessiture, du timbre et de l'équilibre. Avec toutes ces questions en tête, ainsi que les nécessités pratiques de cette édition, notre volume pour voix moyenne présente la mélodie à la fois dans sa tonalité de contralto originale de *mi♭* et en *fa♯* comme dans le manuscrit de Fauré de 1892, tandis que le volume pour voix élevée la présente dans la tonalité conventionnelle pour ce type de voix, *ut*, ainsi qu'en *la♭*, comme dans le recueil pour voix moyenne de 1897.

Notes sur l'interprétation

Les mélodies de ce volume reflètent éloquemment les interactions créatives et professionnelles de Fauré avec des interprètes comme Maurice Bagès, Emma Bardac et Mimi Girette Risler, qui ont tous influencé ses choix de poèmes, de forme et d'écriture vocale. Les partitions annotées de Mimi Risler corroborent en particulier le témoignage d'autres collègues du compositeur, révélant un processus dynamique d'échanges créatifs et pragmatiques – pratique qui sous-tend aussi la philosophie de la présente édition.

Outre les commentaires dans la **Préface générale** ci-dessus, la connaissance des habitudes de Fauré et de ses préférences interprétatives peut éclairer certaines particularités propres à ses mélodies dans la notation et l'édition. Son usage d'*allegretto* est généralement proche d'*allegro*, mais avec plus de légèreté dans la texture et le caractère (le plus en évidence dans les mélodies de *Shylock*, la *Sérénade* et le *Madrigal* op. 35). Son emploi fréquent d'*andante* – souvent nuancé par *quasi allegretto* ou même *quasi adagio* – suggère des tempi modérés, coulants, qui correspondent au sens littéral d'*andante* (« allant ») et d'*adagio* (« à l'aise »).

Dans les mélodies tardives, plus particulièrement, les indications de tempo lentes à modérées supposent un rythme harmonique tendu et nécessitent souvent une diction vocale d'une rapidité trompeuse. La poésie dense de mélodies comme *Le Parfum impérissable*, *Accompagnement* et *Le Don silencieux* exige une élocution précise et vigoureuse, malgré le caractère intime, presque murmuré. Dans une lettre de 1919 à Robert Lortat, Fauré écrivait que *Le Don silencieux* était « surtout à dire, avec son art merveilleux de la couleur des mots [42] ». La nécessité de « jouer le drame » – aspect essentiel de la musique de Fauré, selon son fils Philippe – y est inhérente [43]. Si le drame est manifeste dans *Fleur jetée*, *Au cimetière* ou *La Fleur qui va sur l'eau*, l'intensité tranquille, mue par les mots, des *Présents* et du *Don silencieux* n'est pas moins frappante.

Le souci de la structure dramatique de Fauré est évident dans les substantielles révisions au modelé dynamique qu'il fit pour plusieurs mélodies à un stade tardif, voire parfois après la publication. Une publication précoce d'*Aurore* en feuilleton, apparemment gravée à partir d'une épreuve ou d'un ancien manuscrit, révèle une conception curieusement différente de la forme dynamique de la mélodie, la descente finale mélodique de la mesure 42 étant le sommet *forte* d'un crescendo plutôt que le *subito piano* des sources ultérieures. *Larmes* révèle des révisions similaires, notamment à la mesure 31, où la reprise du début, marquée *forte* dans la première édition, est corrigée en *piano* dans le deuxième recueil de 1897. Les révisions voulues par Fauré, corrompues par des erreurs de gravure, sont clarifiées dans la présente édition.

Certaines parties de piano plus tardives (à partir de *Dans la forêt de septembre*) comportent des crochets embrassant les grands écarts de main gauche : Fauré semble avoir commencé à les utiliser après 1900 à la place de ses signes d'arpègement antérieurs, probablement pour indiquer un arpègement aussi rapide que possible, sans lenteur.

Dans les limites de son solide sens rythmique (voir **Préface générale**), Fauré attendait manifestement une certaine souplesse rythmique à des moments-clefs comme les cadences, revenant normalement au tempo à la résolution cadentielle ou juste avant. Les enregistrements des chanteurs ayant travaillé avec lui en témoignent, tel le remarquable enregistrement de *Clair de lune* fait en 1928 par Jane Bathori (où elle s'accompagne elle-même), autour des mesures 54-55 [44]. En général, toutefois, Fauré demandait un mouvement assuré vers l'avant (ce que Claire Croiza appelait un « allant »), avec une attention stricte aux détails rythmiques. Le pianiste Vlado Perlemuter, qui travailla avec le compositeur dans ses dernières années, le tenait pour « la terreur des chanteurs », car « il voulait que la mélodie fût jouée tout à fait en mesure, sans rubato », au grand dam des chanteurs « qui aiment prendre leurs aises avec le rythme [45] ».

Le 12 janvier 1902, Mimi Girette nota dans son journal :

> Quand [Fauré] m'accompagne nous ne faisons qu'un, il me suit et je sens tout ce qu'il veut cependant. Il se laisse même plus aller à ralentir ou à presser, oh, un rien, parce qu'il sent que je n'exagérerai jamais, que je n'ôterai pas le caractère de sa musique.[46]

Dans les premières années du siècle, Fauré offrit à Mlle Girette non seulement un autographe d'*Accompagnement* (dont elle fit ensuite sa propre copie exemplaire personnel à annoter pour l'exécution), mais aussi ses épreuves corrigées des autres mélodies de cet opus et de *Chanson*. Ces partitions comportent ses indications d'interprétation (voir **Appendice 3**), qu'elle nota presque certainement en travaillant avec le compositeur. Il est significatif pas une seule d'entre elles ne corresponde à une fluctuation de tempo.

Textes et poètes

Couvrant près de quarante ans, le présent volume comprend de grands noms de la poésie comme Verlaine ou Leconte de Lisle, Jean Richepin (surtout passé à la postérité pour sa prose), le populaire Armand Silvestre et l'ésotérique Villiers de L'Isle-Adam, outre de brillantes étoiles poétiques du nouveau siècle comme Henri de Régnier et Marie Closset (Jean Dominique). Fauré connaissait personnellement la plupart de ses poètes ; avec Verlaine et Albert Samain, il envisagea aussi des collaborations théâtrales au début des années 1890. Le catalogue des mélodies de Fauré poursuit donc le parcours du volume 1 des *Complete Songs* en faisant écho à son interaction avec les poètes et les mouvements littéraires.

L'attention soigneuse que Fauré portait au processus de transformation du poème en texte chanté est manifeste dans ses modifications textuelles. Les occasionnels substitutions de mots et changements dans l'ordre des mots visent généralement à rendre les vers plus chantables : *Dans la forêt de septembre* remplace ainsi le « vivace » du poète par « alerte » dans le vers « Je viens d'un pas vivace encore », évitant la répétition maladroite d'une voyelle accentuée [a] ; de manière analogue, dans *Chanson* de Henri de Régnier, la sifflante répétée de « Sur le sable » devient « Dans le sable » [47].

De façon encore plus subtile, Fauré fit souvent de petits ajustements à la ponctuation : les points d'exclamation et les simples points peuvent être échangés, de même que les virgules, points virgules et points de suspension. De tels ajustements ont souvent un but musical, en relation avec la structure de la phrase et de la section, formant d'utiles indications d'interprétation. Les points d'exclamation peuvent renforcer l'intensité dynamique, en particulier avec une note tenue (la fin de *Larmes*, par exemple, où le point d'exclamation du compositeur remplace le simple point du poète), tandis que les virgules peuvent indiquer une respiration ou une non-élision (comme dans les premières mesures de *Au cimetière*) ou servir d'écho à un geste musical[48]. La présente édition respecte ces changements pourvu qu'ils soient cohérents dans les sources musicales, qu'ils expriment une intention perceptible, et qu'ils n'engendrent pas de problèmes syntaxiques ou musicaux.

Remerciements

Nos sincères remerciements vont à tous ceux qui ont aimablement mis des sources à notre disposition pour étude ou qui ont aidé autrement, notamment le personnel musical de la Bibliothèque nationale de France, Paris, la Bibliothèque du Conservatoire royal de Bruxelles, la Bibliothèque François Lang, Royaumont (Valérie De Wispelaere et Thomas Vernet), la Médiathèque musicale Mahler, la Bibliothèque municipale de la ville de Genève, la Bibliotheca Bodmeriana, Cologny (Nicolas Ducimetière), la Morgan Library and Museum, New York (J. Rigbie Turner et Frances Barulich), la Memorial Library of Music, Stanford University, les Beinecke et Irving S. Gilmore Libraries, Yale University, la McLennan Library, McGill University, Montréal, et la Library of Congress, Washington ; les bibliothèques du Conservatoire royal de Bruxelles, du Conservatoire de Genève (Jacques Tchamkerten), du Royal College of Music and Royal Academy of Music, Londres, ainsi que Thierry et Pierrette Bodin, Carlo Caballero, James David Christie, Mary Dibbern, Ulrich Drüner, Judith Gordon, Denis Herlin, Nigel Hughes, Peter Jost, Sylvia Kahan, Robin Lehman, John et Judith Lubrano, Simon Maguire (Sotheby's), Roger Nichols, Robert Orledge, Herbert Schneider et Robin Tait. Les collègues interprètes et enseignants nous ont fait profiter de leur soutien enthousiaste, de leurs compétences et de leurs inestimables réactions musicales lors de stages et de concerts ; nous remercions en particulier Tony Boutté, Mary Dibbern, Guy Flechter, François Le Roux, Rosalind Martin, Jared Schwartz et Christopher Underwood. Basé à la Royal Academy of Music, Londres, le projet éditorial a été soutenu par un Project Grant de l'Arts and Humanities Research Council (Royaume-Uni) ; nous y remercions tout spécialement Nicole Tibbels pour son inestimable collaboration enthousiaste et ses lumières sur les questions pratiques et linguistiques, Richard Stokes pour son aimable autorisation de reproduire ses traductions anglaises des textes chantés, et les étudiants en chant de troisième cycle de l'Academy, ainsi que David Gorton, Neil Heyde et Timothy Jones.

Londres et Paris, 2017   *Roy Howat et Emily Kilpatrick*
                                 (Traduction : Dennis Collins)

---

[1] Les *Cinq mélodies* « de Venise » op. 58 et *La Bonne Chanson* se trouvent dans *Complete Songs* vol. 3, les quatre cycles tardifs dans le volume 4.

[2] Nectoux, *Gabriel Fauré : les voix du clair-obscur*, p. 237-238 ; voir aussi Nectoux (éd.), *Gabriel Fauré : Correspondance* (édition de 1980), chapitre VI.

[3] Montesquiou écrivit le texte pour le chœur *ad libitum* de la *Pavane*, dédiée à la comtesse Greffulhe. Son poème parodie les *Fêtes galantes* de Verlaine, en particulier « Clair de lune » et « Mandoline ». Une reconstitution éditoriale de la *Pavane* pour deux voix, flûte et piano (telle que le compositeur la jouait parfois impromptu) est disponible chez Peters Edition (EP 7526).

[4] Johnson et Stokes, *A French Song Companion*, p. 165. Un compte rendu de la création (*Ménestrel*, 6 mai 1888) fait référence à *Clair de lune* sous le simple titre de « Menuet ».

[5] Pierre de Bréville, « Quelques souvenirs », *La Revue musicale* 201 (septembre 1946), p. 229. Le 2 février 1889, Bagès donna la première audition de deux des *Ariettes* (futures *Ariettes oubliées*) de Debussy et de *Au cimetière* de Fauré, ainsi que de la *Sérénade* de Chausson. Bagès devait également donner la première audition dans un salon et à la Société nationale des mélodies « de Venise » op. 58, la première audition dans un salon de *La Bonne Chanson* en avril 1894, et la création de la transcription faite par Fauré de ce cycle avec quintette à cordes et piano (à Londres) le 1er avril 1898. (Le nom de Breville était habituellement imprimé avec un accent, « Bréville », mais lui-même l'écrivait toujours sans accent.)

[6] Philip Kolb (éd.), *Correspondance de Marcel Proust* (Paris, 1970), i, p. 338 ; cité dans Nectoux, *Gabriel Fauré : les voix du clair-obscur*, p. 257. Certaines des partitions en question sont répertoriées dans les **Commentaires critiques** du présent volume et des *Complete Songs* vol. 3.

[7] Nectoux (éd.), *Gabriel Fauré : Correspondance*, lettre 102.

[8] Johnson, *Gabriel Fauré*, p. 170.

[9] Nectoux, *Gabriel Fauré : les voix du clair-obscur*, p. 257.

[10] Debussy inclut le même poème, avec pour titre son premier vers (« Il pleure dans mon cœur »), ainsi que son pendant « Spleen », dans ses *Ariettes* (ensuite rebaptisées *Ariettes oubliées*), publiées pour la première fois la même année que *Spleen* de Fauré.

[11] Quelques années plus tard (à la fin de 1896 ou au début de 1897), Fauré, exaspéré, rédigea une lettre à Hamelle (qu'il n'a peut-être jamais envoyée) : « Les épreuves des mélodies ne sont pas arrivées encore sans qu'aucun motif puisse justifier ce retard. Il y a trois ans que je vous ai remis les transpositions des mélodies en question. *Trois ans*. Et depuis je vous ai demandé sans cesse de vous en occuper. Il m'est absolument impossible de supporter plus longtemps votre indifférence à l'égard du sort de mes œuvres. » Nectoux (éd.), *Gabriel Fauré : Correspondance*, lettre 189. Les mélodies en question n'étant pas identifiées, il pourrait s'agir de *Nocturne* et *Les Présents*; voir **Commentaire critique**.

[12] Voir Howat et Kilpatrick, « Gabriel Fauré's Middle-Period Songs », p. 330–334.

[13] Nectoux (éd.), *Gabriel Fauré : Correspondance*, lettre 120. Il ne reste aucune trace de cette fin primitive.

[14] *Ibid.*, lettre 107.

[15] Également en collaboration avec Haraucourt ; Fauré n'acheva qu'un Prologue pour chœur et orchestre. Voir Nectoux, *Gabriel Fauré : les voix du clair-obscur*, p. 206.

[16] Nectoux (éd.), *Gabriel Fauré : Correspondance*, lettre 157.

[17] Nectoux, *Gabriel Fauré : les voix du clair-obscur*, p. 211. Voir aussi Orledge, « Fauré's *Pelléas et Mélisande* », *Music and Letters* 56/2 (avril 1975), p. 170–179.

[18] Maeterlinck proposa ce texte comme alternatif à la chanson originale de la pièce, « Mes longs cheveux descendent » (Acte III scène 2), avec laquelle Debussy ouvre l'acte III de son opéra. Pour les représentations londoniennes, « Mélisande's Song » fut déplacé à la fin de la première scène de l'Acte III, où Mélisande est assise à filer ; voir Nectoux, *Gabriel Fauré : les voix du clair-obscur*, p. 220.

[19] Bibliothèque nationale de France, département de la musique, VMD-3211.

[20] Nectoux, *Gabriel Fauré : les voix du clair-obscur*, p. 260.

[21] Nectoux, « Deux interprètes de Fauré : Émilie et Édouard Risler », *Études fauréennes* 18 (1981), p. 10.

[22] *Ibid.*, p. 12.

[23] *Ibid.*, p. 12.

[24] *Ibid.*, p. 13.

[25] Nectoux (éd.), *Gabriel Fauré : Correspondance*, lettre 249.

[26] Nectoux, *Gabriel Fauré : les voix du clair-obscur*, p. 161–162.

[27] La référence à Bach fut notée pour la première fois par Charles Koechlin ; voir Nectoux, *Gabriel Fauré : les voix du clair-obscur*, p. 162.

[28] Fauré-Fremiet (éd.), *Lettres intimes*, p. 121.

[29] Nectoux, *Gabriel Fauré : Correspondance*, lettre 285.

[30] Fauré-Fremiet (éd.), *Lettres intimes*, p. 260.

[31] Il devait encore mettre en musique le cycle *L'Horizon chimérique* en 1921 ; voir *Complete Songs* vol. 4. On sait que cinq autres mélodies du début des années 1900 parfois attribuées à Fauré ne sont pas de lui : *Le Courlis dans les roseaux* et *Cette fille, elle est morte*, qui sont d'Émile Riadis (voir « Carlton Lake : An Inventory of Music in his Collection at the Harry Ransom Humanities Research Center », The University of Texas at Austin, www.hrc.utexas.edu) ; et trois mélodies imprimées vers 1910 par la firme Rouart-Lerolle sous le nom de « G. FAURE » (le seul exemplaire connu de chaque est conservé à la Irving Gilmore Music Library, Yale University), sur des textes de Sully Prudhomme (*Les Yeux*), Theuriet (*Pleurs d'avril*) et « G. FAURE » lui-même (*Souffles de printemps*). D'après cette dernière attribution, et leur langage musical simpliste, leur auteur serait plutôt l'écrivain Gabriel Faure (bon musicien amateur et ami de Fauré) ; il s'agit peut-être d'exemplaires privés publiés à compte d'auteur, bien qu'ils comportent un cotage, un prix et même le cachet de la boutique de l'éditeur Eschig.

[32] Nectoux, *Gabriel Fauré : les voix du clair-obscur*, p. 592-593. Ravel fut à son tour horrifié par le geste chevaleresque de Fauré et proposa de retirer sa propre version ; voir Gustave Samazeuilh, *Musiciens de mon temps* (Paris, Daubin, 1945), p. 430.

[33] Les cotages du recueil, S.B. 2-4, laissent à penser qu'il pourrait s'agir d'une publication à compte d'auteur. Dans sa lettre à Bagès de septembre 1890, citée ci-dessus (voir note 13), Fauré écrit : « J'ai fait une petite mélodie sur des paroles idiotes d'un employé de Durand, Stéphan Bordèse. »

[34] Nectoux (éd.), *Gabriel Fauré : Correspondance*, lettre 291.

[35] *Ibid.*

[36] En 1877, Fauré demanda Marianne Viardot en mariage, mais elle rompit avec lui au bout de quelques mois.

[37] Voir Orledge, *Gabriel Fauré*, p. 52, et Nectoux, *Gabriel Fauré : les voix du clair-obscur*, p. 36 et 61 ; *Pusiqu'ici-bas* figure sur une liste de poèmes de Hugo que Fauré, dit-on, avait mis en musique dès le début de 1864 (voir *Complete Songs*, préface au volume 1). Aucune source ne subsiste (voir **Commentaire critique**) comportant des traces d'une version antérieure à voix seule.

[38] Voir Orledge, *Gabriel Fauré*, p. 87.

[39] Voir le **Commentaire critique** au sujet des tonalités pour *Pusiqu'ici bas toute âme*.

[40] Après la mort de Fauré, Hamelle publia un tiré à part dans la tonalité enharmonique de *sol* ♭. Voir le **Commentaire critique** au sujet des autres tonalités annoncées pour *Nocturne* (et pour « Chanson » de *Shylock*), qui apparemment ne furent jamais publiées.

[41] Nectoux, « Deux interprètes de Fauré », p. 11. Voir Howat et Kilpatrick, « Fauré's Middle-Period Songs », p. 319-325.

[42] Nectoux (éd.), *Gabriel Fauré : Correspondance*, lettre 452.

[43] Fauré-Fremiet, *Gabriel Fauré*, p. 158–162.

[44] *Jane Bathori : The Complete Solo Recordings*, CD, Marston MR 51009 (1999).

[45] Roger Nichols, transcription d'une conversation avec Vlado Perlemuter (années 1970), rapportée dans un courriel à Roy Howat, 12 février 2013.

[46] Nectoux, « Deux interprètes de Fauré », p. 11.

[47] Voir aussi Nectoux, *Gabriel Fauré : les voix du clair-obscur*, p. 448–450.

[48] Pour une étude détaillée de cette question dans les premières mélodies de Fauré, voir Kilpatrick, « Moot point ».

Allgemeines Vorwort

In seinen Liedern bringt Fauré wahrhaftig die Blüte seiner Schöpferkraft zum Vorschein.
— Maurice Ravel[1]

Kein Komponist hat einen wesentlicheren und vielfältigeren Beitrag zum französischen Liedrepertoire geleistet als Gabriel Fauré. Angefangen beim charmanten *Le Papillon et la fleur* aus dem Jahr 1861 bis hin zum meisterhaften, sechzig Jahre später komponierten Zyklus *L'Horizon chimérique* durchzog die Komposition von *Mélodies* sein musikalisches Schaffen. Die Bedeutung seines Beitrags wurde lange Zeit durch die unstete Veröffentlichungsgeschichte beeinträchtigt: Viele der über verschiedene Verleger und Sammel-publikationen verteilten Lieder wurden durch gravierende Druckfehler und widersprüchliche Lesarten innerhalb der unter-schiedlichen Druckfassungen entstellt. Diese erste kritische Gesamtausgabe liefert einen sowohl verlässlichen als auch flexiblen Notentext mit Stücken aus der bekannten dreibändigen Sammlung mit sechzig Liedern (verlegt 1908 von Hamelle) sowie anderen separat veröffentlichten Liedern und Zyklen, darunter drei zu Faurés Lebzeiten unveröffentlichte Lieder und vier Lieder für mehr als eine Stimme. Ein separater Band mit Faurés *Vokalisen* (EP 11385) beinhaltet vierundvierzig erstmals veröffentlichte Vokalisen sowie die 1907 veröffentlichte *Vocalise-Étude*.

Mit ihrem sowohl praktischen als auch wissenschaftlichen Schwerpunkt möchte die vorliegende Ausgabe eine kreative, sichere und sachkundige Aufführung ermöglichen. Sie basiert auf dem Studium hunderter Manuskripte und gedruckter Quellen und wurde international im Rahmen von Meisterklassen, Workshops, Seminaren, Konzerten und Aufnahmen unter Teilnahme professioneller Sänger/-innen, Studierender, Lehrender, Coaches und Spezialisten auf den Prüfstand gestellt. Hierin orientierten sich die Herausgeber am Vorgehen des Komponisten, der seine eigenen Ausgaben auf Grundlage von Aufführungserfahrungen erstellte. Berücksichtigt wurden zudem interpretatorische Einsichten von Musikern, die mit Fauré zusammenarbeiteten, sowie dessen dokumentierte Präferenzen bezüglich der Aufführung.

Quellen und editorische Herangehensweise

Die Hauptverleger der Lieder Faurés waren Choudens (1869–1879), Hamelle (1880–1904), Heugel (1905–1910) und Durand (1915–1921); mehrere seiner Lieder wurden zu unterschiedlichen Zeiten auch von Hartmann, Durand & Schœnewerk, Fromont und dem Londoner Unternehmen Metzler publiziert (hinzu kommen einige von den französischen Originalausgaben abhängige amerikanische Ausgaben). Die meisten seiner Lieder wurden einzeln veröffentlicht, bevor man sie in Sammlungen vereinte. 1879 erschien die erste Sammlung (Choudens), die zweite 1897 (Hamelle) und die dritte im Jahr 1908 (Hamelle).[2] Diese Sammlungen wurden, wie auch die meisten Einzeldrucke, in Tonarten für die hohe und mittlere Stimmlage herausgegeben, einige Lieder wurden in zusätzlichen Transpositionen separat veröffentlicht. Im Gegensatz zu der Vielzahl gedruckter Ausgaben ist die Quellenlage bei den Manuskripten weniger ergiebig. Viele der derzeit ausfindig gemachten Manuskripte sind – insbesondere was die früheren Lieder betrifft – frühe Entwürfe, Widmungsautographe oder Zwischenfassungen.

Der editorische Umgang mit solch unterschiedlichen Quellen erfordert große Sorgfalt. Trotz aller wertvollen Korrekturen, Verifizierungen und Lesarten, die die Manuskripte bieten, müssen sie mit Vorsicht genossen werden, insbesondere dann, wenn sie kein direktes Glied einer zur Veröffentlichung führenden Quellenkette waren. Mittlerweile ist es trotz der Fülle der Quellen häufig unmöglich, eine bestimmte Quelle als den endgültigen oder definitiven Notentext des Komponisten anzusehen und diesem zu folgen. Jede Quelle birgt sowohl wesentliche Informationen als auch Probleme und Verfälschungen (was vor allem die erwähnten früheren Lieder betrifft). Um die im Laufe vieler Jahre vorgenommenen Korrekturen Faurés so getreu wie möglich zu erfassen, mussten hier die besten Quellen ihrer logischen Priorität und ihres musikalischen Sinns entsprechend kombiniert werden. Stets berücksichtigt wurde dabei die Kohärenz einzelner Lieder, Gruppierungen, Zyklen und Sammlungen, ferner sämtliche Kenntnisse über Faurés Kompositions-, Korrektur- und Aufführungsgewohnheiten sowie alle weiteren verfügbaren Indizien. *Ossia*-Versionen sind angegeben, wenn eindeutig mehr als eine Lesart realisierbar ist. Dazu zählen einige frühe Lesarten, die gewisse Aspekte der kompositorischen Absicht Faurés verdeutlichen, beispielsweise Elemente, die mitunter von späteren Korrekturen verdeckt wurden, um die Musik vor unsachgemäßer Aufführung zu „schützen". Ausführliche Erläuterungen finden sich im **Kritischen Kommentar**.

TONARTEN

Es gibt keinerlei Anzeichen dafür, dass Fauré die Transposition seiner Lieder konkret oder prinzipiell ablehnte.[3] Mehrere seiner Lieder existieren in mehr als einer autographen Tonart (darunter einige Transpositionen, die nach der Veröffentlichung vorgenommen wurden), andere erschienen in einer oder mehreren Tonarten, die von den überlieferten Manuskripten abweicht, während es bei den Liedern, deren Manuskripte verschollen sind, manchmal unmöglich ist, anhand der gedruckten Quellen eine Originaltonart oder eine vom Komponisten bevorzugte Tonart zu identifizieren. (Selbst in den Erstausgaben Hamelles sind Kennzeichnungen der „Originaltonart" nicht immer verlässlich.)[4] Als lebenslang ausübender Musiker, Begleiter und ausgebildeter Chorleiter war es Fauré gewohnt, mit verschiedenen Stimmen zu arbeiten. Überlieferte Konzertprogramme bezeugen, dass er seine Lieder regelmäßig mit Sänger/-innen verschiedener Stimmgattungen aufführte, wobei die Umstände – darunter einige wichtige Premieren – häufig das Transponieren von Stücken erforderten. Wie jeder Komponist hatte Fauré für einige Lieder spezifische Präferenzen in Bezug auf Tessitur und Tonartencharakter. Entsprechende Belege sind in dieser Gesamtausgabe zitiert und wurden in dieser Edition berücksichtigt.

Die Herausgeber würdigen insofern die pragmatische Herangehensweise Faurés und machen seine Lieder innerhalb angemessener geschmacklicher Grenzen und im wissenschaftlichen Rahmen für möglichst viele Sänger/-innen zugänglich. Die in den genannten Sammlungen enthaltenen Tonarten für die hohe und mittlere Stimmlage wurden größtenteils beibehalten. Änderungen wurden nur vorgenommen, wenn eine Quelle eine stringentere Option liefert oder auf eine Präferenz Faurés hindeutet, gelegentlich aber auch, um realistischer zwischen hoher und mittlerer Stimmlage zu unterscheiden. Weiterhin wurde die Spielbarkeit auf dem Klavier berücksichtigt. Einige wenige Lieder wurden in eine bestimmte Tonart transponiert, wenn musikalischer Sinn, Tessitur und die Quellenauswertung Anlass dazu gaben. Für die wenigen nur in einer Tonart veröffentlichten oder zu Faurés Lebzeiten noch nicht publizierten Lieder haben die Herausgeber die Transposition nach bestem Wissen bestimmt. Einige wenige ausgewählte Stücke, deren Quellen zusätzliche hilfreiche Tonarten liefern, sind online unter www.fabermusic.com/editionpetersresources in einer dritten Tonart abrufbar. Die vorliegende Ausgabe führt für jedes Lied die bekannte(n) Originaltonart(en) an; war kein Manuskript auffindbar oder unterscheiden sich die gedruckten Originaltonarten, stehen Letztere in runden Klammern, wobei die in den Sammlungen Hamelles angegebenen Originaltonarten **fett** gedruckt sind.

AUFFÜHRUNG

Zeitzeugenberichte über Faurés bevorzugte Spielweise und Inter-pretation lassen darauf schließen, dass er in seinen Liedern den Vorwärtsfluß in den Mittelpunkt stellte und eine strenge Abneigung gegen unnötiges Verlangsamen, Rubato und sentimentale Affek-tiertheit hegte.[5] Sein Tempoverständnis entsprach dem natürlichen Tempo des gesprochenen Gedichts. Faurés gute Kollegin, die berühmte Mezzosopranistin Claire Croiza, betonte, welche Bedeutung er dem Gedicht und dessen Artikulation im Lied beimaß. Croiza erinnerte außerdem:

> Fauré war das personifizierte Metronom. [...] Vor allem das Verlangsamen entstellt ihn [...]. Mehr als bei jedem anderen muss der Ausdruck bei Fauré im Rahmen des vorgegebenen Metrums gefunden werden [...]. Einmal hörte ich, wie ein Sänger *Après un rêve* vortrug und dabei [fast] buchstäblich starb. Beim Essen mit Fauré am selben Abend fragte ich ihn: „Welches Tempo haben Sie tatsächlich für *Après un rêve* vorgesehen, Maître?" Und er sagte: *„Sans ralentir, sans ralentir!"*.[6]

Obwohl Croiza die Intensität tragischer Momente betont (*Chanson du pêcheur* oder *Prison*), warnt sie immer wieder davor, Faurés melancholischere Lieder mit Wehmut zu interpretieren: Die Finesse und Zurückhaltung dieses Stils erreiche man nicht durch Übertreiben und Karikieren, was der Komponist bereits wohl ausbalanciert habe.[7] Besonders unter Faurés frühen Liedern bringt ein offenkundig melancholisches Gedicht wie *Tristesse* bisweilen ein gewisses Maß an Parodie oder Selbstironie mit sich,[8] das Fauré mit leichter Hand quittiert. Zahlreiche Schilderungen seiner Familie und Kollegen über dessen lebendigen Humor und die Fröhlichkeit, die ihm bis in seine späten Jahre erhalten blieb, lassen offensichtliche Parallelen erkennen.[9]

EDITORISCHE GESTALTUNG

Sofern erforderlich, wurden *ossia*-Lesarten von ihren Originaltonarten transponiert. Alle fraglichen musikalischen Varianten wurden mit Fußnoten versehen. Binde- und Haltebögen (sowie vervollständigte Bindebögen) der Herausgeber sind gestrichelt, andere editorische Zusätze stehen in eckigen Klammern. In runden Klammern notierte Warnungsakzidenzien wurden den Quellen entnommen. Rund eingeklammert sind zudem überflüssige Atemzeichen, die sich lediglich in einigen Quellen finden, sowie nützliche Dynamikangaben und andere Angaben aus Sekundärquellen (Ausführungen siehe **Kritischer Kommentar**).

London und Paris, 2017

Roy Howat und Emily Kilpatrick
(Übersetzung: Lore Horlamus)

---

[1] Maurice Ravel, *Les Mélodies de Gabriel Fauré*, La Revue musicale 3 (Oktober 1922), in: Arbie Orenstein (Hrsg.), *Maurice Ravel: Lettres, écrits, entretiens* (Paris: Flammarion 1990), S. 325.

[2] Die Veröffentlichung der dritten Sammlung im Jahr 1908 erfolgte zeitgleich mit der Neuausgabe der ersten und zweiten Sammlung durch Hamelle (1887 hatte dieser die erste Sammlung von Choudens abgekauft und davon 1890 eine Fassung für die hohe Stimmlage herausgegeben), wobei eine gewisse inhaltliche Umverteilung erfolgte; siehe **Kritischer Kommentar**.

[3] Eingehende Erörterungen dessen und anderer für die vorliegende Ausgabe wesentlicher editorischer Aspekte finden sich in den von den Herausgebern dieser Gesamtausgabe verfassten Artikeln *Editorial Challenges in the Early Songs of Gabriel Fauré* und *Gabriel Fauré's Middle-Period Songs*.

[4] Diese finden sich nur in der zweiten und dritten Sammlung Hamelles ab op. 18. Auch war die Tonhöhe zu damaliger Zeit in Europa noch nicht standardisiert – sie unterschied sich über die Ländergrenzen hinweg mitunter um einen Halbton oder mehr –, obwohl sie während Faurés Berufsleben in Frankreich (durch einen Parlamentsbeschluss im Jahr 1859) auf a' = 435 Hz festgelegt wurde, also etwas tiefer als der heutige Standard-Kammerton, der bei 440 Hz oder etwas höher liegt.

[5] Verschiedene dieser Zeitzeugenberichte von Familie und Musikerkollegen Faurés zitiert Roy Howat in: *The Art of French Piano Music* (London und New Haven: Yale UP 2009), S. 247 und im Allgemeinen in den Kapiteln 17, 18 und 21.

[6] Zitiert nach Abraham (Hrsg.), *Un Art de l'interprétation*, S. 199 und 212–13 und teilweise nach Bannerman (Hrsg.), *The Singer as Interpreter*, S. 80–82; Letztere bringt eine spezifische Quelle an, welche die Anweisung „*(sans ralentir)*" in Takt 46 der vorliegenden Ausgabe veranlasst hat. Eine Violinistin und Kollegin Faurés, Hélène Jourdan-Morhange, bekräftigte diese Eigenschaft mit einer Anekdote über eine (nicht namentlich genannte) Sängerin, die an Phrasenenden innehielt und schmachtete: Eines Tages von Fauré bei einem Nachmittagskonzert begleitet, war sie „schockiert, sich vom Klavier angetrieben auf einer wellenlosen Straße wiederzufinden... auf der Autobahn der Zukunft!" (Jourdan-Morhange, *Mes amis musiciens*, S. 22f.).

[7] Vgl. Bannerman (Hrsg.), *The Singer as Interpreter*, S. 84–88 und Abraham, *Un Art de l'interprétation*, S. 31, 40 und 212.

[8] Vladimir Jankélévitch (*Gabriel Fauré et ses mélodies*, S. 49) machte eine ähnliche Beobachtung: „Dennoch ist nichts davon tragisch zu sehen. Fauré war immun gegenüber der Welle der Neurasthenie, die mit Duparc und Chausson über Frankreich hereinzubrechen begann [...] und die Melancholie in *Tristesse* ist nicht allzu ernst."

[9] Die Schwiegertochter des Komponisten erinnerte ihn so: „Als fröhlicher Südländer neigte Fauré zu Scherzen" (*Brève rencontre avec Blanche Fauré-Fremiet*, in: *Journal de Vichy*, 28. Juni 1958). Hélène Jourdan-Morhange beschrieb ihn als jemanden, der im Geiste stets ein „Straßenjunge" [*l'esprit gavroche*] geblieben sei (*Mes amis musiciens*, S. 24). In einigen Erinnerungen, die Fauré mit Ende Siebzig niederschrieb, schildert er mit unverstellter Freude die Jugendstreiche, die er mit seinen Klassenkameraden den Lehrern der École Niedermeyer spielte (*Souvenirs*, in: *La Revue musicale* 4/11, spezielle Fauré-Ausgabe, 1. November 1922, S. 3–9).

Vorwort zu Band 2

Dieser Band umfasst Gabriel Faurés Lieder ab 1884.[1] Angefangen bei den gefälligen Vertonungen der Lyrik Armand Silvestres über die reiche Chromatik der 1890er-Jahre bis hin zur nahezu aphoristischen Kürze einiger seiner letzten Lieder bietet die Sammlung eine faszinierende Reise durch Faurés kreative reife Phase.

Nachdem Faurés Schaffen zwischen 1862 und 1882 vor allem durch die Komposition von Liedern geprägt war, sollten diese erstmals für zwei Jahre in den Hintergrund treten, ehe er sich im Mai 1884 wieder der Liedkomposition widmete. Innerhalb von drei Wochen vollendete er vier Lieder, die er in op. 39 zusammenfasste. Bei den ersten drei Titeln handelt es sich um Vertonungen Armand Silvestres, dessen Lyrik bereits den meisten seiner vorangegangenen Gruppen aus drei Liedern zugrunde lag (op. 18, 23 und 27 aus den Jahren 1878–82; siehe *Complete Songs / Sämtliche Lieder*, Band 1). Das bezaubernd melodische *Aurore* eröffnet den Zyklus, gefolgt vom außerordentlich erregten *Fleur jetée*. Mit *Le Pays de Rêves* kehrt die Ruhe zurück, doch unter der täuschend einfachen Oberfläche des Liedes verbergen sich eine Reihe gewagter harmonischer Ausflüge, die bereits einen Ausblick auf die kommenden drei Jahrzehnte geben. In seinem Text ergründet Silvestre mit der Reise in ein idyllisches Land eine Metapher seiner Epoche: eine Fantasie, die durch Antoine Watteaus berühmtes Gemälde *Einschiffung nach Kythera* aus dem Jahr 1717 beflügelt und in Baudelaires Gedicht „L'Invitation au voyage" („Die Einladung zur Reise"), das Faurés Freunde Duparc und Chabrier 1870 vertont hatten, wiedererweckt wurde. Für das letzte Lied des op. 39 griff Fauré zum wiederholten Mal auf Leconte de Lisle zurück, dessen Vorliebe für das Exotische ihn immer wieder zu konzentrierter Schönheit und harmonischem Reichtum inspirierte.

1886 lernte Fauré einen der berühmtesten Schöngeister der Epoche, Comte Robert de Montesquiou, kennen. Dieser galt als begeisterter Wagnerianer und identifizierte sich stark mit dem französischen Symbolismus. Montesquiou inspirierte zunächst Joris-Karl Huysmans in seinem Roman *À rebours* zur Figur des Des Esseintes und später Marcel Proust in *À la recherche du temps perdu* zur Figur des Baron Charlus. Als ebenso enthusiastischer Bewunderer der Musik Faurés organisierte er im Frühjahr 1887 ein Konzert, das sich ganz dessen Werk widmete. Zudem schien er sich selbst zum informellen literarischen Berater Faurés ernannt zu haben und machte den Komponisten mit der dunkleren, komplexeren Lyrik Villiers de L'Isle-Adams und Paul Verlaines vertraut.[2] Faurés zwei Villiers-Vertonungen, *Nocturne* und *Les Présents* (op. 43 Nr. 2 und op. 46 Nr. 1), entstammen den sieben Gedichten aus Villiers Sammlung *Contes cruels* aus dem Jahr 1883 (die darüber hinaus auch Prosaschriften umfasst). Obwohl diese offenbar als zusammengehörige Lieder gedacht waren – für beide sind zueinander passende Abschriften erhalten, die Fauré 1892 nach der Veröffentlichung mit einem Abstand von wenigen Tagen erstellte – erschienen sie in verschiedenen Opusgruppen. Dies mag daran liegen, dass sie beide eine kontemplative Stimmung vermitteln.

Auf willkürliche Weise wurde *Nocturne* eigentlich unvereinbar mit *Noël* (einer *Cantique*, wie weiter unten ausgeführt) in einem Opus zusammengefasst, während das Montesquiou gewidmete *Les Présents* ein passendes Opuspaar mit Faurés erster Verlaine-Vertonung *Clair de lune* bildet. *Clair de lune* entstand innerhalb weniger Wochen nach der *Pavane* op. 50 im Herbst 1887. Die beiden Stücke wurden erstmals im April 1888 zusammen aufgeführt (und als Zugabe wiederholt).[3] Der Untertitel von *Clair de lune*, „Menuet" – der einzige Tanztitel, den ein Lied Faurés jemals trug –, unterstreicht dessen Ähnlichkeit mit der *Pavane*: Beide Stücke haben eine ausgedehnte instrumentale Einleitung, gefolgt von einer „obligaten Singstimme" (wie Graham Johnson sie treffend beschrieb) über einer im Wesentlichen autonomen Musik, wobei Stimme und Begleitung in den entscheidenden Momenten „wie durch Zufall" verschmelzen.[4]

Die Orchesterpremiere von *Clair de lune* erfolgte mit dem Tenor Maurice Bagès de Trigny, der von Mitte der 1880er-Jahre bis zu seinem frühzeitigen Tod im Jahr 1908 als einer der führenden Liedinterpreten in den Pariser Salons und am Société Nationale tätig war. Der Komponist Pierre de Breville, ein langjähriger Weggefährte von Bagès, erinnerte sich 1946, wie Fauré Bagès bei einer von Henri Duparcs *Soirées* zum ersten Mal *Nell* und *Après un rêve* singen hörte:

> Fauré war bezaubert vom ausdrucksstarken Timbre seiner Stimme, von seinem unvergleichlichen Vortrag, seiner Musikalität. „Singen Sie noch ein weiteres Lied von mir?", fragte er ihn. „Ich liebe und singe sie alle", antwortete Maurice Bagès, und ab diesem Tag wählte Fauré ihn zu seinem besten Interpreten, buchte ihn für die Premieren von *Clair de lune* und *Au cimetière* an der Société nationale und bat ihn, ihn auf seine erste Englandreise nach London zu begleiten, um dort seine Werke bekannt zu machen.[5]

Einen flüchtigen Einblick in diese enge Zusammenarbeit gewährt ein Brief von Marcel Proust an Paul Lavallée vom 30. September 1894: „Bagès hatte seinen gesamten Fauré bei mir liegen lassen, aber die Hälfte waren Manuskripte von Fauré und der Rest gedruckt, jedoch mit Widmungen, und ich hatte solche Angst, diese zu beschädigen, dass ich alles zurückschickte."[6]

Im November 1888 schrieb Fauré an die Comtesse Greffulhe:

Ich habe drei neue, sehr fröhliche Lieder komponiert!!! Die Titel lauten:
1. *Au cimetière*! (Richepin)
2. *Larmes*! id.
3. *Spleen*! (Verlaine)

Für eines von ihnen [*Au cimetière*] habe ich versucht, eine sehr einfache Begleitung nur für die rechte Hand zu schreiben, doch nach zehn Takten wurde die Hilfe der linken Hand notwendig, und nach zwanzig Takten häufen sich die Schwierigkeiten für beide Hände! Ein weiterer Pflasterstein für den Weg in die Hölle![7]

Maurice Bagès' sängerisches Können zeigt sich zweifelsfrei in den Jean-Richepin-Vertonungen *Larmes* und *Au cimetière*, deren ungewöhnlich opernhafter Charakter möglicherweise auf Faurés Wallfahrt nach Bayreuth im Sommer desselben Jahres zurückzuführen ist. Wie Graham Johnson plausibel nahelegt, könnte Faurés Interesse an diesem ungewöhnlichen Lyriker durch dessen Zusammenarbeit mit Emmanuel Chabrier geweckt worden sein, für den Richepin das Libretto zu *La Sulamite* schrieb und jenes zu *Le Roi malgré lui* als Ghostwriter verfasste.[8] *Au cimetière* wurde erstmals in der sehr hohen Tonart e-Moll veröffentlicht. In späteren Ausgaben für die hohe Stimme wurde dies jedoch angesichts der anspruchsvoll hohen Tessitur und des anhaltenden *forte* des *declamato*-Mittelteils zu d-Moll geändert. Wenn Bagès dies auch souverän meisterte, könnte es die Mühe unbedeutenderer Sänger gewesen sein, die den sonst bewundernden Proust dieses Lied als „vraiment affreux" („wirklich scheußlich") empfinden ließ.[9]

Spleen stammt aus Verlaines Sammlung *Romances sans paroles* aus dem Jahr 1874 (in der es keinen Titel trägt; Fauré übernahm den Titel aus einem anderen Gedicht der Sammlung[10]). Versprühten Verlaines *Fêtes galantes* noch eine berauschte, sardonische Stimmung, die sich im metrischen Fluss von *Clair de lune* niederschlug, so besteht *Spleen* aus kurzen, größtenteils monosyllabischen Zeilen, die an das erbarmungslose Ostinato eines prasselnden Regens erinnern, das sich auch in Faurés Vertonung wiederfindet.

La Rose entstand 1890, zwei Jahre nach den anderen Liedern seines Opus. Der Untertitel „Ode anacréontique" ist eine Reminiszenz an den altgriechischen Dichter Anakreon, der in seiner Lyrik die Liebe und den Wein pries (obgleich dem Gedicht nicht das für den anakreontischen Vers charakteristische siebensilbige Versmaß zugrunde liegt). Das Lied ist eine weitere einmalige Vertonung eines Gedichts von Leconte de Lisle und wurde zu op. 51 offenbar noch hinzugefügt, weil sich Hamelle mit der Veröffentlichung der ersten drei Lieder sehr viel Zeit gelassen hatte.[11] Was dieses Lied mit den anderen Titeln des Opus verbindet, wird durch seine Widmung an Bagès ersichtlich. Dass auch *La Rose* zweifelsohne für Bagès' Stimme konzipiert war, wird insbesondere auf der letzten Seite deutlich, wo die gesanglichen Herausforderungen anscheinend die Möglichkeiten anderer früherer Interpreten überstiegen. In der überarbeiteten dritten Sammlung aus dem Jahr 1908 ist dieses Ende gesanglich weniger anspruchsvoll gestaltet, jedoch verursacht diese Fassung neue Probleme: nicht zuletzt einen Bruch in der Harmonieabfolge um Takt 48 herum sowie gelegentliche Unterschiede zwischen den Ausgaben für die hohe und die mittlere Stimme.[12] In der vorliegenden Ausgabe sind sowohl das Ende von 1890 als auch jenes von 1908 abgedruckt. Allerdings war das 1890 entstandene Ende auch nicht Faurés erste Version, wie er Bagès im Herbst desselben Jahres in einem Brief erklärte:

Mein lieber Freund, du hast recht daran getan, mir deine Meinung kundzutun, doch ich glaube, dass ich dir hätte helfen können, das neue Ende anders zu verstehen, hätten wir es uns zusammen angesehen. Zunächst einmal (womöglich gibt es auch einen Fehler in der Abschrift) müssen die Worte „avec la beauté" mit einem Diminuendo gesungen werden.

Sa - lu - a la fleur a - vec la beau - té.

Dann muss die Begleitung <u>voll</u>, jedoch <u>sanft</u> klingen; das Pedal ist notwendig, damit das Bass-Arpeggio richtig fortklingen kann und nur dieses soll beide Male akzentuiert werden:

Das erste Ende hat mich nicht zufriedengestellt: Wäre ich zwei Tage später in Cuy angekommen, hätte ich das Lied nicht in der Form mitgebracht, wie du es dort gesehen hast. Dieses Ende schien mir zu verkürzt und du musst bedenken, dass ich die Periode <u>salua la Fleur</u> [bereits] um einen Takt verlängert hatte. Aber das hat mich nicht zufriedengestellt! Es hat mir zu schaffen gemacht, bis ich die Änderung abgeschlossen hatte.

Ich denke, dass du mir in einer Weile, wenn du die erste Version vergessen hast, zustimmen wirst. Ich muss hinzufügen, dass S[aint-]Saëns nur die zweite Version kennt und nicht geschockt schien: Daher habe ich den Eindruck, dass dich das zweite Ende nicht überrascht hätte, hättest du nicht bereits begonnen gehabt, das erste zu singen.

All dies heißt nicht, dass ich mich nicht irren könnte. Aber was mir diesbezüglich Sicherheit gibt, ist, dass mich dieses beunruhigende Gefühl erst verließ, nachdem ich mein Schlusswort beendet hatte.[13]

Es war zweifelsohne Maurice Bagès, auf den Fauré ein Jahr zuvor in einem Brief an den Dichter Edmond Haraucourt (vom 27. September 1889) angespielt hatte: „Möchten Sie am Sonntag, den 6. Oktober, zum Mittag nach Bougival kommen, wo ein junger Freund von mir die beiden Shylock-Lieder singen wird? Ich habe eine Kopie davon machen und ihm zukommen lassen, damit er an ihnen arbeiten kann."[14]

Obwohl Fauré nur eine Oper vollendete (*Pénélope*, 1913), fühlte er sich wie die meisten französischen Komponisten fortwährend zum Theater hingezogen. Zwischen 1888 und 1898 komponierte er Bühnenmusik für mehrere Theaterstücke: *Caligula* (1888), *Shylock* (1889), *La Passion* (1890),[15] *Le Bourgeois Gentilhomme* (1893) und *Pelléas et Mélisande* (1898). *Shylock*, eine von E. Haraucourt vorgenommene Adaption von Shakespeares *Der Kaufmann von Venedig*, wurde erstmals im Dezember 1889 im Théâtre de l'Odéon aufgeführt. Die Uraufführung der Konzertversion der Bühnenmusik Faurés fand im Mai des folgenden Jahres statt. Die beiden darin enthaltenen Lieder, „Chanson" und „Madrigal", finden keine Entsprechung in Shakespeares Theaterstück. Bei beiden handelt es sich um Serenaden, wobei die erste von einem Sänger hinter den Kulissen für Jessica und die zweite in Akt 2 vom Prinzen von Aragon unter Portias Fenster gesungen wird. (In der abgedruckten Version von „Chanson" wurde die Dynamik für die Stimme zu Beginn des Liedes der Theaterpartitur übernommen. Eine Konzertaufführung kann eine dezente Anpassung erforderlich machen.) Die vorliegende Ausgabe beinhaltet als Option eine verlängerte Einleitung zu „Chanson", die in den Sammlungen Hamelles nicht enthalten ist. Im **Anhang 1** befindet sich ein Auszug für Stimme und Klavier einer bisher unveröffentlichten Zugabeversion von „Chanson" aus den Manuskripten für Orchester, die sich durch eine dritte Strophe mit (leicht gewagten) Wortspielen auszeichnet.

Eine dritte „Sérénade" in diesem Band stammt aus Faurés Bühnenmusik zu Molières *Le Bourgeois Gentilhomme*, einem Auftragswerk, das Saint-Saëns (der zu diesem Zeitpunkt mit der Oper *Phryné* beschäftigt war) seinem ehemaligen Schüler und Freund zuschob. „Ich mag die Idee, aber kann ich das?? Das wird nicht einfach", antwortete Fauré im September 1892.[16] Das Theater (Eden-Théâtre) ging letzten Endes im März 1893 bankrott, doch aus dem abgebrochenen Projekt ging nicht nur dieses Lied hervor, sondern auch eines der bekanntesten kurzen Stücke Faurés, eine *Sicilienne*, die er später für Cello und Klavier umarbeitete und 1898 auch für eine Spielzeit in seine Bühnenmusik zu Maurice Maeterlincks *Pelléas et Mélisande* in London integrierte. Laut englischer Übersetzung von Jack Mackail stammte das Bühnenbild dieser Inszenierung vom präraffaelitischen Künstler Edward Burne-Jones, und die Rolle der Mélisande spielte die überragende Schauspielerin Patrick Campbell [geb. Beatrice Stella Tanner]. Frau Campbell persönlich beauftragte dieses Werk, nachdem sie nach einer ersten Anfrage an Debussy – von dem bekannt war, dass er seine auf Maeterlincks Schauspiel basierende Oper vollendet hatte – eine eindeutige Ablehnung erhalten hatte.[17] Fauré persönlich dirigierte die Uraufführung im Prince of Wales Theatre am 21. Juni 1898, vier Tage nach dem Tod von Burne-Jones. „Mélisande's Song", die einzige Gesangseinlage, stammt aus der „Turm"-Szene im dritten Akt.[18] Fauré vertonte nur den englischen Text, wobei er der Sprache nur rudimentär mächtig war (im Manuskript vertonte er „hope" ursprünglich mit zwei Silben). Die vorliegende Ausgabe bietet entsprechende Lösungen für zwei Stellen, an denen die Textunterlage nicht gebrauchsfähig ist. Maeterlincks französischer Originaltext hat eine so anders geartete Silbentrennung (einschließlich der in der englischen Version nicht vorhandenen Zeilenwiederholungen), dass er nicht mit der Singstimme des Liedes vereinbar ist. 1906 jedoch überarbeitete Fauré dieses Lied und unterlegte es mit einem anderen französischen Text. Diese Fassung trägt den Titel „Crépuscule" und steht als neuntes Lied seines Zyklus *La Chanson d'Ève*, in dem er die Lyrik eines Landsmanns und Freundes von Maeterlinck, Charles van Lerberghe, vertonte.

Prison und *Soir* sind Faurés letzte Kompositionen von 1894 – ein außergewöhnliches Jahr, in dem er *La Bonne Chanson* und drei größere Klavierwerke (die Vierte Valse-Caprice, die Sechste Nocturne und die Fünfte Barcarolle) sowie eine Reihe geistlicher Stücke für Chor vollendete. Die vorliegende Ausgabe enthält wieder die korrekte Opusnummer der Lieder. In späteren Ausgaben hatte Hamelle die Opusnummer aufgrund äußerer Faktoren, die im **Kritischen Bericht (Veröffentlichungsgeschichte)** erläutert sind, mehrere Male geändert. Mit *Prison* vertonte Fauré zum letzten Mal ein Gedicht Paul Verlaines. Es besitzt eine emotionale Sprengkraft, die in den französischen *mélodies* ihresgleichen sucht: die läutende Klavierbegleitung so starr wie die Gitterstäbe eines Gefängnisses. Buchstäblich schlägt sie die Sekunden (entsprechend der Metronomangabe Faurés) bis in die verheerende Schlusslinie „Qu'as-tu fait de ta jeunesse?" hinein.

Soir – Faurés erste Vertonung eines Gedichtes von Albert Samain – bildet ein Pendant zu den Verlaine-Jahren des Komponisten. Es lässt musikalische Parallelen zu zwei kurz zuvor veröffentlichten Werken erkennen: zur *Romance* op. 69 (ein Stück aus früheren Jahren, das Fauré für die Veröffentlichung im Herbst 1894 überarbeitet hatte), und zur Sechsten Nocturne op. 63 (ebenso in des-Moll und mit einem eng verwandten Ende). Wie auch *La Bonne Chanson* ist *Soir* eng mit der Sängerin Emma Bardac verknüpft, mit der Fauré in den frühen 1890er-Jahren eine leidenschaftliche Affäre verband. (Mme Bardac sollte später Claude Debussy heiraten.) Anfang 1894 hatte Fauré ihr eine kurz zuvor veröffentlichte Ausgabe der Gedichte Samains, *Au jardin de l'Infante*, geschenkt, die die Widmung „Ich bitte Sie, dieses Buch anzunehmen und die Gedichte auszuwählen, die Sie singen möchten" trug.[19] Zwei jener Gedichte dieser Ausgabe, die Bleistiftanmerkungen von Mme Bardac enthalten, sind „Élégie" – aus dem Fauré drei Strophen entnahm, die er als *Soir* vertonte – und „Arpège". Als Samain sie Anfang 1896 *Soir* singen hörte, schrieb er an seine Schwester:

Ich traf besagte Mme Bardac bei Fauré, eine junge Frau um die Dreißig. Eine hübsche, elegante Frau von Welt; ihr Mann ist ein Bankier. [...] Nach dem Abendessen sang sie [*Soir*]. Fauré sagte zu mir: „Sie werden es nie besser gesungen hören." Und sie verfügt wahrlich über ein außergewöhnliches Gefühl für Nuancen und hat vor allem einen unverfälschten Ausdruck.[20]

Nahezu drei Jahre unternahm Fauré keinen weiteren Versuch, Samain für eine Stimme zu vertonen (wobei er in der Zwischenzeit das Duett *Pleurs d'or* komponierte). *Arpège* und die im selben Opus enthaltene Vertonung eines Gedichts von Leconte de Lisles, *Le Parfum impérissable*, stammen aus dem Spätsommer 1897. Die flötenähnliche Melodie und die munteren Rhythmen von *Arpège* erinnern an die oben erwähnte *Sicilienne*, *Arpège* wiederum zeigt eine abenteuerlichere Verwendung des Tonmaterials. Im getragenen Tempo von *Le Parfum impérissable* wiederum verdichtet sich eine harmonische Kühnheit ähnlich der von *Prison*, obwohl es anstatt offenkundig dramatisch zu sein eine ruhige Intensität verströmt.

Mit diesem op. 76 kehrte Fauré nur kurzzeitig in die Gefilde der *mélodie* zurück. Abgesehen von „Mélisande's Song" wagte er sich in den kommenden fünf Jahren an kein weiteres Lied. Dies stellte die längste Pause in seinem Liedschaffen dar. Er war nun mit seinen neuen Pflichten als Professor für Komposition am Pariser Konservatorium und der Komposition der „Tragédie lyrique" *Prométhée* (1900, ein opernhaftes Werk) beschäftigt. Mit *Accompagnement* (März 1902) wandte sich Fauré schließlich wieder der Liedkomposition zu. Er komponierte das Stück für Mimi [Émilie] Girette Risler, eine begabte Amateursängerin, die im ersten Jahrzehnt des Jahrhunderts zu seinen Lieblingsinterpretinnen zählte. In ihrem Tagebuch dokumentierte Mlle Girette (die sie damals noch war) neben anderen musikalischen Begegnungen den Fortschritt „ihres" Liedes und bietet einen überraschend intimen Einblick in Faurés Arbeitswelt und kompositorischen Fortschritt:

Dienstag, 7. Januar 1902

Cortot sagte [zu Fauré], dass er etwas für Klavier und Orchester komponieren solle; er [Fauré] sagte zu mir: „Ich werde nichts tun, bis ich ein Lied für Sie geschrieben habe", worauf ich antwortete, dass dies eine der größten Freuden meines Lebens wäre. „Nur habe ich noch nicht die *Lyrik* gefunden, denn ich weiß genau, was Ihnen gefällt", sagte er – und ich antwortete erneut, dass mir der Text ganz egal wäre, dass mir vor allem an der Musik gelegen ist. Doch für ihn bilden Text und Musik eine Einheit, und es sind die Worte, die ihn inspirieren. Das ist offensichtlich in seiner Musik, wo alles bedacht, genau und ausgefeilt ist.[21]

Samstag, 8. März 1902

Er hat mit „meinem Lied" begonnen, obwohl er mir nicht sagen will, welches Gedicht er letztlich ausgewählt hat! Musikalisch gesehen ist es im Stil von *Soir* gehalten. Ich habe ihm gesagt, wie sehr ich diese Art von Liedern mag – er denkt beim Schreiben an mich, an meine Stimme[.] Er hat mir gesagt, dass er zuerst in seinem Kopf komponiert, *von den Worten ausgehend*, es ist die Lyrik, die ihn inspiriert – die Melodie entwickelt sich Stück für Stück in ihm, sie reift nahezu unbewusst, und anschließend kommt die Arbeit, sie niederzuschreiben, was keinesfalls der leichteste Teil ist.[22]

Samstag, 29. März 1902

Welch ein unvergessliches Datum dies für mich ist!! Ich habe „mein Lied" von Fauré erhalten! Er hat es einmal für mich gesungen, dann sang ich es.[23]

2. April

Niemand in der Welt außer ihm und mir kennt *Accompagnement*. Das gefällt mir sehr. Er sagte mir, dass es sich für ihn so anfühle, als wäre es ein kleiner Teil von mir und dass er diesen *in seiner Gänze* integriert habe.[24]

Fauré hatte sicherlich Mimis musikalische Intelligenz im Hinterkopf, als er im November 1902 der Comtesse Greffulhe schrieb: „Ich bin mir sicher, dass es unter meinen Liedern aus den letzten Jahren viele gibt, die Sie noch nicht kennen! Ich träume davon, sie Ihnen mit den perfekten Sängern zu Gehör zu bringen, doch ich kenne keinen aus dem Kreise der Berufsmusiker. Es sind die Amateuere, die mich am besten verstehen und zum Ausdruck bringen können."[25]

Obwohl Fauré das *Accompagnement* als erstes komponierte, wurde es das dritte Stück in seinem op. 85: *Dans la forêt de septembre* und *La Fleur qui va sur l'eau*, beide zu Texten von Catulle Mendès, kamen im September 1902 hinzu. Sowohl von *Dans la forêt de septembre* als auch von *Accompagnement* sind jeweils zwei Autographen erhalten. Offenbar arbeitete Fauré bei beiden Liedern parallel an zwei Manuskripten, denn jedes weist an unterschiedlichen Stellen abgeänderte Lesarten auf. Ein weiteres für diese Gruppe entworfenes Lied, *Dans le ciel clair*, wäre Faurés letzte Vertonung eines Gedichts von Leconte de Lisle gewesen. Er arbeitete im selben Jahr daran, verwarf es jedoch. Eine Übertragung der erhaltenen Fragmente findet sich im **Anhang 2** der vorliegenden Ausgabe.

Mimi Girette inspirierte Fauré zu einem weiteren Geschenk, *Le plus doux chemin* (op. 87 Nr. 1), das anlässlich ihrer Eheschließung mit Édouard Risler entstand. Ebenso wenig wie *Le Ramier*, das Fauré letztlich als zweites Stück in das Opus aufnahm, besitzt *Le plus doux chemin* bei weitem nicht das ausgesprochen chromatische, ausgedehnte Fundament der Lieder des op. 85, doch der schlichtere Satz zeigt Faurés freizügigere Verwendung des Tonmaterials in höchst konzentrierter Form. Mit diesen Liedern widmete sich Fauré ein letztes Mal der Lyrik Armand Silvestres. Beide tragen sie den von Silvestre gewählten gattungsmäßigen Untertitel „Madrigal" und erinnern in dieser Hinsicht an ein früheres Hochzeitsgeschenk, das Fauré seinem Komponistenfreund André Messager machte: dem *Madrigal* op. 35 (1883) für vier Solostimmen, dessen Text aus derselben Silvestre-Sammlung stammt. Später orchestrierte Fauré das *Madrigal*, doch wie Jean-Michel Nectoux bemerkte, blieb er dabei, dieses Stück mit vier Solostimmen aufgeführt wissen zu wollen – auch wenn Hamelle angab, dass eine Aufführung mit vierstimmigem Chor ebenso möglich sei (zu Faurés Lebzeiten wurde es bisweilen mit acht Sängern, jeweils zwei in einer Stimme, aufgeführt).[26] Es mag zu Messagers privater Erheiterung gewesen sein, dass Fauré das Eingangsthema des *Madrigals* Bachs Kantate *Aus tiefer Not schrei' ich zu dir* entnahm (vielleicht mit einem Hauch verschmitzter Ironie), einem Thema, das Bach auch in seiner ersten dis-Moll-Fuge des *Wohltemperierten Klaviers* verwendete.[27]

1906 kündigte Fauré erbittert seinen Vertrag bei Hamelle und unterschrieb einen neuen bei Henri Heugel, ehe er 1910 schließlich zu Jacques Durand wechselte. Seine drei letzten, niemals in die historischen Hamelle-Sammlungen aufgenommenen Lieder sind nach wie vor wenig bekannt. *Le Don silencieux* (op. 92) ging 1906 als Frucht einiger konzentrierter Tage am Ende eines glücklichen Sommeraufenthalts in Vitznau bei Lucerne hervor. An seine Frau schrieb Fauré:

Da es meinen vorangegangen Werken oder irgendetwas anderem, das ich kenne, überhaupt nicht ähnelt, bin ich sehr zufrieden. Außerdem gibt es noch nicht einmal ein Hauptthema. Es ist so frei gestaltet, dass es Théodore Dubois beträchtlich aus der Fassung bringen würde. Es bringt nach und nach die Worte zum Ausdruck, wie sie sich entfalten; es beginnt, es entwickelt sich und endet, nichts weiter; und doch ist es *ein Ganzes*. Aber jetzt werde ich spitzfindig.[28]

In der veröffentlichten Sammlung *L'Anémone des mers* trägt das Gedicht keinen Titel. Fauré gab seiner Vertonung anfangs den Titel *Offrande*. An Octave Maus schrieb er:

Wenn Jean Dominique wegen des Titels, den ich mir aufgrund des nachdrücklichen Wunsches meines Verlegers ausdenken musste, *schmollt*, dann sagen Sie ihm, dass die (im Übrigen sehr schönen) dreizehnfüßigen Zeilen, mit denen er seine Poesie geschmückt hat, mir sehr zu schaffen gemacht haben! Ich hoffe jedoch, sie geschmeidig vertont zu haben.[29]

(Fauré war offenbar noch nicht bewusst, dass Jean Dominique ein Pseudonym der belgischen Dichterin Marie Closset war.)

Mit *Chanson* (1906) kehrte Fauré zum offeneren Satz der späteren Silvestre-„Madrigale" zurück. Dies war Faurés letztes alleinstehendes Lied für Heugel (für den er gerade begonnen hatte, den Zyklus *La Chanson d'Ève* zu schreiben) und sein nahezu letztes Lied überhaupt. 1919 wurde er – mit großem Widerwillen – verpflichtet, das Siegergedicht aus einem von *Le Figaro* veranstalteten Wettbewerb anlässlich des Endes des Ersten Weltkriegs zu vertonen. Das Gedicht rühmte die Tapferkeit der französischen Soldaten (*Poilus*). Seiner Frau beschrieb Fauré den Text als „schreckliches kleines Gedicht" und fügte zwei Tage später hinzu, dass er das „furchtbare Wort" (*poilus*) in *soldats* umgeändert hatte – „Schade für die Dichterin, wenn sie es nicht mag! Ich mache ihr schon genug Ehre damit, wie es ist."[30] Trotz dessen, dass Fauré seinen besten musikalischen Willen demonstrierte und größtmögliche Anstrengungen unternahm (er strich das halbe Gedicht), zeichnet der geschmacklose Text von *C'est la Paix* für ein enttäuschendes Ende hinsichtlich seiner Komposition alleinstehender Lieder verantwortlich.[31] Wir können nur das Übermaß an Bescheidenheit bedauern, das den Komponisten 1924 dazu veranlasste, seine Vertonung von Pierre de Ronsards „Ronsard à son âme" zu zerreißen, als er hörte, dass sein früherer Schüler Maurice Ravel dasselbe Gedicht vertont hatte (beide hatten es als Beitrag für die Sonderausgabe der *La Revue musicale* zu Ehren des 400. Geburtstages des Dichters ausgewählt).[32]

Der vorliegende Band enthält Faurés zwei *Cantiques* zu geistigen Gedichten zweier Zeitgenossen des Komponisten: von Stéphan Bordèse (*En prière*) und vom Musikschriftsteller Victor Wilder (*Noël*). *En prière* wurde zuerst von Durand in *Les Contes mystiques*, einer Sammlung mit Vertonungen geistlicher Gedichte von Bordèse (einem Mitarbeiter Durands) aus dem Jahr 1890, veröffentlicht, ehe es 1897 in Hamelles zweite Sammlung der Lieder Faurés aufgenommen wurde.[33] Das 1885 komponierte *Noël* wurde erst 1908 als Lückenbüßer in die deutlich früher erschienene erste Sammlung integriert (von der Hamelle in einem komplizierten Versuch, drei Bände mit je 20 Liedern Faurés zusammenzustellen, willkürlich das frühere Lied *Barcarolle* herausgenommen hatte; siehe **Kritischen Bericht** unter **Veröffentlichungsgeschichte**). In einem langen Brief aus dem August 1907 protestierte Fauré vehement gegen die von Hamelle vorgenommene Umverteilung der Lieder: „Welchen Unterschied macht es aus, welche Bedeutung kann es haben, ob der 3. Band vierzehn oder fünfzehn Lieder umfasst?"[34] Fauré hätte *Noël* lieber ausgeklammert – teils wegen seines „hybriden Charakters" und teils „wegen seines Stils, der allem, was im 3. Band enthalten sein wird, sehr hinterher ist." Der dritte Band sollte seinem Wunsch zufolge nur Lieder ab op. 57 enthalten. (Dass Hamelle *Noël* schließlich in die erste Sammlung aufnahm, war vermutlich sein Versuch, dies zu berücksichtigen.) Gegen einen vorübergehenden Vorschlag Hamelles, Wilders „jämmerliche" Zeilen für *Noël* durch einen neuen Text von Charles Grandmougin (dessen Lyrik Fauré zuvor bereits in *Poème d'un jour* vertont hatte) zu ersetzen, legte der Komponist sein Veto ein:

> Die Lyrik Grandmougins [...] passt überhaupt nicht zur Musik. Ob gut oder mittelmäßig: Dies ist *Weihnachts*musik. Ihr naiver, ausdrucksloser Charakter, ihre Begleitung, die Ausdruck anhaltend *klingender* GLOCKEN ist, passt zu den ziemlich jämmerlichen Versen von Wilder, da diese letztendlich den *Charakter* der Musik inspiriert haben, ihre *Physiognomie*, ihr *Aussehen*.[35]

Im selben Brief betonte Fauré, dass die in der Einzelausgabe mit *ad libitum* überschriebene Harmoniumbegleitung „wirklich notwendig" war (womit er vermutlich bezweckte, dass Hamelle diese Stimme entweder mit abdruckt oder das Lied überhaupt nicht in die Sammlung aufnimmt). Die in der Hamelle-Sammlung fehlende Harmoniumstimme wurde in der vorliegenden Ausgabe wieder hinzugefügt.

Den Abschluss des vorliegenden Bandes bilden Faurés weltliche Lieder für mehr als eine Solostimme. Die Duette *Puisqu'ici bas toute âme* und *Tarentelle* wurden 1875 von Claudie Chamerot und Marianne Viardot, den Töchtern der großen Mezzosporanistin Pauline Viardot, uraufgeführt. Diese waren selbst exzellente Interpretinnen, wie die virtuose Singstimme von *Tarentelle* deutlich macht (der Text stammt von Marc Monnier, einem Dichter aus dem Bekanntenkreis der Viardots).[36] Obwohl vorgebracht wurde, dass Fauré *Puisqu'ici bas* – eine Vertonung eines Gedichts von Victor Hugo – auf Grundlage einer früheren Version für nur eine Singstimme für die Viardot-Schwestern adaptierte hat, sind die Kompositionsweise der vorliegenden Singstimmen und die Struktur des Stückes der eines Duetts eigen.[37] Das deutlich später komponierte *Pleurs d'or* besitzt die gleiche fließende Chromatik wie Faurés andere Samain-Vertonung aus dieser Zeit, *Arpège*. Es wurde im Mai 1896 für ein Konzert in London komponiert, in dem Berichten zufolge eine obligate Violinstimme beteiligt war. Diese ist jedoch nicht mehr auffindbar.[38] Die zwei unterschiedlichen Opusnummern, die das Lied erhielt, resultieren aus Missverständnissen zwischen den beiden ursprünglichen Verlegern (siehe **Kritischen Bericht**, **Veröffentlichungsgeschichte**).

Musikalische Quellen

Für die Mehrheit der Lieder des vorliegenden Bandes dienten die 1908 von Hamelle herausgebrachte dritte sowie die überarbeitete erste und zweite Sammlung der Lieder Faurés als Hauptquellen für die Editionsarbeit, wobei andere Quellen wichtige Details ergänzen. Für die aus den Ausflügen in die Theaterwelt stammenden Lieder wurden darüber hinaus überlieferte Orchesterfassungen sowie einige Lieder, die Fauré für andere Zwecke orchestrierte, hinzugezogen. Für die nicht in den Hamelle-Sammlungen enthaltenen Lieder diente die jeweils erste Ausgabe als Hauptquelle, mit Ausnahme der zwei Lieder, die zu Faurés Lebzeiten nicht veröffentlicht wurden.

Aufeinanderfolgende Notenstiche und überarbeitete Neuausgaben verschiedener Lieder haben – insbesondere Dynamik und Artikulation betreffend – zu unzähligen Diskrepanzen zwischen den Ausgaben für die hohe und mittlere Stimme der Sammlungen Hamelles geführt, sodass keine einzige Quelle als maßgeblich stimmige Version angesehen werden kann. Ob in der vorliegenden Ausgabe in der jeweiligen Version für die hohe oder mittlere Stimmlage der Vorrang gegeben wurde, erfolgte in Abhängigkeit davon, welche der Quellen eine sorgfältigere Erstellung oder Revision erkennen ließ. Die jeweils gewählte Ausgangsquelle wurde durch Korrekturen und Revisionen aus anderen Quellen ergänzt.

Autographen sind für knapp über die Hälfte der im vorliegenden Band versammelten Lieder überliefert. Von ihnen dienten sechzehn für den Notenstich oder als wahrscheinliche Quellen für Abschriften, die ihrerseits dem Notenstich dienten. Zu weiteren autographen Quellen zählen Entwürfe (*Clair de lune*), Manuskripte für Orchester, Abschriften mit Anmerkungen Faurés und korrigierte Druckfahnen. Obwohl die meisten Manuskripte im Grunde durch die veröffentlichten Versionen abgelöst wurden, helfen sie, Druckfehler aufzuklären und Details bezüglich der Stimmführung und -anordnung aufzudecken.

Im gesamten Band sind stimmige Lesarten in *ossia*-Notenlinien oder Fußnoten angegeben; andere Varianten von Interesse sind im **Anhang 2** oder im **Kritischen Bericht** angeführt. Bot eine andere relevante Quelle wesentliche Korrekturen, so wurden diese in den Notentext aufgenommen; weniger grundlegende, jedoch nützliche Musizierhinweise aus Sekundärquellen (darunter Orchesterversionen) sind in Klammern notiert.

Tonarten

Alle von Hamelle veröffentlichten Sololieder Faurés bis op. 87 sowie das Duett *Pleurs d'or* sind in Ausgaben für die mittlere und hohe Stimme erschienen. In der vorliegenden Ausgabe wurden die Tonarten übernommen, die in den Hamelle-Sammlungen von 1908 festgelegten wurden. Das *Madrigal* op. 35 erfordert keine Transposition; für *Tarentelle* wiederum ist im Grunde keine möglich, da die hohe Tessitur den Charakter des Stückes bestimmt, während die zweite Stimme mehr zwischen Mezzosopran und Bariton angesiedelt ist.[39] Für die übrigen in nur einer Tonart veröffentlichten Lieder sowie für die zwei zu Faurés Lebzeiten unveröffentlicht gebliebenen Lieder haben die Herausgeber eine zweite Tonart gewählt.

Viele Lieder Faurés erschienen bei Hamelle einzeln in zusätzlichen Transpositionen: *Les Roses d'Ispahan* zum Beispiel wurde neben dem in Hamelles zweiter Sammlung gedruckten D- und E-Dur auch in B- und Des-Dur veröffentlicht. Der faszinierende Fall von *Nocturne* beleuchtet Faurés proaktive Herangehensweise beim Transponieren. Das Lied wurde 1886 zunächst in Es-Dur mit einem Einband, der ungewöhnlicherweise mit „pour / Contralto ou Basse" untertitelt ist, veröffentlicht. In einem späteren Autograph von 1892 steht es in Fis-Dur. Obwohl das Manuskript Hamelles Verlagsstempel trägt, wurde das Lied jedoch nie in dieser Tonart veröffentlicht.[40] Stattdessen erschien *Nocturne* in der zweiten Sammlung von 1897 für die mittlere Stimme in As und für die hohe Stimme in C, also eine Quarte beziehungsweise Sexte höher als im Original. Nirgendwo anders in Faurés Schaffen begegnen wir einer so weit auseinanderliegenden Transposition. Diese mit Sorgfalt ausgearbeiteten Transpositionen enthalten neue Elemente wie Anweisungen zum Pedalgebrauch und Metronomangaben sowie Phrasierungen in der Singstimme und andere Varianten bezüglich Dynamik und Satz, darunter einige hinzugefügte Ziernoten im Klavierbass. Am bemerkenswertesten und wiederum einzigartig in Faurés Liedschaffen ist jedoch, dass die Klavierstimme nicht auch nach oben, sondern nach unten transponiert wurde, wo sie die Singstimme folglich eine Oktave tiefer begleitet.

1902 notierte Mimi Girette in ihrem Tagebuch: „Niemand singt ihm [Fauré] jemals die *Nocturne* vor, und er mag sie; ich werde mit ihm daran arbeiten, doch er wird versuchen, mich dazu zu bringen, dass ich sie in der Originaltonart singe, die sehr tief ist, denn er mag sie im Kontraalt."⁴¹ Das mag der Grund sein, weshalb die Fassung für die mittlere Stimme in der Neuausgabe der zweiten Sammlung von 1908 wieder in der Ursprungstonart Es-Dur abgedruckt ist. Diese vielen Versionen von *Nocturne* bezeugen Faurés ernsthafte kompositorische Auseinandersetzung mit der Praxis (oder Kunst) der Liedtransposition, im Zuge derer er Tessitur, Timbre und Balance sehr überlegt ergründete. Vor dem Hintergrund der dargestellten Problematik und aufgrund der in der vorliegenden Ausgabe verfolgten Praktikabilität ist das Lied in der Ausgabe für die mittlere Stimme sowohl in der ursprünglichen, für den Kontraalt vorgesehenen Tonart Es-Dur als auch in Fis-Dur, wie es in Faurés Manuskript von 1892 zu finden ist, abgedruckt. In der Ausgabe für die hohe Stimme wiederum steht es in der Standardtonart für die hohe Stimme, C-Dur, sowie in jenem As-Dur, das der Sammlung für die mittlere Stimme von 1897 entnommen wurde.

AUFFÜHRUNGSHINWEISE

Die Lieder des vorliegenden Bandes spiegeln auf eindrucksvolle Weise Faurés kreative und professionelle Interaktionen mit Interpreten wie Maurice Bagès, Emma Bardac und Mimi Girette Risler, die allesamt seine Auswahl der Gedichte, seine Wahl der Form und die Gestaltung der Singstimme beeinflussten. Insbesondere die mit Anmerkungen versehenen Partituren Mimi Rislers bekräftigen die Aussagen anderer Kollegen Faurés und offenbaren einen dynamischen Kompositionsprozess mit kreativem und praktischem Austausch – eine Praxis, die die Philosophie der vorliegenden Ausgabe untermauert.

Neben den Bemerkungen im **Allgemeinen Vorwort** oben können Kenntnisse über Faurés Gewohnheiten und Aufführungspräferenzen einige Eigenarten bezüglich Notation und Edition seiner Lieder beleuchten. Er verwendet das *Allegretto* üblicherweise nahezu wie ein *Allegro*, wobei ersterem ein weniger kompakter Satz und ein leichterer Charakter zugrunde liegt (am deutlichsten zeigen dies die *Shylock*-Lieder, *Sérénade* und das *Madrigal* aus op. 35). Faurés häufige Verwendung des *Andante* – oft relativiert durch ein *quasi allegretto* oder gar ein *quasi adagio* – lässt auf moderate, fließende Tempi schließen, die das *andante* wörtlich als „gehend" und das *adagio* wörtlich als „gemächlich" verkörpern.

Insbesondere in den späteren Liedern bedingen die mit langsam bis moderat bezeichneten Tempi einen straffen harmonischen Rhythmus und erfordern häufig eine täuschend schnelle Gesangsdarbietung. Die dichten Verse von Liedern wie *Le Parfum impérissable*, *Accompagnement* und *Le Don silencieux* erfordern trotz ihres intimen, nahezu murmelnden Charakters eine fokussierte, energische Artikulation. In einem Brief an Robert Lortat schrieb Fauré 1919, dass *Le Don silencieux* vor allem „mit seiner wunderbaren Kunst der Wortfärbung" vorzutragen sei.⁴² Dem wohnt die Notwendigkeit inne, das Drama umzusetzen (*jouer le drame*), das Faurés Sohn Philippe als wesentlich für die Musik seines Vaters erachtete.⁴³ In *Fleur jetée*, *Au cimetière* oder *La fleur qui va sur l'eau* ist das *drame* offensichtlich, doch die ruhige, durch die Worte bestimmte Intensität von *Les Présents* und *Le Don silencieux* ist nicht weniger bemerkenswert.

Dass sich Fauré eingehend mit der Dramaturgie der Lieder befasste, wird in den umfangreichen Änderungen deutlich, die er zu einem späteren Zeitpunkt (bisweilen sogar nach Veröffentlichung) an der dynamischen Gestaltung einiger Lieder vornahm. In einer frühen Feuilleton-Veröffentlichung von *Aurore*, die offensichtlich auf Grundlage eines Korrekturabzugs oder eines frühen Manuskripts gestochen wurde, weist das Lied eine verblüffend andere dynamische Gestaltung auf. Der letzte melodische Abstieg ab Takt 42 ist mit der *forte*-Gabel eines Crescendos versehen, anstatt dass hier, wie in späteren Quellen, ein unerwartetes *piano* vorgeschrieben ist. Im Fall von *Larmes* wiederum wurde das *forte* aus der ersten Ausgabe in der zweiten Sammlung von 1897 zu einem *piano* geändert. Die vorliegende Ausgabe bietet Aufschluss über die Überarbeitungen, die Fauré in diesem Lied vorgenommen hatte, die jedoch durch Fehler beim Notenstich verfälscht wurden.

In manchen späteren Liedern (ab *Dans la forêt de septembre*) ist neben Akkorden in weiter Lage in der linken Hand der Klavierstimme eine angeschrägte eckige Klammer abgedruckt. Fauré begann diese offenbar nach 1900 anstelle seiner früher verwendeten Arpeggio-Symbole zu notieren und wollte damit wahrscheinlich ein möglichst knappes Arpeggio ohne Verweilen kennzeichnen.

Im Rahmen seines strengen Rhythmusverständnisses (siehe **Allgemeines Vorwort**) erwartete Fauré bei Schlüsselmomenten wie Kadenzen ein gewisses Maß an rhythmischer Flexibilität, wobei das Tempo üblicherweise mit oder kurz vor Auflösung der Kadenz wieder aufzunehmen ist. Aufnahmen von Sänger/-innen, die mit dem Komponisten zusammenarbeiteten, bestätigen dies: was die Takte 54–55 von *Clair de lune* betrifft zum Beispiel die bemerkenswerte Aufnahme von Jane Bathori aus dem Jahr 1928 (bei der sie sich selbst begleitete).⁴⁴ Im Allgemeinen verlangte Fauré jedoch eine entschlossene Vorwärtsbewegung (Claire Croiza nannte sie ein „*allant*") mit strenger Beachtung rhythmischer Details. Der Pianist Vlado Perlemuter, der mit dem Komponisten in dessen letzten Lebensjahren zusammenarbeitete, nannte ihn den „Schrecken der Sänger", da er zum Unbehagen jener, „die den Rhythmus gern locker nehmen, das Lied möglichst genau im Takt, ohne Rubato, gespielt wissen wollte".⁴⁵

Am 12. Januar 1902 notierte Mimi Girette in ihrem Tagebuch:

> Wenn [Fauré] mich begleitet, sind wir eine Person, obwohl er mir folgt, kann ich auch alles spüren, was er möchte. Er erlaubt mir sogar, das Tempo ein winziges bisschen zu verlangsamen oder zu beschleunigen, da er spürt, dass ich nie übertreiben würde, dass ich seiner Musik den Charakter nicht nehmen würde.⁴⁶

Zu Beginn des Jahrhunderts gab Fauré Mlle Girette nicht nur ein Autograph von *Accompagnement* (von dem sie zwecks Anmerkungen für die Aufführung eine Kopie für sich erstellte), sondern auch seine korrigierten Korrekturabzüge der anderen Lieder des Opus sowie von *Chanson*. In diesen Partituren finden sich ihre Vortragsangaben (siehe **Anhang 3**), die sie mit hoher Wahrscheinlichkeit eintrug, als sie mit dem Komponisten an den Liedern arbeitete. Bezeichnenderweise lässt keine dieser Angaben Temposchwankungen zu.

TEXTE UND DICHTER

Der einen Zeitraum von nahezu vierzig Jahren umspannende vorliegende Band beinhaltet unter anderem Gedichte der Berühmtheiten Verlaine, Leconte de Lisle und Jean Richepin (der vor allem für seine Prosa bekannt ist), des populären Armand Silvestres und des esoterischen Villiers de L'Isle-Adam sowie von gefeierten Lyrikern des neuen Jahrhunderts, namentlich Henri de Régnier und Marie Closset (Jean Dominique). Die meisten seiner Dichter kannte Fauré persönlich; mit Verlaine und Albert Samain erwägte er in den frühen 1890er-Jahren auch in puncto Bühnenmusik eine Zusammenarbeit. Die Reihe an Liedern ist daher insofern eine Fortsetzung der Erzählung der *Complete Songs / Sämtliche Lieder* Band 1, als dass sie Faurés fortdauernde Interaktion mit Lyrikern und literarischen Bewegungen widerspiegelt.

In seinen textlichen Änderungen werden die sorgfältigen Überlegungen, die er bei der Umwandlung der Lyrik in einen gesungenen Text anstellte, deutlich. In *Dans la forêt de septembre* ersetzte er in der Zeile „Je viens d'un pas vivace encore" das „vivace" durch „alerte" und vermied somit die unschöne Wiederholung eines betonten Vokals [a]. Analog dazu änderte er in Henri de Régniers *Chanson* die Textstelle „Sur le sable" aufgrund des wiederholten Zischlauts in „Dans le sable".[47]

Kleinere Änderungen wiederum nahm Fauré an der Interpunktion vor: Er ersetzte zum Teil Ausrufezeichen und Punkte sowie Kommata, Semikola und Ellipsen. Solcherlei Anpassungen haben häufig einen musikalischen Zweck in Hinblick auf die Phrasen- und Absatzstruktur und dienen als nützliche Interpretationshinweise. Ausrufezeichen können die dynamische Intensität steigern, insbesondere durch eine gehaltene Note (am Ende von *Larmes* zum Beispiel, wo das Ausrufezeichen des Komponisten den Punkt des Dichters ersetzt). Kommata wiederum können ein Atemhinweis oder ein Hinweis darauf sein, Silben nicht zu verschmelzen (wie in den Anfangstakten von *Au cimetière*). Auch können sie dazu dienen, eine musikalische Geste wiederzugeben.[48] In der vorliegenden Ausgabe wurden diese Änderungen respektiert, vorausgesetzt, sie wurden in den entsprechenden musikalischen Quellen einheitlich verwendet, dienen einem erkennbaren Zweck und verursachen keine syntaktischen oder musikalischen Probleme.

Danksagung

Der herzliche Dank der Herausgeber gilt all jenen, die uns für die wissenschaftliche Untersuchung freundlicherweise Quellen zur Verfügung gestellt oder auf praktische Weise Unterstützung geleistet haben: insbesondere den Mitarbeitern der Musikabteilung der Bibliothèque nationale de France, Paris, der Bibliothèque François Lang, Royaumont (Valérie De Wispelaere und Thomas Vernet), der Médiathèque musicale Mahler, Paris, der Bibliothèque municipale de la ville de Genève, der Bibliotheca Bodmeriana, Cologny (Nicolas Ducimetière), der Morgan Library and Museum, New York (J. Rigbie Turner und Frances Barulich), der Memorial Library of Music, Stanford University, der Beinecke and Irving S. Gilmore Libraries, Yale University, der McLennan Library, McGill University, Montreal und der Library of Congress, Washington; den Bibliotheken des Conservatoire Royal de Bruxelles, Conservatoire de Genève (Jacques Tchamkerten), Royal College of Music und der Royal Academy of Music, London sowie Thierry und Pierrette Bodin, Carlo Caballero, James David Christie, Mary Dibbern, Ulrich Drüner, Judith Gordon, Denis Herlin, Nigel Hughes, Peter Jost, Sylvia Kahan, Robin Lehman, John und Judith Lubrano, Dr. Simon Maguire (Sothebys), Roger Nichols, Robert Orledge, Herbert Schneider und Robin Tait. Musiker- und Lehrerkollegen sowie Studenten unterstützten uns in Workshops und Konzerten mit ihrem Enthusiasmus, ihrer Fachkompetenz und ihrem unschätzbaren musikalischen Feedback; der besondere Dank der Herausgeber gilt Tony Boutté, Mary Dibbern, Guy Flechter, François Le Roux, Rosalind Martin, Jared Schwartz und Christopher Underwood. Der Standort dieses Editionsprojekts, die Royal Academy of Music, London, wurde durch eine Projektförderung des Arts and Humanities Research Councils (GB) unterstützt; unser spezieller Dank gilt Nicole Tibbels für ihre grenzenlose enthusiastische Mitarbeit sowie ihre Einsichten bezüglich praktischer und linguistischer Fragen, des Weiteren Richard Stokes für die freundliche Genehmigung des Nachdrucks seiner englischen Übersetzungen der Liedtexte, den Gesangsstudenten im Aufbaustudium der Royal Academy sowie David Gorton, Neil Heyde und Timothy Jones.

London und Paris 2017 *Roy Howat und Emily Kilpatrick*
(Übersetzung: Lore Horlamus)

---

[1] Die fünf „venezianischen" Lieder op. 58 und *La Bonne Chanson* finden sich in *Complete Songs / Sämtliche Lieder*, Band 3, die vier letzten Zyklen in Band 4.

[2] Nectoux, *Gabriel Fauré : les voix du clair-obscur*, S. 237f.; siehe auch Nectoux (Hrsg.), *Gabriel Fauré : Correspondance*, Ausgabe von 1890, Kapitel VI.

[3] Montesquiou lieferte die Textvorlage für den *Ad-libitum*-Refrain der *Pavane*, die der Comtesse Greffulhe gewidmet war. Sein Text ist eine Parodie auf die *Fêtes galantes* von Verlaine, insbesondere auf „Clair de lune" und „Mandoline". Eine editorische Neueinrichtung der *Pavane* für zwei Stimmen, Flöte und Klavier (wie mitunter vom Komponisten aus dem Stegreif aufgeführt) ist als Edition Peters EP 7526 erhältlich.

[4] Johnson und Stokes, *A French Song Companion*, S. 165. In einer Rezension der Premiere (*Ménestrel*, 6 Mai 1888) wird *Clair de lune* schlichtweg als „Menuet" bezeichnet.

[5] Pierre de Bréville, *Quelques souvenirs*, in: *La Revue musicale* 201 (September 1946), S. 229. Mit einer Uraufführung vom 2. Februar 1889 präsentierte Bagès zwei der *Ariettes* von Debussy (später *Ariettes oubliées* genannt), Faurés *Au cimetière* und Chaussons *Sérénade*. Auch präsentierte Bagès erstmals Faurés „venezianische" Lieder op. 58 in einem Salon sowie in der Société Nationale. *La Bonne Chanson* führte er erstmalig im April 1894 in einem Salon auf und war an der Premiere dieses von Fauré für Streichquartett und Klavier transkribierten Zyklus am 1. April 1898 (in London) beteiligt. (Brevilles Nachname wurde für gewöhnlich als „Bréville" gedruckt, obwohl er selbst durchgehend ohne Akzent unterschrieb).

[6] Philip Kolb (Hrsg.), *Correspondance de Marcel Proust*, Paris 1970, Bd. I, S. 338; zitiert nach: Nectoux, *Gabriel Fauré : les voix du clair-obscur*, S. 257. Einige der betreffenden Partituren sind im **Kritischen Bericht** des vorliegenden Bandes und jenem der *Complete Songs / Sämtliche Lieder*, Band 3 aufgeführt.

[7] Nectoux (Hrsg.), *Gabriel Fauré : Correspondance*, Brief 102.

[8] Johnson, *Gabriel Fauré*, S. 170.

[9] Nectoux, *Gabriel Fauré : les voix du clair-obscur*, S. 257.

[10] Debussy nahm dasselbe, mit der ersten Zeile („Il pleure dans mon cœur") betitelte Gedicht sowie das aus derselben Sammlung stammende „Spleen" in seine *Ariettes* auf (welche später in *Ariettes oubliées* umbenannt wurden). Diese wurden erstmals im selben Jahr wie Faurés *Spleen* veröffentlicht.

[11] In einem Brief, den Fauré Mitte der 1890er-Jahre entwarf (doch möglicherweise nicht abschickte), schrieb er erzürnt an Hamelle: „Die Korrekturabzüge der Lieder sind noch nicht eingetroffen, obwohl es überhaupt keinen Grund für eine Verspätung geben kann. Vor drei Jahren habe ich Ihnen die transponierte Abschrift für die betreffenden Lieder gegeben. *Vor drei Jahren*. Und ich habe Sie seitdem unaufhörlich gebeten, sich ihnen anzunehmen. Es ist absolut unmöglich, Ihre Gleichgültigkeit bezüglich der Veröffentlichung meiner Werke hinzunehmen." Nectoux (Hrsg.), *Gabriel Fauré : Correspondance*, Brief 189. Bei den nicht benannten Liedern könnte es sich um *Nocturne* und *Les Présents* handeln; siehe **Kritischen Bericht**.

[12] Siehe Howat und Kilpatrick, *Gabriel Fauré's Middle-Period Songs*, S. 330–34.

[13] Nectoux (Hrsg.), *Gabriel Fauré : Correspondance*, Brief 120. Von diesem ursprünglichen Ende fehlt jegliche Spur.

[14] Ebd., Brief 107.

[15] Auch eine Zusammenarbeit mit Haraucourt. Fauré vollendete nur einen „Prologue" für Chor und Orchester. Siehe Nectoux, *Gabriel Fauré: A Musical Life*, S. 146.

[16] Nectoux (Hrsg.), *Gabriel Fauré : Correspondance*, Brief 157.

[17] Nectoux, *Gabriel Fauré: A Musical Life*, S. 149f. Siehe auch Orledge, *Fauré's Pelléas et Mélisande*, in: *Music and Letters* 56/2 (April 1975), S. 170–79.

[18] Maeterlincks Text ersetzte an dieser Stelle das ursprünglich im publizierten Drama abgedruckte Lied „Mes longs cheveux descendent" (Akt III 2. Szene), mit dem Debussy den dritten Akt seiner Oper eröffnet. Für die Aufführungen in London wurde „Mélisande's Song" an das Ende der ersten Szene im dritten Akt verschoben; siehe Nectoux, *Gabriel Fauré: A Musical Life*, S. 156.

[19] Bibliothèque nationale de France, Paris, Musikabteilung, VMD-3211.

[20] Nectoux, *Gabriel Fauré : les voix du clair-obscur*, S. 260.

[21] Nectoux, *Deux interprètes de Fauré : Émilie et Édouard Risler*, in: *Études fauréennes* 18 (1981), S. 10.

[22] Ebd., S. 12.

[23] Ebd., S. 12.

[24] Ebd., S. 13.

²⁵ Nectoux (Hrsg.), *Gabriel Fauré : Correspondance*, Brief 249.

²⁶ Nectoux, *Gabriel Fauré : les voix du clair-obscur*, S. 161f.

²⁷ Wie in Nectoux, *Gabriel Fauré: A Musical Life*, S. 108 hervorgehoben, bemerkte Charles Koechlin als erster die Anspielung auf Bach.

²⁸ Fauré-Fremiet (Hrsg.), *Gabriel Fauré : Lettres intimes*, S. 121.

²⁹ Nectoux, *Gabriel Fauré : Correspondance*, Brief 285.

³⁰ Fauré-Fremiet (Hrsg.), *Gabriel Fauré : Lettres intimes*, S. 260.

³¹ 1921 vertonte er jedoch noch den Zyklus *L'Horizon chimérique*; siehe *Complete Songs / Sämtliche Lieder*, Band 4. Von fünf weiteren Liedern aus den frühen 1900er-Jahren, die ihm gelegentlich zugeschrieben werden, wissen wir, dass sie nicht von ihm stammen: *Le Courlis dans les roseaux* und *Cette fille, elle est morte* wurde von Émile Riadis komponiert (siehe „Carlton Lake: An Inventory of Music in his Collection at the Harry Ransom Humanities Research Center", The University of Texas at Austin, www.hrc.utexas.edu); und drei um 1910 von der Firma Rouart-Lerolle gedruckte Lieder von „G. FAURE" (das jeweils einzige bekannte Exemplar befindet sich im Besitz der Irving Gilmore Music Library, Yale University), zu Texten von Sully Prudhomme (*Les Yeux*), Theuriet (*Pleurs d'avril*) und „G. FAURE" persönlich (*Souffles de printemps*). Diese Zuschreibung sowie die allzu simple musikalische Sprache der drei Lieder legen nahe, dass es sich bei dem Urheber um den Schriftsteller Gabriel Faure (ein eifriger Amateurmusiker und Freund Faurés) handelte. Obwohl sie möglicherweise Selbstpublikationen sind, enthalten sie nichtsdestotrotz Plattennummern, Preise und den Ladenstempel des Verlegers Eschig.

³² Nectoux, *Gabriel Fauré : les voix du clair-obscur*, S. 592f. Ravel wiederum war entsetzt von Faurés ritterlicher Geste und bat ihm an, seine eigene Vertonung zurückzuziehen; siehe Gustave Samazeuilh, *Musiciens de mon temps*, Daubin: Paris 1945, S. 430.

³³ Die Plattennummern der Sammlung, S.B. 2–4, legen nahe, dass es sich um eine Selbstpublikation gehandelt haben könnte. In seinem oben zitierten Brief an Bagès aus dem September oder Oktober 1890 (siehe Endnote 13) schrieb Fauré „Ich habe ein kleines Lied zu einem idiotischen Text von einem Mitarbeiter von Durand, Stéphan Bordèse, geschrieben."

³⁴ Nectoux (Hrsg.), *Gabriel Fauré : Correspondance*, Brief 291.

³⁵ Ebd.

³⁶ 1877 machte Fauré Marianne Viardot einen Heiratsantrag, sie kündigte die Verlobung jedoch nach ein paar Monaten auf.

³⁷ Siehe Orledge, *Gabriel Fauré*, S. 52 und Nectoux, *Gabriel Fauré : les voix du clair-obscur*, S. 36 und 61; *Puisqu'ici-bas* steht auf einer Liste von Hugo-Vertonungen, die Fauré 1864 angefertigt haben soll (siehe *Complete Songs / Sämtliche Lieder*, Vorwort zu Band 1). Unter dem überlieferten Quellenmaterial (siehe **Kritischen Bericht**) ist keine frühere Vertonung für Solostimme auffindbar.

³⁸ See Orledge, *Gabriel Fauré*, S. 87.

³⁹ Eine Erläuterung zu den Tonarten für *Pusiqu'ici bas toute âme* findet sich im **Kritischen Bericht**.

⁴⁰ Nach Faurés Tod gab Hamelle einen Sonderdruck im enharmonisch umgedeuteten Ges-Dur heraus. Siehe **Kritischen Bericht** bezüglich weiterer beworbener Tonarten für *Nocturne* (und „Chanson" aus *Shylock*), die offensichtlich nie herausgegeben wurden.

⁴¹ Nectoux, *Deux interprètes de Fauré*, S. 11. Siehe Howat und Kilpatrick, *Gabriel Fauré's Middle-Period Songs*, S. 319–25.

⁴² Nectoux (Hrsg.), *Gabriel Fauré : Correspondance*, Brief 452.

⁴³ Fauré-Fremiet, *Gabriel Fauré*, S. 158–62.

⁴⁴ *Jane Bathori: The Complete Solo Recordings*, CD, Marston MR 51009, 1999.

⁴⁵ Roger Nichols, Abschrift einer Unterhaltung mit Vlado Perlemuter (in den 1970er-Jahren), von der er Roy Howat am 12. Februar 2013 in einer E-Mail berichtete.

⁴⁶ Nectoux, *Deux interprètes de Fauré*, S. 11.

⁴⁷ Siehe auch Nectoux, *Gabriel Fauré : les voix du clair-obscur*, S. 448ff.

⁴⁸ Eine detaillierte Besprechung dieses Themas findet sich, insbesondere in Hinblick auf die frühen Lieder Faurés, bei Kilpatrick, *Moot point*.

Index of Songs / Table des mélodies / Liederverzeichnis

			Key *Tonart*	Range *Umfang*	Page *Seite*
1.	*Aurore* (Op. 39 No. 1)	Armand Silvestre	F		2
2.	*Fleur jetée* (Op. 39 No. 2)	Armand Silvestre	d		6
3.	*Le Pays des Rêves* (Op. 39 No. 3)	Armand Silvestre	G♭		10
4.	*Les Roses d'Ispahan* (Op. 39 No. 4)	Leconte de Lisle	D		15
5a.	*Nocturne* (Op. 43 No. 2), original version for contralto or bass	Villiers de L'Isle-Adam	E♭		20
5b.	*Nocturne* (Op. 43 No. 2), version for mezzo-soprano or baritone	Villiers de L'Isle-Adam	F♯		23
6.	*Les Présents* (Op. 46 No. 1)	Villiers de L'Isle-Adam	E♭		26
7.	*Clair de Lune (Menuet)* (Op. 46 No. 2)	Paul Verlaine	b♭		28
8.	*Larmes* (Op. 51 No. 1)	Jean Richepin	b♭		32
9.	*Au Cimetière* (Op. 51 No. 2)	Jean Richepin	c		36
10.	*Spleen* (Op. 51 No. 3)	Paul Verlaine	d		40
11.	*La Rose (ode anacréontique)* (Op. 51 No. 4)	Leconte de Lisle	E♭		44
12a.	*Prélude* to *Chanson (Shylock)* (Op. 57 No. 1)		A♭		50
12b.	*Chanson (Shylock)* (Op. 57 No. 1)	Edmond Haraucourt	A♭		51
13.	*Madrigal (Shylock)* (Op. 57 No. 3)	Edmond Haraucourt	E♭		54
14.	*Sérénade (Le Bourgeois Gentilhomme)*	Molière	d		57
15.	*Prison* (Op. 68 No. 1)	Paul Verlaine	e♭		60
16.	*Soir* (Op. 68 No. 2)	Albert Samain	D♭		62
17.	*Le Parfum impérissable* (Op. 76 No. 1)	Leconte de Lisle	E		65
18.	*Arpège* (Op. 76 No. 2)	Albert Samain	e		68

			Key *Tonart*	Range *Umfang*	Page *Seite*
19.	*Mélisande's Song (Pelléas et Mélisande)* (from Op. 80)	Maurice Maeterlinck	d		72
20.	*Dans la forêt de septembre* (Op. 85 No. 1)	Catulle Mendès	G♭		74
21.	*La Fleur qui va sur l'eau* (Op. 85 No. 2)	Catulle Mendès	b		78
22.	*Accompagnement* (Op. 85 No. 3)	Albert Samain	G♭		82
23.	*Le plus doux chemin (Madrigal)* (Op. 87 No. 1)	Armand Silvestre	f		88
24.	*Le Ramier (Madrigal)* (Op. 87 No. 2)	Armand Silvestre	e		90
25.	*Le Don silencieux* (Op. 92)	Jean Dominique	E		92
26.	*Chanson* (Op. 94)	Henri de Régnier	e		95
27.	*C'est la Paix* (Op. 114)	Georgette Debladis	G		97

Cantiques

28.	*Noël* (Op. 43 No. 1)	Victor Wilder	F		99
29.	*En prière*	Stéphan Bordèse	E♭		104

Vocal duets

30.	*Puisqu'ici-bas toute âme ...* (Op. 10 No. 1)	Victor Hugo	B♭		107
31.	*Tarentelle* (Op. 10 No. 2)	Marc Monnier	f		113
32.	*Pleurs d'or* (Op. 71/72)	Albert Samain	E♭		120

4 voices (SATB)

33.	*Madrigal* (Op. 35)	Armand Silvestre	d		124

Poetic texts / Textes poétiques des mélodies / Liedtexte

The French texts follow the layout, wording and punctuation of the poetic sources, as listed in the **Critical Commentary**.
Fauré's textual modifications are shown in [ ]; […] indicates omitted stanzas.

Le texte français suit les sources poétiques, citées dans le **commentaire critique**, y compris dans leur disposition et leur ponctuation.
Les modifications textuelles de Fauré sont placées entre crochets; les strophes omises sont indiquées par […].

Die französischen Texte stimmen in Layout, Wortlaut und Interpunktion mit der im **Kritischen Bericht** aufgeführten dichterischen Vorlage überein.
Faurés Änderungen am Text sind in [ ] angegeben; […] signalisiert ausgelassene Strophen.

English translations by Richard Stokes / Deutsche Übersetzung von Klaus Strobel

1. [Aurore]
Armand Silvestre

Des jardins de la nuit s'envolent les étoiles.
Abeilles d'or qu'attire un invisible miel,
Et l'aube, au loin tendant la candeur de ses toiles,
Trame de fils d'argent le manteau bleu du ciel.

Du jardin de mon cœur qu'un rêve lent enivre
S'envolent mes désirs sur les pas du matin,
Comme un essaim léger qu'à l'horizon de cuivre
Appelle un chant plaintif, éternel et lointain.

Ils volent à tes pieds, astres chassés des nues,
Exilés du ciel d'or où fleurit ta beauté
Et, cherchant jusqu'à toi des routes inconnues,
Mêlent au jour naissant leur mourante clarté.

1. [Dawn]
Armand Silvestre

Stars take wing from the gardens of night.
Golden bees tempted by invisible honey,
And the distant dawn, stretching its guileless veils,
Weaves silver threads through the sky's blue cloak.

From the garden of my dream-enraptured soul
My desires take wing as morning appears,
Like a delicate swarm called to the copper horizon
By a sad, never-ending and distant song.

They fly to your feet, stars banished from the sky,
Exiled from the golden heavens where your beauty thrives
And, seeking to reach you by untried paths,
They mingle their dying light with the dawning day.

1. [Morgenröte]
Armand Silvestre

Aus den Gärten der Nacht fliegen die Sterne davon.
Goldene Bienen, die ein unsichtbarer Honig anzieht,
Und die Morgendämmerung, in der Ferne die
Arglosigkeit ihrer Tücher spannend,
Durchwirkt mit silbernen Fäden den blauen Mantel
des Himmels.

Vom Garten meines Herzens, das ein langsamer
Traum berauscht,
Entfliehen meine Wünsche an der Schwelle des
Morgens,
Wie ein leichter Schwarm, den am kupfernen Horizont
Ein klagender, ewiger und entfernter Gesang ruft.

Sie fliegen zu deinen Füßen, von den Wolken
verjagte Sterne,
Vom goldenen Himmel verbannt, wo deine
Schönheit blüht,
Und, zu dir unbekannte Straße suchend,
Mischen sie in den neuen Tag ihre sterbende Helligkeit.

2. Fleur jetée
Armand Silvestre

Emporte ma folie
    Au gré du vent,
Fleur en chantant cueillie
Et jetée en rêvant.
    – Emporte ma folie
    Au gré du vent!

Comme la fleur fauchée
    Périt l'amour.
La main qui t'a touchée
Fuit ma main sans retour[.]
    – Comme la fleur fauchée,
    Périt l'amour!

Que le vent qui te sèche,
    Ô pauvre fleur,
Tout à l'heure si fraîche
Et demain sans couleur!
    – Que le vent qui te sèche,
    Sèche mon cœur!

2. Discarded flower
Armand Silvestre

Bear away my folly
    At the whim of the wind,
Flower plucked while singing
And discarded while dreaming.
    – Bear away my folly
    At the whim of the wind!

Like a scythed flower
    Love perishes.
The hand that touched you
Shuns my hand for ever.
    – Like a scythed flower,
    Love perishes!

May the wind that withers you,
    O poor flower,
So fresh just now
But tomorrow faded,
    – May the wind that withers you,
    Wither my heart!

2. Hingeworfene Blume
Armand Silvestre

Nimm meinen den Launen des Windes
ausgesetzten Wahnsinn weg,
Singend gepflückte Blume
Und träumend hingeworfen.
    – Nimm meinen den Launen des Windes
    ausgesetzten Wahnsinn weg!

Wie die abgemähte kleine Blume
    Geht die Liebe zugrunde.
Die Hand, die Dich berührt hat,
Flieht meine Hand für immer.
    – Wie die abgemähte kleine Blume
    Geht die Liebe zugrunde!

Daß der Wind, der dich trocknet,
    O arme Blume,
Eben noch so frisch,
Und morgen ohne Farbe!
    – Daß der Wind, der dich trocknet
    Mein Herz trockne!

3. Le Pays de Rêves
Armand Silvestre

Veux-tu qu'au beau pays des Rêves
Nous allions la main dans la main ?
Plus haut [loin] que l'odeur du jasmin [des jasmins],
Plus loin [haut] que la plainte des grèves,
Veux-tu, du beau pays des Rêves,
Tous les deux chercher le chemin ?

J'ai taillé dans l'azur les toiles
Du vaisseau qui nous portera,
Et doucement nous conduira
Jusqu'au verger d'or des étoiles.
J'ai taillé dans l'azur les toiles
Du vaisseau qui nous conduira.

Mais combien la terre est lointaine
Que poursuivent ses blancs sillons !
Au caprice des papillons
Demandons la route incertaine :
Ah ! combien la terre est lointaine
Où fleurissent nos visions !

Vois-tu : – le beau pays des Rêves
Est trop haut pour les pas humains.
Respirons à deux les jasmins
Et chantons encor sur les grèves.
– Vois-tu : – du beau pays des Rêves,
L'amour seul en sait les chemins !

4. Les Roses d'Ispahan
Leconte de Lisle

Les roses d'Ispahan dans leur gaine de mousse,
Les jasmins de Mossoul, les fleurs de l'oranger
Ont un parfum moins frais, ont une odeur moins douce,
Ô blanche Leïlah ! que ton souffle léger.

Ta lèvre est de corail, et ton rire léger
Sonne mieux que l'eau vive et d'une voix plus douce,
Mieux que le vent joyeux qui berce l'oranger,
Mieux que l'oiseau qui chante au bord d'un nid de mousse.

[…]

Ô Leïlah ! depuis que de leur vol léger
Tous les baisers ont fui de ta lèvre si douce,
Il n'est plus de parfum dans le pâle oranger,
Ni de céleste arome aux roses dans leur mousse.

[…]

Oh ! que ton jeune amour, ce papillon léger,
Revienne vers mon cœur d'une aile prompte et douce,
Et qu'il parfume encor les fleurs [la fleur] de l'oranger,
Les roses d'Ispahan dans leur gaine de mousse !

5. Éblouissement
[Nocturne]
Villiers de L'Isle-Adam

La Nuit, sur le grand mystère,
Entr'ouvre ses écrins bleus :
Autant de fleurs sur la terre
Que d'étoiles dans les cieux !

On voit ses ombres dormantes
S'éclairer, à tous moments,
Autant par les fleurs charmantes
Que par les astres charmants.

Moi, ma nuit au sombre voile
N'a, pour charme et pour clarté,
Qu'une fleur et qu'une étoile :
Mon amour et ta beauté !

3. The land of Dreams
Armand Silvestre

Shall we go to the land of Dreams,
Holding each other's hand?
Higher than the scent of jasmine,
Farther than the shore's lament,
Shall we together seek the road
To the lovely land of Dreams?

I have cleaved the blue sky with the sails
Of the ship that will bear us,
And gently lead us
To the golden orchard of the stars.
I have cleaved the blue sky with the sails
Of the ship that will bear us.

But how distant the land is
That these white furrows seek out!
Let us, with the impulse of butterflies,
Ask how to find the uncertain road:
Ah! how distant the land is
Where our visions can bear fruit!

You see: the lovely land of dreams
Is too high for human steps.
Let us both breathe in the jasmine
And sing again on the shore.
– You see: – love alone knows the path
To the lovely land of dreams!

4. Roses of Isfahan
Leconte de Lisle

The roses of Isfahan in their mossy sheaths,
The jasmines of Mosul, the orange blossom
Have a fragrance less fresh and a scent less sweet,
O pale Leilah, than your soft breath!

Your lips are of coral and your light laughter
Rings brighter and sweeter than running water,
Than the blithe wind rocking the orange-tree boughs,
Than the singing bird by its mossy nest.

[…]

O Leilah! ever since on light wings
All kisses have flown from your sweet lips,
The pale orange-tree fragrance is spent,
And the heavenly scent of moss-clad roses.

[…]

Oh! may your young love, that airy butterfly,
Wing swiftly and gently to my heart once more,
To scent again the orange blossom,
The roses of Isfahan in their mossy sheaths!

5. Illumination
[Nocturne]
Villiers de L'Isle-Adam

Onto a landscape of great mystery
Night half-opens its blue caskets:
As many flowers on earth
As stars in the sky!

Its sleeping shadows are seen
Brightening every moment,
As much by charming flowers
As by charming stars.

My own darkly veiled night
Has, for charm and light,
But one flower and one star:
My love and your beauty!

3. Das Land der Träume
Armand Silvestre

Willst du, daß wir ins schöne Land der Träume
Hand in Hand gehen?
Weiter als der Duft der Jasminblüten,
Höher als die Klage der Strände,
Willst du zum schönen Land der Träume
Zu zweit den Weg suchen?

Ich schnitt in das Azur die Segel
Des Schiffes, das uns tragen
Und sanft geleiten wird
Bis zum goldenen Obstgarten der Sterne.
Ich schnitt in das Azur Segel
Des Schiffes, das uns tragen wird.

Doch wie entfernt das Land ist,
Das seine weißen Strahlen fortsetzen!
Fragen wir die Launen der Schmetterlinge
Nach dem unsicheren Weg;
Ah! Wie entfernt das Land ist,
Wo unsere Visionen blühn!

Siehst du: – das schöne Land der Träume
Ist zu hoch für den menschlichen Schritt.
Atmen wir zu zweit den Jasmin
Und singen wir noch an den Ufern.
– Siehst du: – zum schönen Land der Träume,
Kennt allein die Liebe den Weg!

4. Die Rosen von Ispahan
Leconte de Lisle

Die Rosen von Ispahan in ihrem Saum von Moos,
Der Jasmin von Mossoul, die Blüten des Orangenbaums
Haben einen weniger frischen Duft, einen weniger lieblichen Geruch,
O weiße Leïlah! als dein leichter Atem.

Deine Lippe ist aus Korallen, und dein leichtes Lachen
Klingt schöner und mit einer lieblicheren Stimme als das sprudelnde Wasser,
Schöner als der fröhliche Wind, der den Orangenbaum wiegt,
Schöner als der Vogel, der am Rand des Nestes aus Moos singt.

[…]

O Leïlah! seit mit ihrem leichten Flug
alle Küsse deiner so süßen Lippe entflohen sind,
Gibt es keinen Duft mehr in dem blassen Orangenbaum,
Noch himmlischen Wohlgeruch an den Rosen in ihrem Saum.

[…]

Oh! daß deine junge Liebe, dieser leichte Schmetterling,
Zurückkomme zu meinem Herzen mit rascher und süßer Schwinge,
Und daß er die Blüten des Orangenbaums noch mit Duft erfülle,
Die Rosen von Ispahan in ihrem Saum von Moos.

5. Illumination
[Nocturne]
Villiers de L'Isle-Adam

Die Nacht über dem großen Geheimnis
Öffnet ihre blauen Schmuckkästchen:
So viele Blumen auf Erden
Wie Sterne am Himmel!

Man sieht ihre schlafenden Schatten
Sich immerzu erhellen,
Sowohl durch die bezaubernden Blumen
Als auch durch die reizenden Sterne.

Meine Nacht mit dunklen Schleiern
Hat als Zauber und als Licht
Nur eine Blume und einen Stern:
Meine Liebe und deine Schönheit!

6. Les Présents
Villiers de L'Isle-Adam

Si tu me parles [Si tu demandes], quelque soir,
Le secret de mon cœur malade,
Je te dirai, pour t'émouvoir,
Une très ancienne ballade !

Si tu me parles de tourment [tourments],
D'espérance désabusée,
J'irai te cueillir, seulement,
Des roses pleines de rosée.

Si, pareille à la fleur des morts
Qui fleurit dans l'exil des tombes,
Tu veux partager mes remords…
Je t'apporterai des colombes !

7. Clair de lune
Paul Verlaine

Votre âme est un paysage choisi
Que vont charmant masques et bergamasques
Jouant du luth et dansant et quasi
Tristes sous leurs déguisements fantasques.

Tout en chantant sur le mode mineur
L'amour vainqueur et la vie opportune,
Ils n'ont pas l'air de croire à leur bonheur
Et leur chanson se mêle au clair de lune,

Au calme clair de lune triste et beau,
Qui fait rêver les oiseaux dans les arbres
Et sangloter d'extase les jets d'eau,
Les grands jets d'eau sveltes parmi les marbres.

8. Larmes
Jean Richepin

Pleurons nos chagrins, chacun le nôtre.
Une larme tombe, puis une autre.
Toi, qui pleures-tu ? Ton doux pays,
Tes parents lointains, ta fiancée.
Moi, mon existence dépensée
    En vœux trahis.

Pleurons nos chagrins, chacun le nôtre.
Une larme tombe, puis une autre.
Semons dans la mer ces pâles fleurs.
À notre sanglot qui se lamente
Elle répondra par la tourmente
    Des flots hurleurs[.]

[…]

Pleurons nos chagrins, chacun le nôtre.
Une larme tombe, puis une autre.
Peut-être toi-même, ô triste mer,
Mer au goût de larme âcre et salée,
Es-tu de la terre inconsolée
    Le pleur amer.

---

6. The gifts
Villiers de L'Isle-Adam

If you should ask, one evening,
The secret of my sick heart,
I shall tell you, to move you,
A very ancient ballad!

If you talk to me of torments,
Of shattered hopes,
I shall simply pick for you
Roses full of dew!

If, like the flower of the dead,
Which blossoms only in the exile of the grave,
You should wish to share my remorse…
I shall bring you doves!

7. Moonlight
Paul Verlaine

Your soul is a chosen landscape
Bewitched by masquers and bergamaskers
Playing the lute and dancing and almost
Sad beneath their fanciful disguises.

Singing as they go in a minor key
Of conquering love and life's favours,
They do not seem to believe in their fortune
And their song mingles with the light of the moon,

The calm light of the moon, sad and fair,
That sets the birds dreaming in the trees
And the fountains sobbing in their rapture,
Tall and svelte amid marble statues.

8. Tears
Jean Richepin

Let us mourn our sorrows, each his own.
One tear fails, another follows.
You, who do you mourn? Your sweet native land,
Your distant family, your betrothed.
And I – my existence, wasted
    On vows betrayed.

Let us mourn our sorrows, each his own.
One tear falls, another follows.
Let us bestrew the sea with these pale flowers.
To our sobbing lament
It will reply with the storm
    Of howling waves.

[…]

Let us mourn our sorrows, each his own.
One tear falls, another follows.
Perhaps you yourself, O dismal sea,
That tastes of acrid and salty tears,
Are the inconsolable earth's
    Bitter weeping.

---

6. Die Geschenke
Villiers de L'Isle-Adam

Wenn du mich eines Abends fragst
Nach dem Geheimnis meines kranken Herzens,
Werde ich dir erzählen, um dich zu bewegen,
Eine sehr alte Ballade.

Wenn du mir von Qual sprichst,
Von enttäuschter Hoffnung,
Werde ich dir nur pflücken
Rosen voll von Tau.

Wenn, gleich der Blume der Toten,
Die in der Verbannung der Gräber blüht,
Du meine Gewissensbisse teilen willst…
Werde ich dir Tauben bringen.

7. Mondschein
Paul Verlaine

Eure Seele ist eine ausgewählte Landschaft,
Wo reizende Masken und Bergamasken gehen,
Laute spielend und tanzend und fast
Traurig unter ihren wunderlichen Verkleidungen.

Obgleich sie in Moll besingen
Die siegreiche Liebe und das günstige Leben,
Sehen sie nicht so aus, als ob sie an ihr Glück glaubten,
Und ihr Lied verschmilzt mit dem Mondschein,

Mit dem stillen, traurig-schönen Mondschein,
Der die Vögel in den Bäumen träumen
Und die Brunnen vor Verzückung schluchzen läßt,
Die großen schlanken Springbrunnen zwischen dem
    Marmor.

8. Tränen
Jean Richepin

Beweinen wir unseren Kummer, jeder den unseren.
Eine Träne fällt, dann eine andere.
Wen beweinst du? Dein liebliches Land,
Deine fernen Eltern, deine Verlobte.
Ich mein verschwendetes Leben
    Und verratene Gelübde.

Beweinen wir unseren Kummer, jeder den unseren.
Eine Träne fällt, dann noch eine.
Säen wir diese blassen Blumen ins Meer.
Unserem klagenden Schluchzen
Wird sie durch den Sturm
    Der heulenden Fluten antworten.

[…]

Beweinen wir unseren Kummer, jeder den unseren.
Eine Träne fällt, dann noch eine.
Vielleicht du selbst, trauriges Meer,
Meer mit dem Geschmack herber und salziger Tränen,
Bist du der ungetrösteten Erde
    Bitteres Weinen.

9. Au cimetière
Jean Richepin

Heureux qui meurt ici
    Ainsi
Que les oiseaux des champs !
Son corps près des amis
    Est mis
Dans l'herbe et dans les chants.

Il dort d'un bon sommeil
    Vermeil
Sous le ciel radieux.
Tous ceux qu'il a connus,
    Venus,
Lui font de longs adieux.

À sa croix les parents
    Pleurants
Restent agenouillés ;
Et ses os, sous les fleurs,
    De pleurs
Sont doucement mouillés.

Chacun sur le bois noir
    Peut voir
S'il était jeune ou non,
Et peut avec de vrais
    Regrets
L'appeler par son nom.

Combien plus malchanceux
    Sont ceux
Qui meurent à la mé,
Et sous le flot profond
    S'en vont
Loin du pays aimé !

Ah ! pauvres, qui pour seuls
    Linceuls
Ont les goëmons verts
Où l'on roule inconnu,
    Tout nu,
Et les yeux grands ouverts.

Heureux qui meurt ici
    Ainsi
Que les oiseaux des champs !
Son corps près des amis
    Est mis
Dans l'herbe et dans les chants.

10. [Spleen]
Paul Verlaine

Il pleure dans mon cœur
Comme il pleut sur la ville,
Quelle est cette langueur
Qui pénètre mon cœur ?

Ô bruit doux de la pluie
Par terre et sur les toits !
Pour un cœur qui s'ennuie
Ô le chant de la pluie !

Il pleure sans raison
Dans ce [mon] cœur qui s'écœure.
Quoi ! nulle trahison ?
Ce [Mon] deuil est sans raison.

C'est bien la pire peine
De ne savoir pourquoi,
Sans amour et sans haine,
Mon cœur a tant de peine !

9. In the cemetery
Jean Richepin

Happy he who dies here
    Even
As the birds of the fields!
His body near his friends
    Is laid
Amid the grass, amid the songs.

He sleeps a good sleep,
    Crimson
Beneath the radiant sky.
All those he has known
    Are come
To bid him a long farewell.

By the cross his weeping
    Parents
Remain kneeling;
And his bones, beneath the flowers,
    With tears
Are gently watered.

On the black wood all
    Can see
If he was young or not,
And can with true
    Regret
Call him by his name.

How much more unfortunate
    Are they
Who die at sea,
And beneath deep waters
    Drift
Far from their beloved land!

Ah! poor souls, whose only
    Shroud
Is the green seaweed
Where they roll unknown,
    Unclothed,
And with wide-open eyes.

Happy he who dies here
    Even
As the birds of the fields!
His body near his friends
    Is laid
Amid the grass, amid the songs.

10. [Spleen]
Paul Verlaine

Tears fall in my heart
As rain falls on the town,
What is this torpor
Pervading my heart?

Ah, the soft sound of rain
On the ground and roofs!
For a listless heart,
Ah, the song of the rain!

Tears fall without reason
In this disheartened heart.
What! Was there no treason?
This grief's without reason.

And the worst pain of all
Must be not to know why,
Without love and without hate,
My heart has so much pain.

9. Auf dem Friedhof
Jean Richepin

Glücklich, wer hier stirbt
    So wie
Die Vögel auf den Feldern!
Sein Körper, nahe seiner Freunde,
    Wird gebettet
Ins Gras und in die Gesänge.

Er schläft einen guten Schlaf,
    Leuchtendrot
Unter dem strahlenden Himmel.
Alle, die er kannte,
    Sind gekommen
Und verabschieden sich lange von ihm.

An seinem Kreuz die weinenden
    Verwandten
Bleiben knieen;
Und seine Knochen, unter den Blumen,
    Werden von Tränen
Sanft benetzt.

Jeder kann auf dem schwarzen Holz
    Sehen,
Ob er jung war oder nicht,
Und kann mit wahrem
    Bedauern
Ihn bei seinem Namen rufen.

Wieviel unglücklicher
    Sind die,
die im Elend sterben
Und unter tiefem Wasser
    Forttreiben,
Weit vom geliebten Land!

Ach! Arme, die als einziges
    Leichentuch
Den grünen Tang haben,
In dem man unbekannt dahintreibt,
    Ganz nackt
Und die Augen weit offen.

Glücklich, wer hier stirbt
    So wie
Die Vögel auf den Feldern!
Sein Körper, nahe seiner Freunde,
    Wird gebettet
Ins Gras und in die Gesänge.

10. [Spleen]
Paul Verlaine

Es weint in meinem Herzen
So wie es auf die Stadt regnet;
Was ist das für eine Wehmut,
Die mein Herz durchdringt?

O süßes Geräusch des Regens
Am Boden und auf den Dächern!
Für ein Herz, das sich langweilt,
O der Gesang des Regens!

Es weint ohne Grund
In meinem Herzen, das sich anwidert.
Was! Kein Verrat?
Meine Trauer hat keinen Grund.

Es ist wohl die schlimmste Qual,
Nicht zu wissen warum,
Ohne Liebe und ohne Haß,
Mein Herz hat soviel Kummer!

11. La Rose
Leconte de Lisle

Je dirai la rose aux plis gracieux.
La rose est le souffle embaumé des Dieux,
Le plus cher souci des Muses divines.
Je dirai ta gloire, ô charme des yeux,
Ô fleur de Kypris, reine des collines !
Tu t'épanouis entre les beaux doigts
De l'Aube écartant les ombres moroses ;
L'air bleu devient rose, et roses les bois ;
La bouche et le sein des Nymphes [vierges] sont roses !
Heureuse la vierge aux bras arrondis
Qui dans les halliers humides te cueille !
Heureux le front jeune où tu resplendis !
Heureuse la coupe où nage ta feuille !
Ruisselante encor du flot paternel,
Quand de la mer bleue Aphrodite éclose
Étincela nue aux clartés du ciel,
La Terre jalouse enfanta la rose ;
Et l'Olympe entier, d'amour transporté,
Salua la fleur avec la Beauté !

12–13. Shylock
Edmond Haraucourt

Chanson[1]

Oh, les filles ! Venez, les filles aux voix douces !
C'est l'heure d'oublier l'orgueil et les vertus,
Et nous regarderons éclore dans les mousses
    La fleur des baisers défendus.

Les baisers défendus, c'est Dieu qui les ordonne.
Oh, les filles ! Il fait le printemps pour les nids,
Il fait votre beauté pour qu'elle nous soit bonne,
    Nos désirs pour qu'ils soient unis.

Oh, les filles ! Vos cœurs vont mourir dans les jeûnes ;
Vos seins sont de beaux fruits promis aux beaux péchés,
Puisqu'il faudra mourir et que vous êtes jeunes,
    Cueillez les pêches aux pêchers.

Oh, filles ! Hors l'amour, rien n'est bon sur la terre
Et depuis les soirs d'or jusqu'aux matins rosés
Les morts ne sont jaloux, dans leur paix solitaire,
    Que du murmure des baisers.

Madrigal

Celle que j'aime a de beauté
Plus que Flore et plus que Pomone,
Et je sais, pour l'avoir chanté,
Que sa bouche est le soir d'automne,
Et son regard la nuit d'été.

Pour marraine elle eut Astarté,
Pour patronne elle a la Madone,
Car elle est belle autant que bonne
    Celle que j'aime.

Elle écoute, rit et pardonne,
N'écoutant que par charité :
Elle écoute, mais sa fierté
N'écoute ni moi ni personne,
Et rien encore n'a tenté
    Celle que j'aime.

---

[1] La 3e strophe ne paraît que dans la version de l'**Appendice 1**.

11. The rose
Leconte de Lisle

I shall speak of the rose with its graceful petals.
The rose is the scented breath of the gods,
The most cherished care of the divine Muses.
I shall speak of your glory, O delight of the eyes,
O flower of Cypris, queen of the hills!
You bloom between the beautiful fingers
Of dawn, brushing gloomy shadows aside;
The blue air turns rose, and rose the woods;
The lips and breasts of virgins are pink!
Happy the virgin with rounded arms
Who gathers you in moist thickets!
Happy the young brow that you adorn!
Happy the cup where your leaves float!
Streaming still from the paternal waters,
When from the blue sea Aphrodite emerged
Glistening naked in the brilliant sky,
Jealous Earth gave birth to the rose;
And all Olympus, transported by love,
Greeted the flower with Beauty!

12–13. Shylock
Edmond Haraucourt

Song[1]

Oh, girls! Come, girls with the sweet voices!
It is time to forget your pride and virtue,
And we shall watch forbidden kisses
    Flower among the mosses.

Forbidden kisses – it's God that orders them.
Oh, girls! He creates springtime for nesting,
He creates your beauty so that it seems good to us,
    And our desires that they might be joined.

Oh, girls! Your hearts will die in fasting;
Your breasts are beautiful fruits promised for delightful sins,
Since one must die, and as you are young,
    Gather the peaches from the peach trees.

Oh, girls! Except for love, there is nothing good on earth,
And from the gold of evening to the pink of dawn,
The dead, in their solitary peace, are jealous only
    Of murmured kisses.

Madrigal

She whom I love has more beauty
Than Flora and Pomona,
And I know, for having sung it,
That her mouth is an autumn evening
And her gaze a summer night.

Astarte was her godmother,
Madonna her patroness,
For she is as lovely as she is good,
    She whom I love.

She listens, laughs and forgives,
Listening only from charity:
She listens, but her pride
Listens neither to me nor anyone,
And nothing yet has tempted
    She whom I love.

---

[1] Strophe 3 figures only in the present **Appendix 1**

11. Die Rose
Leconte de Lisle

Ich werde die Rose mit anmutigen Falten besingen.
Die Rose ist der duftende Atem der Götter,
Die teuerste Sorge der göttlichen Musen.
Ich werde deinen Ruhm besingen, o Zauber der Augen,
O Blume der Kypris, Königin der Hügel!
Du erblühst zwischen den schönen Fingern
Des Morgengrauens, das die verdrießlichen Stunden
    verdrängt;
Die blaue Luft wird rosa und rosa die Wälder;
Der Mund und die Brust der Jungfrauen sind rosa!
Glücklich die Jungfrau mit gerundeten Armen,
Die dich im feuchten Dickicht pflückt!
Glücklich die junge Stirn, wo du schimmerst!
Glücklich die Trinkschale, worin dein Blatt schwimmt!
Noch triefend von den väterlichen Fluten,
Als die aus dem blauen Meer aufgestiegene Aphrodite
Nackt im Licht des Himmels funkelte,
Brachte die eifersüchtige Erde die Rose hervor;
Und der ganze Olymp, von Liebe überwältigt,
Grüßt die Blume nebst der Schönheit.

12–13. *Shylock*
Edmond Haraucourt

Lied[1]

Oh Mädchen! Kommt, Mädchen mit den süßen
    Stimmen!
Es ist die Zeit, Stolz und Tugenden zu vergessen.
Und wir werden schauen, wie im Moos aufblüht
    Die Blume der verbotenen Küsse.

Es ist Gott, der die verbotenen Küsse befiehlt.
Oh Mädchen! Er macht für die Nester den Frühling,
Er macht eure Schönheit, damit sie uns zugute kommt,
    Unsere Leidenschaft, auf daß sie vereint seien.

Ach, Mädchen! Einst stirbt euer Herz in enthaltsamer
    Tugend;
Eure Busen sind köstliche Früchte, berufen zu
    köstlicher Sünd,
Da wir sterblich sind und ihr voller Jugend,
Pflückt die Pfirsiche, die so köstlich sind.

Oh Mädchen! Außer der Liebe ist nichts auf Erden gut,
Und von den goldenen Abenden bis zu den zartrosa
    Morgen
Sind die Toten in ihrem einsamen Frieden
    Nur auf das Murmeln der Küsse eifersüchtig.

Madrigal

Die ich liebe, hat mehr Schönheit
Als Flore und mehr als Pomone,
Und ich weiß, weil ich es besungen habe,
Daß ihr Mund der Herbstabend
Und ihr Blick die Sommernacht ist.

Als Patin hatte sie Astarté,
Als Patronin hat sie die Madonna,
Denn sie ist ebenso schön wie gut,
    Diejenige, die ich liebe.

Sie hört zu, lacht und vergibt,
Denn sie hört nur aus Barmherzigkeit zu:
Sie hört zu, aber ihr Stolz
Hört weder mir noch sonst jemandem zu,
Und nichts hat sie bisher in Versuchung geführt,
    Diejenige, die ich liebe.

---

[1] Strophe 3 nur in **Anhang 1** enthalten

14. *Sérénade* du *Bourgeois gentilhomme*
Molière

Je languis nuit et jour et mon mal [ma peine] est extrême
Depuis qu'à vos rigueurs vos beaux yeux m'ont soumis ;
Si vous traitez ainsi, belle Iris, qui vous aime,
Hélas ! que pourriez-vous faire à vos ennemis ?

15. {Prison}
Paul Verlaine

Le ciel est, par-dessus le toit,
    Si bleu, si calme !
Un arbre, par-dessus le toit
    Berce sa palme.

La cloche dans le ciel qu'on voit
    Doucement tinte.
Un oiseau sur l'arbre qu'on voit
    Chante sa plainte.

Mon Dieu, mon Dieu, la vie est là,
    Simple et tranquille.
Cette paisible rumeur-là
    Vient de la ville.

– Qu'as-tu fait, ô toi que voilà
    Pleurant sans cesse,
Dis, qu'as-tu fait, toi que voilà,
    De ta jeunesse ?

16. Élégie
{Soir}
Albert Samain

Voici que les jardins de la Nuit vont fleurir.
Les lignes, les couleurs, les sons deviennent vagues.
Vois, le dernier rayon agonise à tes bagues.
Ma sœur, entends-tu pas quelque chose mourir ?...

Mets sur mon front tes mains fraîches comme une eau pure,
Mets sur mes yeux tes mains douces comme des fleurs ;
Et que mon âme, où vit le goût secret des pleurs,
Soit comme un lys fidèle et pâle à ta ceinture.

C'est la Pitié qui pose ainsi son doigt sur nous ;
Et tout ce que la terre a de soupirs qui montent,
Il semble qu'à mon cœur enivré le racontent
Tes yeux levés au ciel, si tristes et si doux.

---

14. *Serenade* from *Le Bourgeois gentilhomme*
Molière

I languish night and day, and my pain is extreme,
Since your lovely eyes have subjected me to your severity:
If, lovely Iris, you treat him who loves you thus,
How, alas, would you treat your enemies?

15. {Prison}
Paul Verlaine

The sky above the roof,
    So blue, so calm!
A tree, above the roof,
    Waves its crown.

The bell, in the sky that you see,
    Gently rings.
A bird, on the tree that you see,
    Plaintively sings.

My God, my God, life is there,
    Simple and serene.
That peaceful murmur there
    Comes from the town.

O you, what have you done,
    Weeping without end,
Say, what have you done
    With your young life?

16. Elegy
{Evening}
Albert Samain

Now the gardens of Night begin to flower.
Lines, colours and sounds begin to blur.
See the last rays fade on your rings.
My sister, can you not hear something dying?…

Place on my brow your hands, cool as pure water,
Place on my eyes your hands as sweet as flowers;
And let my soul, with its secret taste of tears,
Be like a lily at your waist, faithful and pale.

It is Pity that lays thus its finger on us;
And all the sighs that rise from the earth
Seem uttered to my enraptured heart
By your sad sweet eyes raised to the skies.

---

14. *Serenade* aus *Der Bürger als Edelmann*
Molière

Ich verzehre mich Tag und Nacht, und mein Schmerz ist extrem,
Seit Eure schönen Augen mich Euren Launen unterwarfen;
Wenn Ihr den, der Euch liebt, so behandelt, schöne Iris,
Ach! was könntet Ihr Euren Feinden antun?

15. {Prison}
Paul Verlaine

Der Himmel über dem Dach ist
    So blau, so ruhig!
Ein Baum über dem Dach
    Wiegt seinen Palmenzweig.

Die Glocke am Himmel, den man sieht,
    Läutet sanft.
Ein Vogel auf dem Baum, den man sieht,
    Singt seine Klage.

Mein Gott, mein Gott, das Leben ist da,
    Einfach und ruhig.
Dieser friedliche Lärm da
    Kommt aus der Stadt.

Was hast du gemacht, o du, der du hier bist,
    Unaufhörlich weinend,
Sag, was hast du gemacht, o du, der du hier bist,
    Aus deiner Jugend?

16. Elegie
{Abend}
Albert Samain

Jetzt ist die Zeit, da die Gärten der Nacht blühen.
Die Linien, die Farben, die Klänge werden undeutlich.
Sieh, der letzte Strahl erstirbt auf deinen Ringen.
Meine Schwester, hörst du nicht etwas sterben?

Leg auf meine Stirn deine wie reines Wasser kühlen Hände,
Leg auf meine Augen deine wie Blumen sanften Hände;
Und daß meine Seele, wo der heimliche Gefallen an den Tränen lebt,
Wie eine treue und bleiche Lilie an deinem Gürtel sei.

Es ist das Mitleid, das so seinen Finger auf uns legt;
Und alles, was die Erde an aufsteigenden Seufzern hat,
Es scheint, als ob es meinem trunkenen Herzen erzählten
Deine zum Himmel erhobenen, so traurigen und so weichen Augen.

17. Le Parfum impérissable
Leconte de Lisle

Quand la fleur du soleil, la rose de Lahor,
De son âme odorante a rempli goutte à goutte
La fiole d'argile ou de cristal ou d'or,
Sur le sable qui brûle on peut l'épandre toute.

Les fleuves et la mer inonderaient en vain
Ce sanctuaire étroit qui la tint enfermée;
Il garde en se brisant son arome divin,
Et sa poussière heureuse en reste parfumée.

Puisque par la blessure ouverte de mon cœur
Tu t'écoules de même, ô céleste liqueur,
Inexprimable amour, qui m'enflammais pour elle!

Qu'il lui soit pardonné, que mon mal soit béni!
Par delà l'heure humaine et le temps infini
Mon cœur est embaumé d'une odeur immortelle!

17. Inextinguishable perfume
Leconte de Lisle

When the flower of the sun, the rose of Lahore,
Has drop by drop from her scented soul
Filled the phial of day or crystal or gold,
It can all be scattered on the burning sands.

Rivers and oceans would flood in vain
This narrow sanctuary where it was confined;
On shattering it keeps its heavenly scent,
Which still perfumes its happy dust.

Since through the gaping wound of my heart
You likewise flow, O heavenly nectar,
Ineffable love which inflamed me for her!

May she be pardoned and my pain be blessed!
Beyond this world and infinity
My heart is embalmed with immortal fragrance!

17. Der unvergängliche Duft
Leconte de Lisle

Wenn die Blume der Sonne, die Rose von Lahor,
Mit ihrer duftenden Seele Tropfen für Tropfen
                              gefüllt hat
Die Fiole aus Ton oder Kristall oder Gold,
Kann man sie auf dem Sand, der brennt,
                            vollständig ausgießen.

Die Flüsse und das Meer überschwemmten vergeblich
Dieses enge Heiligtum, das sie eingeschlossen hatte:
Es behält seinen Duft, während es zerbricht,
Und sein glücklicher Staub bleibt davon durchduftet.

Da durch die offene Wunde meines Herzens
Du ebenso dahinfließt, o himmlischer Saft,
Unaussprechliche Liebe, die mich für sie entflammte.

Auf daß es ihr verziehen sei, auf daß mein Leiden
                            gesegnet sei!
Über die menschliche Stunde und die unendliche
                            Zeit hinaus
Ist mein Herz durchströmt von einem unsterblichen
                            Duft!

18. Arpège
Albert Samain

L'âme d'une flûte soupire
Au fond du parc mélodieux;
Limpide est l'ombre où l'on respire
Ton poème silencieux,

Nuit de langueur, nuit de mensonge,
Qui poses d'un geste ondoyant
Dans ta chevelure de songe
La lune, bijou d'Orient.

Sylva, Sylvie et Sylvanire,
Belles au regard bleu changeant,
L'étoile aux fontaines se mire,
Allez par les sentiers d'argent,

Allez vite – l'heure est si brève!
Cueillir au jardin des aveux
Les cœurs qui se meurent du rêve
De mourir parmi vos cheveux…

18. Arpeggio
Albert Samain

The soul of a flute is sighing
Deep in the melodious park;
The shade is limpid where one breathes
Your silent poem,

Night of languor, night of delusion,
That with a flowing gesture
Sets in your dreamy hair
The moon, that Orient jewel.

Sylva, Sylvie and Sylvanire,
Beauties with eyes of shimmering blue,
Fountains reflect the morning star –
Go along the silvery paths,

Go quickly – time is so short!
To gather in the garden of vows
The hearts which are dying of the dream
Of dying enveloped in your hair…

18. Arpeggio
Albert Samain

Die Seele einer Flöte seufzt
Tief im melodischen Park;
Klar ist der Schatten, wo man einatmet
Dein stilles Gedicht,

Nacht der Wehmut, Nacht der Lüge,
Die mit einer wiegenden Gebärde legt
In dein Traumhaar
Den Mond, Schmuck des Orients.

Sylva, Sylvie und Sylvanire,
Schöne mit dem blauen schillernden Blick,
Der Stern spiegelt sich in den Brunnen,
Geht auf den silbernen Pfaden,

Geht schnell – die Stunde ist so kurz!
Im Garten der Geständnisse pflückt
Die Herzen, die in dem Traum,
Zwischen Euren Haaren zu sterben, zugrunde gehen…

19. Chanson de Mélisande
Maurice Maeterlinck[2]

Les trois sœurs aveugles,
(Espérons encore).
Les trois sœurs aveugles,
Ont leurs lampes d'or.

Montent à la tour,
(Elles, vous et nous).
Montent à la tour,
Attendent sept jours.

Ah! dit la première,
Espérons encore,
Ah! dit la première,
J'entends nos lumières.

Ah! dit la seconde,
(Elles, vous et nous).
Ah! dit la seconde,
C'est le roi qui monte.

Non, dit la plus sainte,
(Espérons encore).
Non, dit la plus sainte,
Elles se sont éteintes…

19. Mélisandes Lied
Maurice Maeterlinck, trans. Jack Mackail

The King's three blind daughters
Sit locked in a hold.
In the darkness their lamps
Make a glimmer of gold.

Up the stairs of the turret
The sisters are gone,
Seven days they wait there
And the lamps they burn on.

What hope? Says the first
And leans o'er the flame.
I hear our lamps burning,
O yet! if he came!

O hope! says the second
Was that the lamp's flare
Or a sound of low footsteps? –
The Prince on the stair!

But the holiest sister
She turns her about:
Oh no hope now for ever,
Our lamps are gone out.

19. Mélisandes Lied
Maurice Maeterlinck

Des Königs drei blinde Töchter
Sitzen eingesperrt in einem Gefängnis.
Ihre Lampen schimmern in der Dunkelheit
Wie Gold.

Die Treppen zum Türmchen hinauf
Sind die Schwestern gegangen,
Sieben Tage warten sie da
und die Lampen brennen weiter.

Was besteht für Hoffnung? sagt die erste,
Und lehnt sich über die Flamme.
Ich höre unsere Lampe brennen,
O wenn er doch käme!

O Hoffnung! sagt die zweite,
Das war das Flackern der Lampe
Oder der Klang von leisen Schritten?
Der Prinz auf der Treppe!

Aber die heiligste Schwester
Sie dreht sich herum:
O nun ist die Hoffnung für immer verloren,
Unsere Lampen sind ausgegangen.

---

[2] Original French from *Pelléas et Mélisande* (see **Preface**)

20. Dans la forêt de septembre
Catulle Mendès

Ramure aux rumeurs amollies,
Troncs sonores que l'âge creuse,
L'antique forêt douloureuse
S'accorde à nos mélancolies.

Ô sapins agriffés au gouffre,
Nids déserts des [aux] branches brisées,
Halliers brûlés, fleurs sans rosées,
Vous savez bien comme l'on souffre !

Et lorsque l'homme, passant blême,
Pleure dans le bois solitaire,
Des plaintes d'ombre et de mystère
L'accueillent en pleurant de même.

II

Bonne forêt ! promesse ouverte
De l'exil que la vie implore !
Je viens d'un pas vivace [alerte] encore
Dans ta profondeur encor verte,

Mais, d'un fin bouleau de la sente,
Une feuille, un peu rousse, frôle
Ma tête, et tremble à mon épaule ;
C'est que la forêt vieillissante,

Sachant l'hiver où tout avorte
Déjà proche en moi comme en elle,
Me fait l'aumône fraternelle
De sa première feuille morte.

21. La Belle dans la nuit et la fleur qui va sur l'eau
{La Fleur qui va sur l'eau}
Catulle Mendès

Sur la mer voilée
D'un brouillard amer,
La Belle est allée,
La nuit, sur la mer !

Elle avait aux lèvres
D'un air irrité
La Rose des fièvres,
La Rose Beauté.

D'un souffle farouche
L'ouragan hurleur
Lui baisa la bouche
Et lui prit la fleur.

Dans l'océan sombre,
Moins sombre déjà,
Où le trois-mâts sombre
La fleur surnagea.

L'eau s'en est jouée,
Dans ses noirs sillons ;
C'est une bouée
Pour les papillons.

Et l'embrun, la houle,
Depuis cette nuit,
Les brisants où croule
Un sauvage bruit,

L'alcyon, la voile,
L'hirondelle autour,
Et l'ombre et l'étoile
Se meurent d'amour.

Et l'aurore éclose
Dans [Sur] le gouffre clair,
Pour la seule rose
De toute la mer !

20. In the September forest
Catulle Mendès

Foliage of deadened sound,
Resonant trunks hollowed by age,
The ancient, mournful forest
Blends with our melancholy.

O fir-trees, clinging to chasms,
Abandoned nests in broken branches,
Burnt-out thickets, flowers without dew,
You well know our suffering!

And when man, that pale wanderer,
Weeps in the lonely wood,
Shadowy, mysterious laments
Greet him, likewise weeping.

II

Good forest! Open promise
Of exile that life implores!
I come with a step still brisk
Into your ever-green depths,

But, from a slender birch by the path,
A reddish leaf brushes
My head, and quivers on my shoulder;
For the ageing forest,

Knowing that winter, when all withers,
Is already close for me as for her,
Bestows on me the fraternal gift
Of its first dead leaf.

21. The Fair Lady in the night, and the flower on the water
{The flower on the water}
Catulle Mendès

On the sea
A bitter fog has veiled,
The Fair Lady set out,
At night, on the sea!

Between her lips,
Indignantly, she held
The Rose of Fevers,
The Rose of Beauty.

With its savage breath
The shrieking storm
Kissed her mouth
And took the flower.

In the sombre ocean,
Less sombre now,
Where the three-master sinks
The flower floated.

The waves toyed with it,
In their black furrows;
Like a buoy
Attracting butterflies.

And since that night,
The spray, the swell,
The breakers crashing
With a savage roar,

The halcyon, the sails,
The circling swallows,
The shadows and the stars
All have been dying with love.

And the dawn breaking
Over the clear depths,
For the only rose
In all the sea!

20. Im Septemberwald
Catulle Mendès

Geäst mit weichem Geräusch,
Tönende Stämme, die das Alter höhlt,
Der altertümliche schmerzhafte Wald
Harmoniert mit unserer Schwermut.

O am Schlund sich klammernde Tannen,
Verwaiste Nester auf geknickten Ästen,
Verbranntes Dickicht, Blumen ohne Tau,
Ihr wißt genau, wie sehr man leidet!

Und wenn der bleich Vorübergehende
Im einsamen Wald weint,
Klagen von Schatten und von Geheimnis
Empfangen auch ihn weinend.

II

Guter Wald! offenes Versprechen
Der Verbannung, die das Leben erfleht!
Ich komme noch mit raschem Schritt
In deine noch grüne Tiefe.

Aber von einer zarten Birke des kleinen Pfades
Streift ein etwas rötliches Blatt
Meinen Kopf und zittert an meiner Schulter;
Das bedeutet, daß der alternde Wald,

Der den Winter, wo alles verkümmert,
Schon nahe weiß in mir wie in ihm,
Mir sein erstes welkes Blatt
Als brüderliches Almosen gibt.

21. Die Schöne in der Nacht und die Blume auf dem Wasser
{Die Blume auf dem Wasser}
Catulle Mendès

Auf das Meer, verschleiert
Von einem bitteren Nebel,
Ist die Schöne gegangen,
Nachts, auf das Meer!

Sie hatte auf den Lippen,
Mit ärgerlicher Miene,
Die Rose des Fiebers,
Die Rose der Schönheit.

Mit heftigem Atem
Küßte der brüllende Sturm
Ihr den Mund
Und nahm ihr die Blume.

Im düsteren Ozean,
Weniger düster schon,
Wo der Dreimaster versinkt,
Schwimmt die Blume oben.

Das Wasser hielt sie zum Besten,
In seinen schwarzen Furchen;
Es ist eine Boje
Für die Schmetterlinge.

Und die Gischt, die Dünung,
Seit dieser Nacht,
Die Klippen, auf die einstürzt
Ein wilder Lärm.

Der Eisvogel, das Segel,
Die Schwalbe darum herum,
Und der Schatten und der Stern
Sterben vor Liebe.

Und die Morgenröte erblüht
Über dem hellen Schlund
Für die einzige Rose
Auf dem ganzen Meer.

22. Accompagnement
Albert Samain

Tremble argenté, tilleul, bouleau…
La lune s'effeuille sur l'eau…

Comme de longs cheveux peignés au vent du soir,
L'odeur des nuits d'été parfume le lac noir.
Le grand lac parfumé brille comme un miroir.

    La [Ma] rame tombe et se relève,
    Ma barque glisse dans le rêve.

    Ma barque glisse dans le ciel
    Sur le lac immatériel…

    […]

    En cadence, les yeux fermés,
    Rame, ô mon cœur, ton indolence
    À larges coups lents et pâmés.

Là-bas, la lune écoute, accoudée au coteau,
Le silence qu'exhale en glissant le bateau…
Trois grands lys frais-coupés meurent sur mon manteau.

Vers tes lèvres, ô Nuit voluptueuse et pâle,
Est-ce leur âme, est-ce mon âme qui s'exhale ?
Cheveux des nuits d'argent peignés aux longs roseaux…

    Comme la lune sur les eaux,
    Comme la rame sur les flots,
    Mon âme s'effeuille en sanglots !

22. Accompaniment
Albert Samain

Silver aspen, lime, birch…
The moon sheds itself on the water…

Like long hair combed by the evening breeze,
The scent of summer nights perfumes the black lake.
The great perfumed lake gleams like a mirror.

    My oar dips and rises,
    My boat glides in the dream.

    My boat glides in the sky
    On the insubstantial lake…

    […]

    In cadence, with closed eyes,
    Row, O my heart, your indolence
    In broad slow swooning strokes.

Over there the moon, against the hillside, listens
To the silence of the gliding boat…
Three large fresh-cut lilies die on my cape.

Is it their soul or mine that rises
To your lips, O pale and voluptuous night?
Hair of silver nights combed by tall reeds…

    Like the moon on the waters,
    Like the oar on the waves,
    My soul sheds itself in sobs!

22. Begleitung
Albert Samain

Versilberte Espe, Linde, Birke…
Der Mond entlaubt sich über dem Wasser…

Wie lange Haare, gekämmt mit dem Abendwind,
Umhüllt der Geruch der Sommernächte den
    schwarzen See mit seinem Duft.

    Mein Ruder fällt und hebt sich,
    Mein Boot gleitet in den Traum.

    Mein Boot gleitet in den Himmel
    Über den erdentrückten See.

    […]

    Rhythmisch, die Augen geschlossen,
    Rudert, o mein Herz, deine Trägheit
    Mit weiten Schlägen, langsam und erstarrt.

Dort hört der Mond, mit den Ellenbogen auf den
    Hügel gestützt,
Der Stille zu, die das gleitende Boot verströmt…
Drei große, frisch geschnittene Lilien sterben auf
    meinem Mantel.

Ist es ihre Seele, ist es meine Seele, die sich aushaucht
Zu deinen Lippen, o sinnliche und blasse Nacht?
Silberne Haare der Nacht, gekämmt mit langem Schilf…

    Wie der Mond über den Wassern,
    Wie das Ruder auf den Fluten,
    Entblättert sich meine schluchzende Seele!

23. {Le plus doux chemin}
Armand Silvestre

À mes pas le plus doux chemin
Mène à la porte de ma belle,
– Et, bien qu'elle me soit rebelle,
J'y veux encor passer demain.

Il est tout fleuri de jasmin
Au temps de la saison nouvelle,
– Et, bien qu'elle me soit rebelle [cruelle],
J'y passe, des fleurs à la main.

Pour toucher son cœur inhumain
J'y [Je] chante ma peine cruelle,
– Et, bien qu'elle me soit rebelle,
C'est pour moi le plus doux chemin !

23. {The sweetest path}
Armand Silvestre

The sweetest path for me
Leads to the door of my fair one,
– And, although she resists me,
I shall tomorrow pass by once more.

It is all a-bloom with jasmine
When the new season arrives,
– And, although she resists me,
I go there bearing flowers.

To touch her inhuman heart
I sing of my cruel pain,
– And, although she resists me,
It is for me the sweetest path!

23. {Der süßeste Weg}
Armand Silvestre

Meine Schritte führt der süßeste Weg
Zur Tür meiner Schönen,
– Und, obwohl sie sich mir widersetzt,
Will ich dort morgen nochmals vorbeigehen.

Er ist ganz geschmückt mit Jasmin
In der neuen Jahreszeit,
– Und, obowohl sie grausam zu mir ist,
Gehe ich dort mit Blumen in der Hand vorbei.

Um ihr unmenschliches Herz zu berühren,
Singe ich mein grausames Leid,
– Und, obwohl sie sich mir widersetzt,
Ist es für mich der süßeste Weg.

24. {Le Ramier}
Armand Silvestre

Avec son chant doux et plaintif,
Ce ramier blanc te fait envie :
S'il te plaît l'avoir pour captif,
J'irai te le chercher, Sylvie.

Mais là, près de toi, dans mon sein,
Comme ce ramier mon cœur chante :
S'il t'en plaît faire le larcin,
Il sera mieux à toi, méchante !

Pour qu'il soit tel qu'un ramier blanc,
Le prisonnier que tu recèles,
Sur mon cœur, oiselet tremblant,
Pose tes mains comme deux ailes.

24. {The ring-dove}
Armand Silvestre

With its gentle plaintive song,
This white ring-dove makes you envious:
If you want it as a captive,
I'll go and seek it for you, Sylvie.

But there, near you, in my breast,
Like this ring-dove, my heart sings:
If you would like to steal it,
It will be better for you, wicked girl!

For it to be like a white ring-dove,
The prisoner that you conceal,
Place your hands like two wings
On my heart, a trembling little bird.

24. {Die Ringeltaube}
Armand Silvestre

Mit ihrem lieblichen und klagenden Gesang
Macht dir diese weiße Ringeltaube Lust;
Wenn du sie als Gefangene haben willst,
Werde ich sie dir holen, Sylvie.

Aber da, nahe bei dir, in meiner Brust,
Singt mein Herz wie diese Ringeltaube:
Wenn es dir gefällt, daraus Diebesbeute zu machen,
Wird er dir besser gehören, Böse!

Damit er so ist wie eine weiße Ringeltaube,
Der Gefangene, den du verbirgst,
Auf mein Herz, zitterndes Vöglein,
Lege deine Hände wie zwei Flügel.

25. {Le Don silencieux}
Jean Dominique

Je mettrai mes deux mains sur ma bouche, pour taire
Ce que je voudrais tant vous dire, âme bien chère !

Je mettrai mes deux mains sur mes yeux, pour cacher
Ce que je voudrais tant que pourtant vous cherchiez.

Je mettrai mes deux mains sur mon cœur, chère vie,
Pour que vous ignoriez de quel cœur je vous prie !

Et puis je les mettrai doucement dans vos mains,
Ces deux mains-ci qui meurent d'un fatigant chagrin !...

Elles iront à vous, pleines de leur faiblesse,
Toutes silencieuses et même sans caresse,

Lasses d'avoir porté tout le poids d'un secret
Dont ma bouche, [et] mes yeux et mon cœur [front]
              parleraient.

Elles iront à vous, légères d'être vides,
Et lourdes d'être tristes, tristes d'être timides ;

Malheureuses et douces et si découragées
Que peut-être, mon Dieu, vous les recueillerez !...

25. {The silent gift}
Jean Dominique

I shall place my two hands over my mouth, to silence
What I so wish to tell you, dearest soul!

I shall place my two hands over my eyes, to hide
What I still so wish you to seek.

I shall place my two hands over my heart, dear life,
That you may not know with how much heart I entreat!

And then I shall place them gently in your hands,
These two hands that die of a wearying sorrow!...

They will come to you, full of their weakness,
All silent and even without a caress,

Weary of having borne all the weight of a secret
That my lips and eyes and heart would reveal.

They will come to you, light at being empty,
Heavy at being sad, sad at being shy;

Unhappy and gentle and so downcast
That maybe, my God, you will gather them up!...

25. {Die stille Gabe}
Jean Dominique

Ich werde meine beiden Hände auf meinen Mund
              legen, um zu verschweigen,
Was ich Euch so gerne sagen möchte, gute, liebe Seele!

Ich werde meine zwei Hände auf meine Augen legen,
              um das zu verstecken,
Von dem ich so gerne möchte, daß Ihr es dennoch sucht.

Ich werde meine beiden Hände auf mein Herz legen,
              liebes Leben,
Damit Ihr nicht wißt, mit welchem Herzen ich
              Euch bitte!

Und dann werde ich sie zärtlich in Eure Hände legen,
Diese beiden Hände hier, die eines ermüdenden
              Kummers sterben!...

Sie werden zu Euch gehen, voll ihrer Schwäche,
Ganz leise und selbst ohne Zärtlichkeit,

Müde, das ganze Gewicht eines Geheimnisses
              getragen zu haben,
Das mein Mund und meine Augen und mein Herz
              ausgeplaudert hätten.

Sie werden zu Euch gehen, leicht, weil sie leer sind,
Und schwer, weil sie traurig sind, traurig,
              weil sie schüchtern sind;

Unglücklich und sanft und so entmutigt,
Daß vielleicht, mein Gott, Ihr sie aufnehmt!...

26. Chanson
Henri de Régnier

Que me fait toute la terre
Inutile où tu n'as pas
En marchant marqué tes [ton] pas
Sur [Dans] le sable ou la poussière !

Il n'est de fleuve attendu
Par ma soif qui s'y étanche
Que l'eau qui sourd et s'épanche
De la source où tu as bu ;

La seule fleur qui m'attire
Est celle où je trouverai
Le souvenir empourpré
De ta bouche et de ton rire ;

Et, sous la courbe des cieux,
La mer pour moi n'est immense
Que parce qu'elle commence
À la couleur de tes yeux.

26. Song
Henri de Régnier

What use to me is all the earth
Where you have not left
The imprint of your steps
In the sand or the dust!

I await no river
To quench my thirst
But the waters that well and flow
From the spring where you have drunk;

The only flower which attracts me
Is that on which I'll find
The crimson memory
Of your lips and your laughter;

And beneath the sweep of the sky,
The sea for me is only immense
Because it begins
With the colour of your eyes.

26. Lied
Henri de Régnier

Was kümmert mich die ganze Erde;
Unnütz, wo du nicht
Laufend deinen Fußstapfen abgedrückt hast
In den Sand oder den Staub!

Es wird kein Fluß erwartet
Von meinem Durst, der sich daran stillt,
Als nur das Wasser, das hervorquillt und sich ergießt
Aus der Quelle, an der du getrunken hast;

Die einzige Blume, die mich anzieht,
Ist die, in der ich finden werde
Die purpurne Erinnerung
Deines Mundes und deines Lachens;

Und unter der Wölbung des Himmels
Ist das Meer für mich nur unermeßlich,
Weil es beginnt
In der Farbe deiner Augen.

27. C'est la Paix
Gilette de Besgador [Georgette Debladis]

Pendant qu'ils étaient partis pour la guerre
On ne dansait plus, on ne parlait guère,
    On ne chantait pas.
Mes sœurs ! c'est la paix ! la guerre est finie ;
Allons, au devant, dans la paix bénie
           [Dans la paix bénie courons au devant]
De nos chers Poilus [soldats].

[…]

Nous les bercerons avec sa cadence
           [Et joyeusement, toutes en cadence,]
Et nous danserons avec eux la danse [Nous irons vers eux en dansant la danse]
    Qu'on danse chez nous.

[…]

Nous les aimerons ! la guerre est finie.
Ils seront aimés dans la paix bénie
    Sitôt leur retour ;
Pour avoir chassé la horde germaine
Ils auront nos cœurs ; au lieu de la haine
    Ils auront l'amour.

27. Peace has come
Georgette Debladis

As long as they were at the wars
We danced no more, we hardly spoke,
    We did not sing.
My sisters, peace has come! The war is over;
In this blessed peace,
    Let us run to meet our dear soldiers.

[…]

And joyfully, keeping time,
We shall all move towards them, dancing
    The dance we dance at home.

[…]

We shall love them! The war is over.
They shall be loved in this blessed peace,
    As soon as they return;
For having routed the German hordes,
They shall have our hearts; – instead of hate,
    They shall have love.

27. Es ist Frieden
Georgette Debladis

Während sie in den Krieg gezogen waren,
Tanzte man nicht mehr, man sprach kaum,
    Man sang nicht.
Meine Schwestern, es ist Frieden! Der Krieg ist zu Ende,
Im gesegneten Frieden
    Laufen wir unseren lieben Soldaten entgegen.

[…]

Und alle glücklich, im Takt,
Gehen wir zu ihnen und tanzen den Tanz,
    Den man bei uns tanzt.

[…]

Wir werden sie lieben! Der Krieg ist aus.
Sie werden geliebt sein im gesegneten Frieden,
    Sobald sie zurück sind;
Dafür, daß sie die germanische Horde davongejagt haben,
Werden sie unsere Herzen besitzen; anstatt Haß
    Werden sie Liebe haben.

28. Noël
Victor Wilder

La nuit descend du haut des cieux,
Le givre au toit suspend ses franges.
Et, dans les airs, le vol des anges
Éveille un bruit mystérieux.

L'étoile qui guidait les mages
S'arrête enfin dans les nuages,
Et fait briller un nimbe d'or
Sur la chaumière où Jésus dort.

Alors, ouvrant ses yeux divins,
L'enfant couché dans l'humble crèche,
De son berceau de paille fraîche,
Sourit aux nobles pèlerins.

Eux, s'inclinant, lui disent : – Sire,
Reçois l'encens, l'or et la myrrhe,
Et laisse-nous, ô doux Jésus,
Baiser le bout de tes pieds nus.

Comme eux, ô peuple, incline-toi,
Imite leur pieux exemple,
Car cette étable, c'est un temple,
Et cet enfant sera ton roi !

28. Christmas
Victor Wilder

Night falls from the sky,
Frost hangs its fringes along the roofs.
And the flight of angels in the sky
Creates a mysterious sound.

The star that led the Magi
Stops at last in the clouds,
And casts a golden halo
Above the humble dwelling where Jesus sleeps.

Then, opening His divine eyes,
From His crib of fresh hay
The Child, lying in the humble manger,
Smiles at the noble pilgrims.

They, bowing down, address Him: Sire,
Receive the incense, gold and myrrh,
And allow us, gentle Jesus,
To kiss the tips of your naked feet.

Bow down like them, O people,
Follow their devout example,
For this stable is a temple,
And this Child shall be your king!

28. Weihnachten
Victor Wilder

Die Nacht steigt von den Höhen des Himmels hernieder,
Der Frost hängt seine Fransen ans Dach,
Und in den Lüften erweckt der Flug der Engel
Ein geheimnisvolles Geräusch.

Der Stern, der die Weisen führte,
Hält endlich in den Wolken an
Und läßt einen goldenen Schein erstrahlen
Über der Hütte, wo Jesus schläft.

Nun, jetzt, da es seine göttlichen Augen öffnet,
lächelt das Kind, in der bescheidenen Krippe liegend,
Aus seiner Wiege aus frischem Stroh
Den edlen Pilgern zu.

Sie verbeugen sich und sagen: Herr,
Empfange den Weihrauch, das Gold und die Myrrhe
Und lass uns, o süßer Jesus,
die Spitze deiner nackten Füße küssen.

Wie sie, o Volk, verneige dich,
Ahme dieses fromme Beispiel nach,
Denn dieser Stall ist ein Tempel,
Und dieses Kind wird dein König sein!

29. En prière
Stéphan Bordèse

Si la voix d'un enfant peut monter jusqu'à Vous,
    Ô mon Père,
Écoutez de Jésus, devant Vous à genoux,
    La prière !

Si Vous m'avez choisi pour enseigner vos lois
    Sur la terre,
Je saurai Vous servir, auguste Roi des rois,
    Ô Lumière !

Sur mes lèvres, Seigneur, mettez la vérité
    Salutaire,
Pour que celui qui doute, avec humilité
    Vous révère !

Ne m'abandonnez pas, donnez-moi la douceur
    Nécessaire,
Pour apaiser les maux, soulager la douleur,
    La misère.

Révélez-Vous à moi, Seigneur en qui je crois
    Et j'espère :
Pour Vous je veux souffrir et mourir sur la croix,
    Au Calvaire !

29. In prayer
Stéphan Bordèse

If a child's voice may rise up to You,
    O my Father,
Hear the prayer of Jesus who kneels before You
    In prayer!

If You have chosen me to teach Your laws
    On earth,
I shall serve You, august King of Kings,
    O light!

On my lips, O Lord, place truth that is
    Salutary,
So that he who doubts may with humility
    Revere You!

Do not abandon me, give me the kindness
    Required,
To ease pain, console sorrow
    And misery.

Reveal Yourself to me, Lord, in whom I believe
    And hope:
For you I would suffer and die on the Cross,
    On Calvary!

29. Im Gebet
Stéphan Bordèse

Wenn die Stimme eines Kindes bis zu Euch
    aufsteigen kann,
    O mein Vater,
Hört von Jesus, der vor Euch kniet,
    Das Gebet!

Wenn Ihr mich auserwählt habt, um Eure Gesetze
    zu lehren
    Auf Erden,
Wüßte ich Euch zu dienen, erhabener König der Könige,
    O Licht!

Auf meine Lippen, Herr, legt die heilsame Wahrheit.
Damit der, der zweifelt, mit Demut
    Euch verehrt!

Verlaßt mich nicht, gebt mir die nötige
    Milde,
Um die Leiden zu stillen, die Schmerzen zu lindern,
    Das Elend!

Offenbart Euch mir, Herr, an den ich glaube,
    Und ich hoffe.
Für Euch will ich leiden und sterben am Kreuz,
    Auf dem Kalvarienberg!

30. {Puisqu'ici-bas toute âme}
Victor Hugo

Puisqu'ici-bas toute âme
    Donne à quelqu'un
Sa musique, sa flamme,
    Ou son parfum ;

Puisqu'ici toute chose
    Donne toujours
Son épine ou sa rose
    À ses amours ;

Puisqu'avril donne aux chênes
    Un bruit charmant ;
Que la nuit donne aux peines
    L'oubli dormant ;

[…]

Puisque, lorsqu'elle arrive
    S'y reposer,
L'onde amère à la rive
    Donne un baiser ;

Je te donne à cette heure,
    Penché sur toi,
La chose la meilleure
    Que j'aie en moi !

Reçois donc ma pensée,
    Triste d'ailleurs,
Qui, comme une rosée,
    T'arrive en pleurs !

Reçois mes vœux sans nombre,
    Ô mes amours !
Reçois la flamme ou l'ombre
    De tous mes jours !

Mes transports pleins d'ivresses,
    Purs de soupçons,
Et toutes les caresses
    De mes chansons !

Mon esprit qui sans voile
    Vogue au hasard,
Et qui n'a pour étoile
    Que ton regard !

[…]

Reçois, mon bien céleste,
    Ô ma beauté !
Mon cœur dont rien ne reste,
    L'amour ôté !

30. {Since here on earth each soul}
Victor Hugo

Since here on earth each soul
    Gives someone
Its music, its ardour,
    Or its perfume;

Since here all things
    Will always give
Their thorns or roses
    To those they love;

Since April gives the oaks
    A sound that charms;
And night gives suffering
    Drowsy oblivion;

[…]

Since when they come
    To settle there,
The briny waves
    Give the shore a kiss;

I give you, at this hour,
    Inclining over you,
The finest things
    I have in me!

Accept, then, my thoughts,
    Sad though they be,
Which, like drops of dew,
    Come to you as tears!

Accept my countless vows,
    O my loves!
Accept the flame and the shade
    Of all my days!

My frenzied rapture,
    Devoid of all distrust,
And all the caresses
    Of my songs!

My spirit that floats at random
    Without a sail,
And has no lodestar
    But your gaze!

[…]

Take all my celestial qualities,
    O my beauty,
My heart, of which nothing remains,
    When there's no love!

30. {Da hienieden}
Victor Hugo

Da hienieden jede Seele
    Jemandem
Ihre Musik, ihre Flamme
    Oder ihren Duft gibt;

Da hier jedes Ding
    Immer
Seinen Stachel oder seine Rose
    Seinen Liebsten gibt;

Da der April den Eichen
    einen reizenden Klang verleiht;
Auf daß die Nacht der Pein
    Das schlafende Vergessen gebe;

[…]

Da, während sie ankommt,
    Um sich an ihm auszuruhen,
Die bittere Welle dem Ufer
    Einen Kuss gibt;

Gebe ich dir zu dieser Stunde,
    Über dich gebeugt,
Das Beste,
    Das ich in mir habe!

Empfang' denn mein Denken,
    Traurig übrigens,
Welches wie ein Tau
    Zu dir in Tränen kommt!

Empfang' meine zahlreichen Gelübde,
    O meine Liebe!
Empfange die Flamme oder den Schatten
    All meiner Tage!

Meinen Trunkenheitstaumel,
    Bar jeden Argwohns,
Und all die Zärtlichkeiten
    Meiner Lieder!

Meinen Geist, der ohne Segel
    Zufällig dahingleitet,
Und der als Stern
    Nur deinen Blick hat!

[…]

Empfange, mein himmlisches Gut,
    O meine Schönheit,
Mein Herz, von dem nichts mehr bleibt,
    Wenn man die Liebe wegnimmt!

31. Tarentelle
Marc Monnier

Aux cieux la lune monte et luit.
Il fait grand jour en plein minuit.
Viens avec moi, me disait-elle,
Viens sur le sable grésillant
Où saute et glisse [brille] en frétillant
    La tarentelle.

Sus, les danseurs ! En voilà [voici] deux :
Foule sur l'eau, foule autour d'eux ;
L'homme est bien fait, la fille est belle ;
Mais gare à vous ! Sans y penser,
C'est jeu d'amour que de danser
    La tarentelle.

[…]

Doux est le bruit du tambourin !
Si j'étais fille de marin
Et toi pêcheur, me disait-elle,
Toutes les nuits joyeusement
Nous danserions en nous aimant
    La tarentelle.

31. Tarantella
Marc Monnier

The moon rises bright in the sky,
Turning midnight into day.
Come with me, she said,
Come to the whirling sands
And the leaping, flashing and turning
    Tarantella.

Come! Here are two dancers,
Thronged around in the water;
The man is well-built, the girl beautiful;
But look out! Before you are aware,
You'll be playing with love if you dance
    The tarantella.

[…]

Sweet is the sound of the drum!
If I were a sailor's daughter
And you a fisherman, she said,
Every night, full of joy,
We'd love each other and dance
    The tarantella.

31. Tarantella
Marc Monnier

Der Mond steigt in den Himmel auf und leuchtet,
Es ist taghell inmitten der Nacht.
Komm mit mir, sagte sie zu mir,
Komm auf den knisternden Sand,
Wo zappelnd springt und strahlt
    Die Tarantella.

Los, ihr Tänzer! Da sind zwei:
Menge auf dem Wasser, Menge um sie;
Der Mann ist wohlgestaltet, das Mädchen ist schön;
Aber paßt auf! Ohne daß man sich dessen bewußt ist,
Ist es Liebesspiel zu tanzen
    Die Tarantella.

[…]

Lieblich ist der Lärm des Tamburins!
Wenn ich ein Seemannsmädchen wäre
Und du Fischer, sagte sie,
Würden wir jede Nacht fröhlich
Uns liebend tanzen
    Die Tarantella.

32. Larmes
{Pleurs d'or}
Albert Samain

Larmes aux fleurs suspendues,
Larmes aux sources perdues
Aux mousses des rochers creux ;

Larmes d'automne épandues,
Larmes de cors entendues
Dans les grands bois douloureux ;

Larmes des cloches latines,
Carmélites, Feuillantines…
Voix des beffrois en ferveur ;

[…]

Larmes des nuits étoilées,
Larmes des flûtes voilées
Au bleu du parc endormi ;

Larmes aux longs [grands] cils perlées,
Larmes d'amantes coulées
Jusqu'à l'âme de l'ami ;

Gouttes [Larmes] d'extase, éplorement délicieux,
Tombez des nuits ! Tombez des fleurs ! Tombez des yeux !

[…]

32. Tears
{Golden tears}
Albert Samain

Tears clinging to flowers,
Tears from springs lost
In the moss of hollowed rocks;

Tears shed by autumn,
Tears from horns sounding
In great doleful forests;

Tears of church bells,
Of Carmelite and Feuillantine convents…
Devout belfry voices;

[…]

Tears of starlit nights,
Tears of muffled flutes
In the blue of the sleeping park;

Pearly tears on long lashes,
A beloved's tears flowing
To her friend's soul;

Tears of rapture, delicious weeping,
Fall at night! Fall from the flowers! Fall from these eyes!

[…]

32. Tränen
{Goldene Tränen}
Albert Samain

An Blumen hängende Tränen,
Tränen von Quellen, verloren
Im Moos hohler Felsen.

Vergessene Herbsttränen,
Tränen von Hörnern vernommen
In den großen schmerzhaften Wäldern.

Tränen lateinischer Glocken,
Karmeliter, Feuillanten…
Stimmen eifriger Glockentürme;

[…]

Tränen sternenübersäter Nächte,
Tränen verletzter Flöten
Im Blau des verschlafenen Parks;

Perlenförmige Tränen an großen Wimpern,
Tränen der Geliebten, geflossen
Bis zur Seele des Freundes;

Tränen der Verzückung, tränenerstickt köstlich,
Fallt vom Nachthimmel! Fallt von den Bäumen!
Fallt aus den Augen!

[…]

33. {Madrigal}
Armand Silvestre

LES JEUNES GENS
– Inhumaines qui, sans merci,
Vous raillez de notre souci,
Aimez ! aimez quand on vous aime !

LES JEUNES FILLES
– Ingrats qui ne vous doutez pas
Des rêves éclos sur vos pas,
Aimez ! aimez quand on vous aime !

LES JEUNES GENS
– Sachez, ô cruelles Beautés,
Que les jours d'aimer sont comptés.
Aimez ! aimez quand on vous aime !

LES JEUNES FILLES
– Sachez, amoureux inconstants,
Que le bien d'aimer n'a qu'un temps.
Aimez ! aimez quand on vous aime !

ENSEMBLE
Le [Un] même destin nous poursuit
Et notre folie est la même :
C'est celle d'aimer qui nous fuit,
C'est celle de fuir qui nous aime !

33. {Madrigal}
Armand Silvestre

YOUNG MEN
– You cruel women who, mercilessly,
Mock our turmoil,
Love! Love when you are loved!

YOUNG WOMEN
– You ungrateful men, heedless
Of the dreams that blossom in your footsteps,
Love! Love when you are loved!

YOUNG MEN
– Know, oh cruel beauties,
That the days of loving are numbered
Love! Love when you are loved!

YOUNG WOMEN
– Know, inconstant lovers,
That love flowers for but a single season.
Love! Love when you are loved!

TOGETHER
The same fate purses us
And our folly is the same:
That of loving those we flee,
And fleeing those we love!

(Translation: Roy Howat / Emily Kilpatrick)

33. {Madrigal}
Armand Silvestre

DIE JUNGEN
– Ihr Unbarmherzigen, die ihr ohne Gnade
Uunser Leiden nur belacht,
Liebet! Liebet, wenn man euch liebt!

DIE MÄDCHEN
– Ihr Undankbaren, die ihr nicht ahnt,
Dass Träume erblühen, wo ihr geht,
Liebet! Liebet, wenn man euch liebt!

DIE JUNGEN
– Wisset, ihr grausamen Schönen,
Dass die Tage des Liebens gezählt sind.
Liebet! Liebet, wenn man euch liebt!

DIE MÄDCHEN
– Wisset, ihr unstet Liebenden:
Das Gut der Liebe kehrt nicht wieder.
Liebet! Liebet, wenn man euch liebt!

ALLE
Uns verfolgt das gleiche Schicksal
Und gleich ist unser Wahn:
Zu lieben, wer uns flieht,
Zu fliehen, wer uns liebt!

(Übersetzung: Arne Muus)

Select Bibliography / Bibliographie sélective / Auswahlbibliographie

Abraham, Hélène (ed.). *Un Art de l'interprétation : Claire Croiza : les cahiers d'une auditrice*. Paris : Office de centralisation d'ouvrages, 1954

Bannerman, Betty (ed. & trans.). *The Singer as Interpreter: Claire Croiza's Master Classes*. London: Gollancz, 1989

Bernac, Pierre. *The Interpretation of French Song*. Translations of song texts by Winifred Radford. London: Gollancz, 1970

Duchen, Jessica. *Gabriel Fauré*. London: Phaidon, 2000

Fauré-Fremiet, Philippe. *Gabriel Fauré*. Paris : Albin Michel, 1957 (revised edition)
— (ed.). *Gabriel Fauré : Lettres intimes*. Paris : Grasset, 1951

Grubb, Thomas. *Singing in French: A Manual of French Diction and French Vocal Repertoire*. New York: Schirmer, 1979

Howat, Roy and Emily Kilpatrick. "Gabriel Fauré's Middle-Period Songs, Editorial Quandaries, and the Chimera of the 'Original Key'", *Journal of the Royal Musical Association* 139:2 (autumn 2014), pp. 303–37

Hunter, David. *Understanding French Verse: A Guide for Singers*. New York: Oxford UP, 2005

Jankélévitch, Vladimir. *Gabriel Fauré et ses mélodies*. Paris : Plon, 1938

Johnson, Graham. *Gabriel Fauré: The Songs and their Poets*. Aldershot: Ashgate, 2009
— and Richard Stokes. *A French Song Companion*. New York: Oxford UP, 2002

Jones, J. Barrie (ed. and trans.). *Gabriel Fauré: A Life in Letters*. London: Batsford, 1988

Jourdan-Morhange, Hélène. *Mes amis musiciens*. Paris: Les Éditeurs français réunis, 1955

Kilpatrick, Emily. "Moot Point: Editing Poetry and Punctuation in Fauré's Early Songs". *Nineteenth-Century Music Review* 9:2 (December 2012), pp. 213–235

Nectoux, Jean-Michel. *Gabriel Fauré : les voix du clair-obscur*. Paris : Fayard, 2008 (revised edition).
English edition: *Gabriel Fauré: A Musical Life*, transl. Roger Nichols. Cambridge: Cambridge UP, 1991

— (ed.). *Gabriel Fauré : Correspondance, suivie de Lettres à Madame H.* Paris: Fayard, 2015

— (ed.). *Gabriel Fauré: His Life through his Letters*, trans. J. A. Underwood. London and New York: Marion Boyars, 1984
English edition of *Gabriel Fauré : Correspondance*. Paris: Flammarion, 1980

Orledge, Robert. *Gabriel Fauré*. London: Eulenburg, 1979

Phillips, Edward. *Gabriel Fauré: A Research and Information Guide*. 2nd edn. New York & London: Routledge, 2010

Le Roux, François and Romain Reynaldy. *Le Chant intime : de l'interprétation de la mélodie française*. Paris: Fayard, 2004

Strobel, Klaus. *Das Liedschaffen Gabriel Faurés*. Hamburg: Verlag Dr Kovač, 2000

On questions of pronunciation, see *inter alia* the guidelines and observations by Roger Nichols in the Peters Editions *The Art of French Song* (EP 7519–7120) and collected songs of Duparc (EP 7778), in addition to Bernac, *The Interpretation of French Song* and Grubb, *Singing in French*.

Richtlinien und Betrachtungen zur Aussprache finden sich u. a. bei Roger Nichols in den bei Edition Peters erschienenen Ausgaben *The Art of French Song* (EP 7519–7120) und den sämtlichen Liedern Duparcs (EP 7778) sowie bei Pierre Bernac, *The Interpretation of French Song* und Thomas Grubb, *Singing in French*.

À Madame H. Roger-Jourdain

1. Aurore

(Armand Silvestre)

Gabriel Fauré (1845–1924)
Op. 39 No. 1

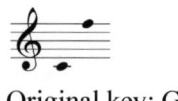
Original key: G

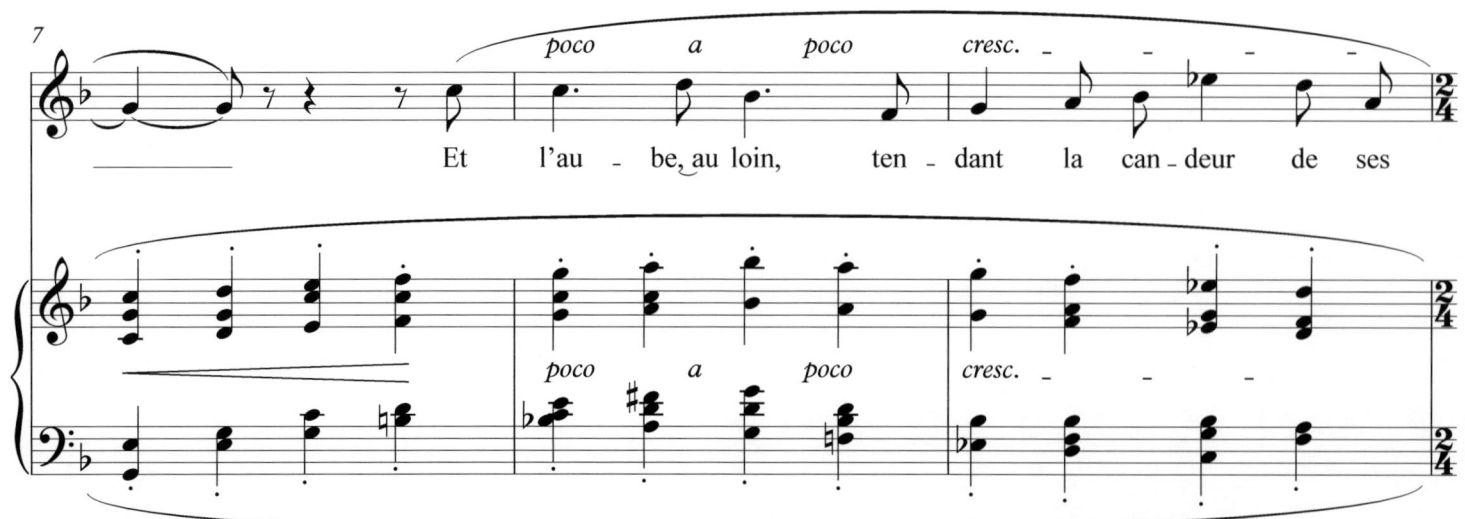

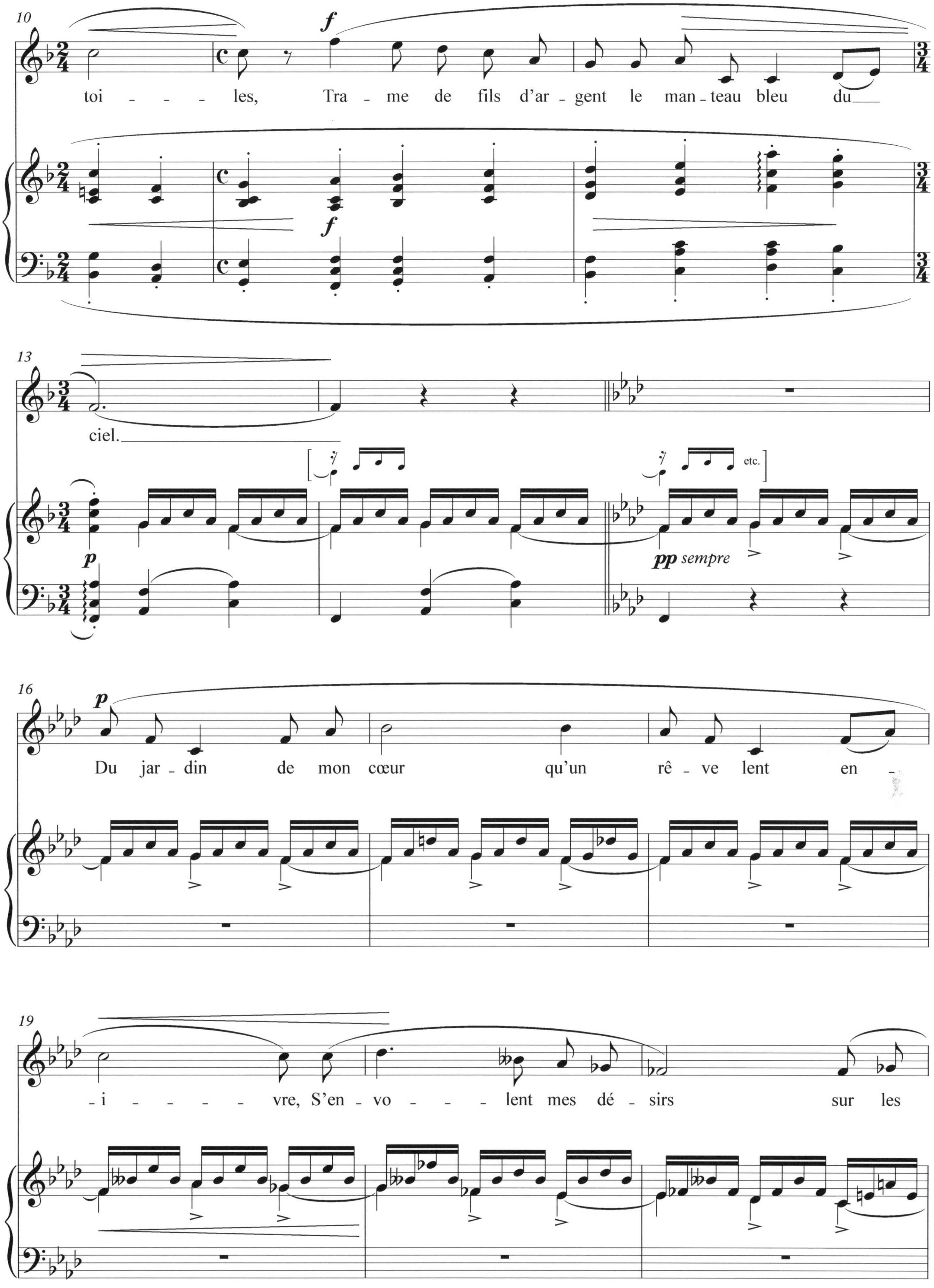
10
f
toi - - - les, Tra - me de fils d'ar - gent le man - teau bleu du
13
ciel.
p
etc.
pp sempre
16
p
Du jar - din de mon cœur qu'un rê - ve lent en -
19
- i - - - - vre, S'en - vo - - - lent mes dé - sirs sur les

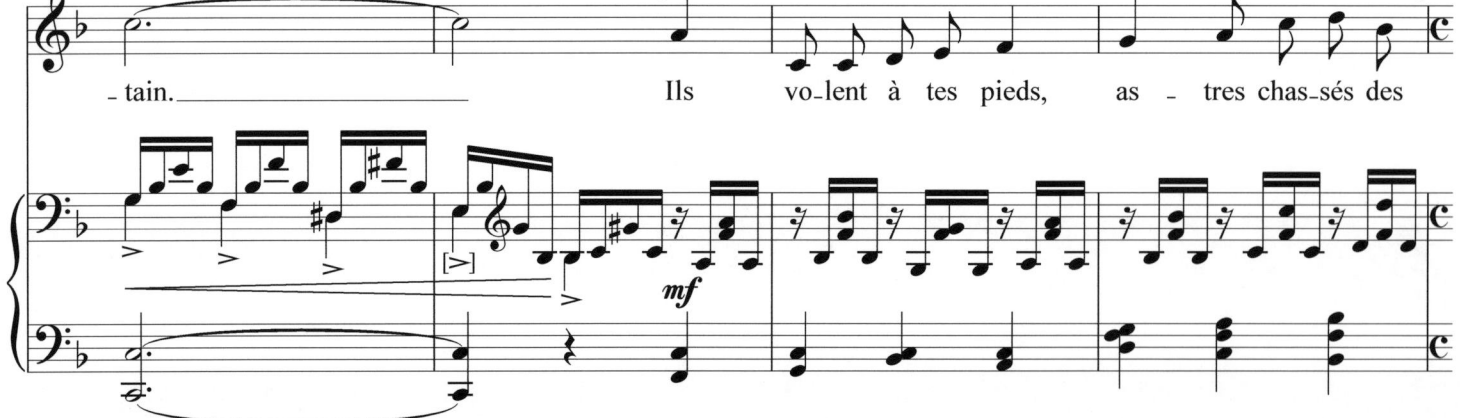

1) See Critical commentary regarding dynamics up to bar 46 / Voir Commentaire critique à propos des dynamiques jusqu'à la mes. 46 / Zur Dynamik bis Takt 46 siehe Kritischen Bericht

À Madame Jules Gouïn

2. Fleur jetée

(Armand Silvestre)

Op. 39 No. 2

Original key: f

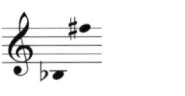

Allegro energico (♩. = 72)

Em - por - te ma fo - li - e
Au gré du vent, Fleur en chan - tant cueil - li - e
Et je - tée en rê - vant! Em - por - te ma fo - li - e, Au
gré du vent.

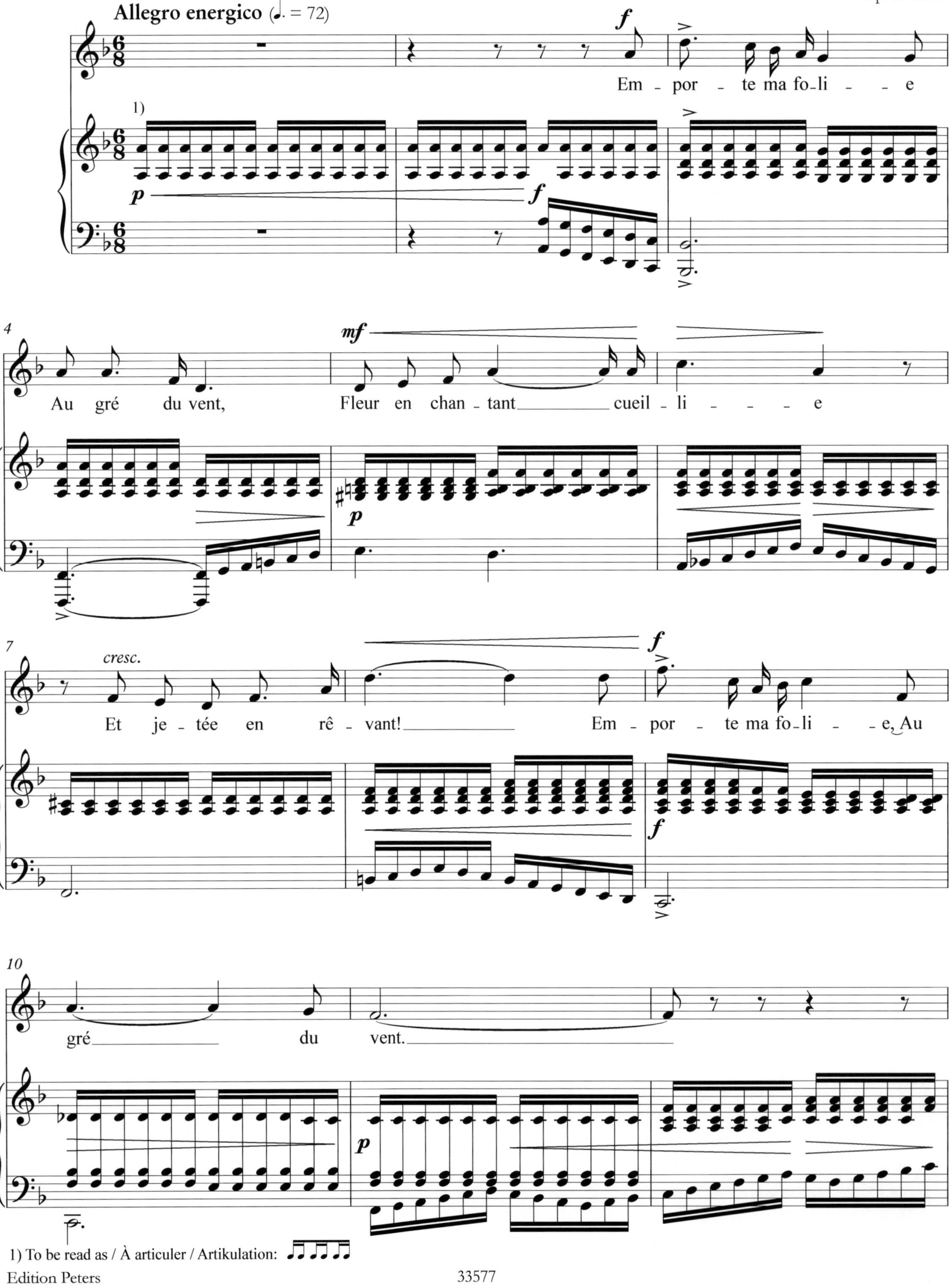

1) To be read as / À articuler / Artikulation: ♫♫♫♫

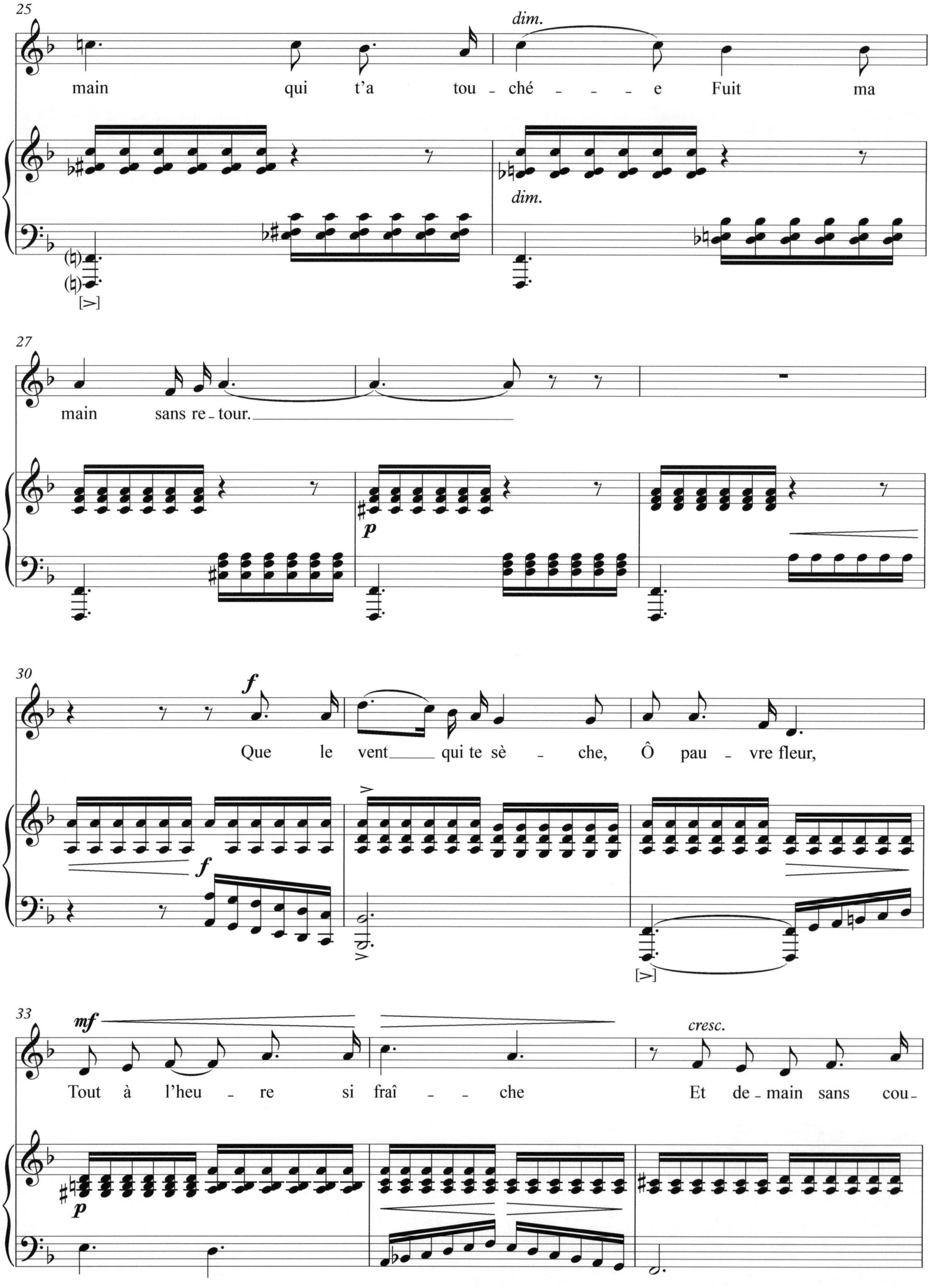
25
dim.
main qui t'a tou - ché - - - e Fuit ma
dim.
[>]
27
main sans re - tour.
p
30
f
Que le vent qui te sè - che, Ô pau - vre fleur,
f
[>]
33
mf
Tout à l'heu - re si fraî - - - che
cresc.
Et de - main sans cou -
p

1) Beat 2 perhaps intended an 8ᵛᵉ higher, or an error for
2ᵉ temps peut-être voulu une 8ᵛᵉ plus haut, ou une erreur pour
2. Schlag vielleicht eine 8ᵛᵉ höher vorgesehen, oder Irrtum für

À Mademoiselle Thérèse Guyon

3. Le Pays des Rêves
(Armand Silvestre)

Original key: A♭

Op. 39 No. 3

Andante quasi allegretto ♩. = 84

Veux - tu___ qu'au beau pa-ys_ des rê _ ves Nous al_lions la main dans la main?

Plus loin___ que l'o_deur des jas-mins, Plus haut___ que la plain-te des grè _ _ ves,

Veux - tu,___ du beau pa-ys_ des rê _ _ ves,

1) **Es-g:** *pp*

À Mademoiselle Louise Collinet

4. Les Roses d'Ispahan

(Leconte de Lisle)

Original key: D

Op. 39 No. 4

20

À Madame H. Roger-Jourdain

5a. Nocturne

(Villiers de L'Isle-Adam)

Original version, contralto or bass

Original key: E♭

[1] Op. 43 No. 2

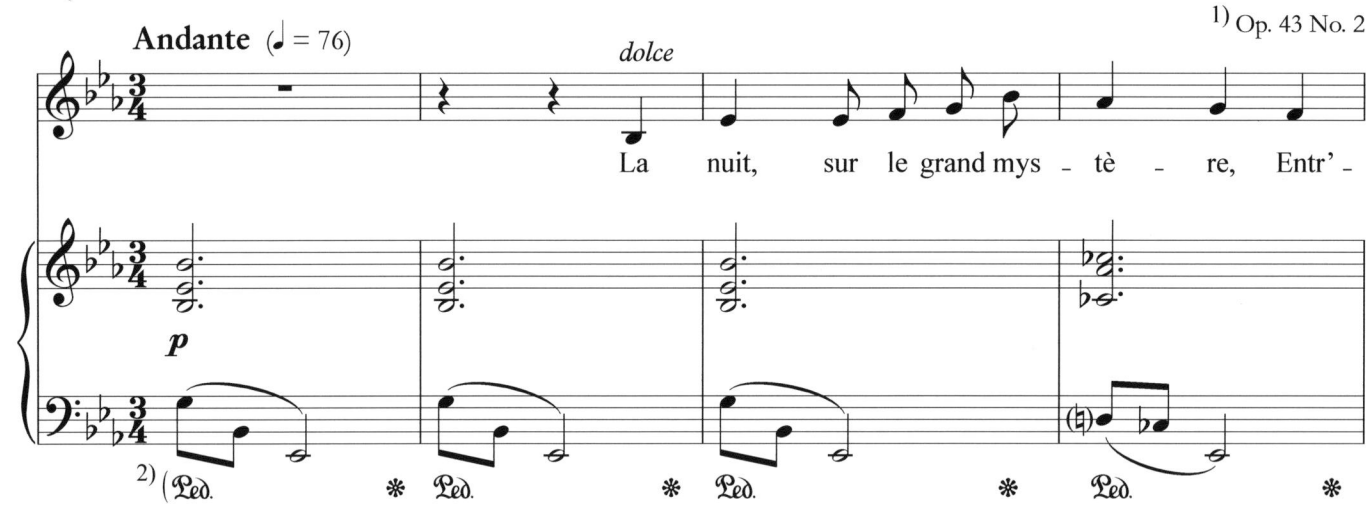

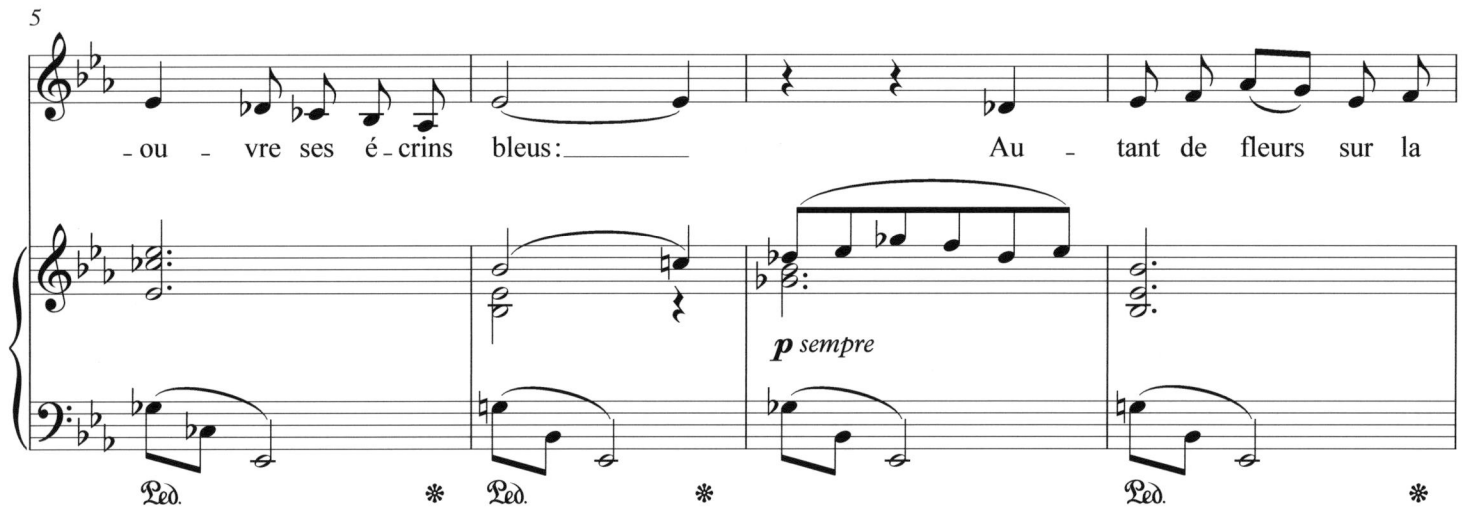

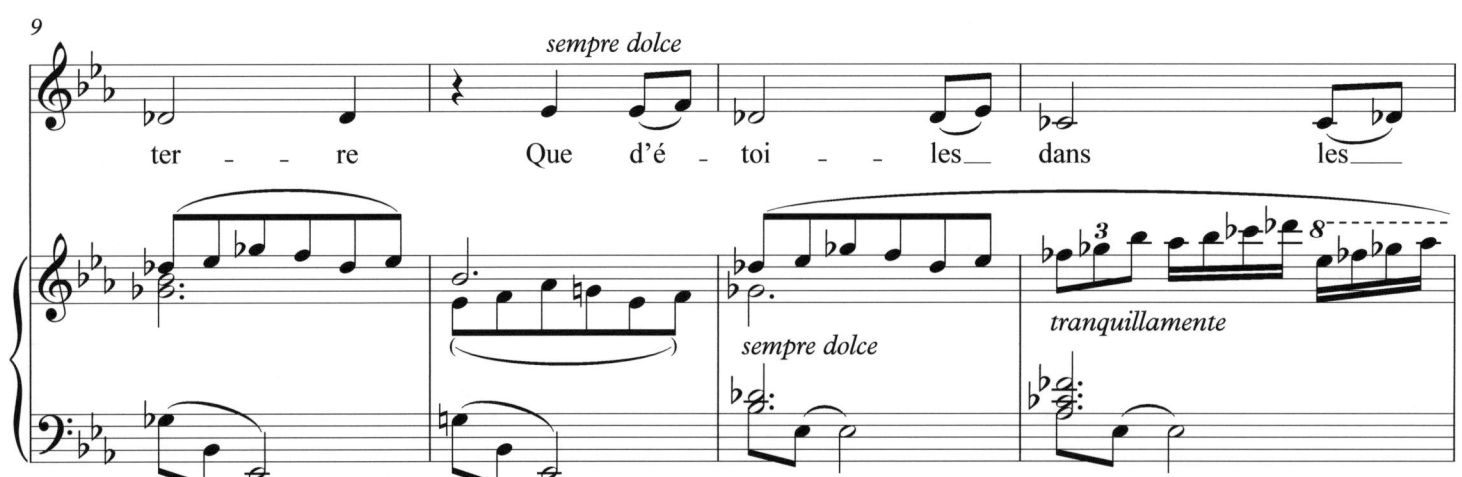

1) For Op. 43 No. 1 see p. 99 and Preface / Pour l'Op. 43 N° 1 voir p. 99 et Préface / Für Op. 43 Nr. 1 siehe S. 99 und Vorwort

2) Pedalling and metronome indication from later versions; see Critical commentary
   Pédale et indication métronomique provenant de versions ultérieures; voir Commentaire critique
   Pedal und metronomische Angabe stammen aus späteren Bearbeitungen; siehe Kritischen Bericht

Edition Peters   33577

1) Grace note added to this version in 1908 / Petite note rajoutée dans cette version en 1908 / Kleine Note 1908 in diese Fassung eingefügt

5b. Nocturne

(Villiers de L'Isle-Adam)

Version II, manuscript, mezzo-soprano or baritone [1]

Original key of this version: F#

Op. 43 No. 2

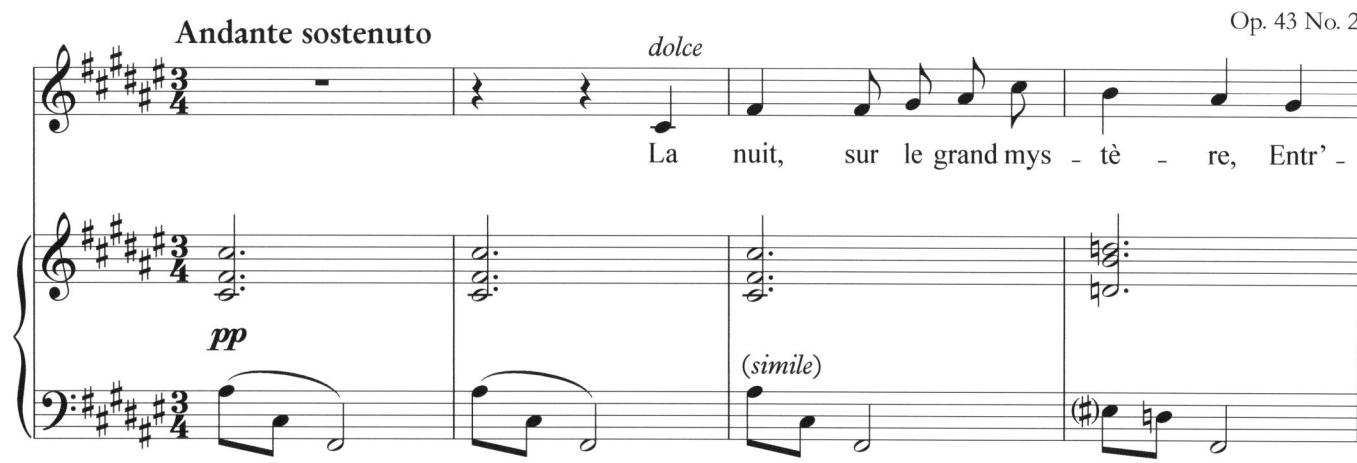

[1] See the present high voice edition for a version in A♭
   Pour une version en *la♭* voir la présente édition pour voix élevées
   Siehe die aktuelle Ausgabe für hohe Stimme für eine andere Fassung in As

À Monsieur le Comte Robert de Montesquiou-Fezensac

6. Les Présents

(Villiers de L'Isle-Adam)

Original keys: E♭, F

Op. 46 No. 1

À Emmanuel Jadin

7. Clair de Lune (Menuet)

(Paul Verlaine)

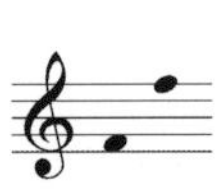

Original keys: g [sketches] / b♭ / c

Op. 46 no. 2

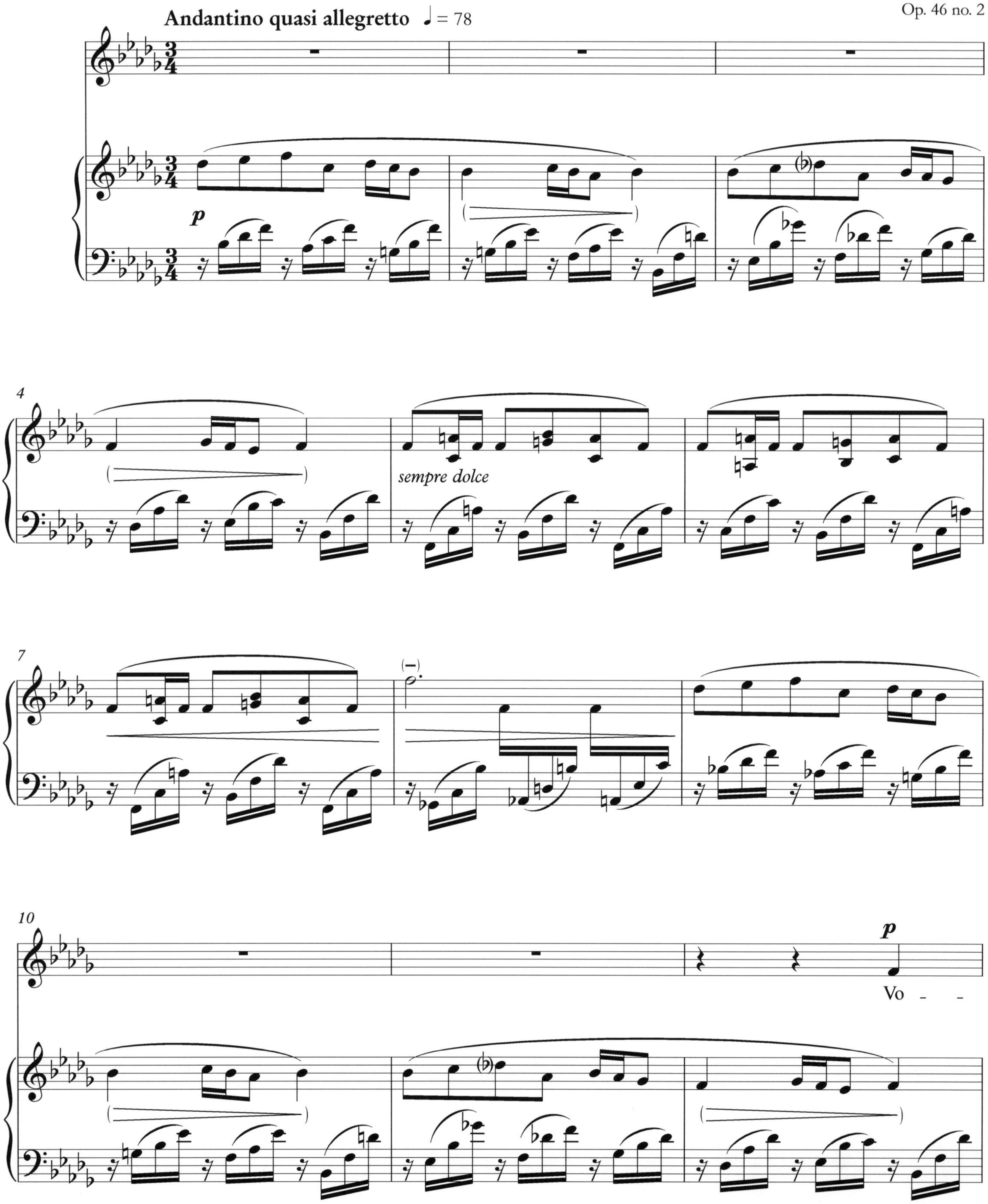
Andantino quasi allegretto ♩ = 78
p
sempre dolce
p
Vo - -

32

Original key: c

À Madame la Princesse Edmond de Polignac

8. Larmes

(Jean Richepin)

Op. 51 No. 1

1) See Appendix 2 for original dynamics to bar 34 / Voir Appendice 2 pour la version originale des dynamiques jusqu'à la mesure 34
Siehe Anhang 2 zur Originaldynamik bis Takt 34
2) **A** und **Es** maintain *p* until bar 42 / **A** et **Es** maintiennent *p* jusqu'à mesure 42 / **A**, **Es**: *p* bleibt bis Takt 42

À Madame Maurice Sulzbach

9. Au Cimetière

(Jean Richepin)

Original key: e

Op. 51 No. 2

À Madame Henry Cochin

10. Spleen

(Paul Verlaine)

Original key: d

Op. 51 no. 3

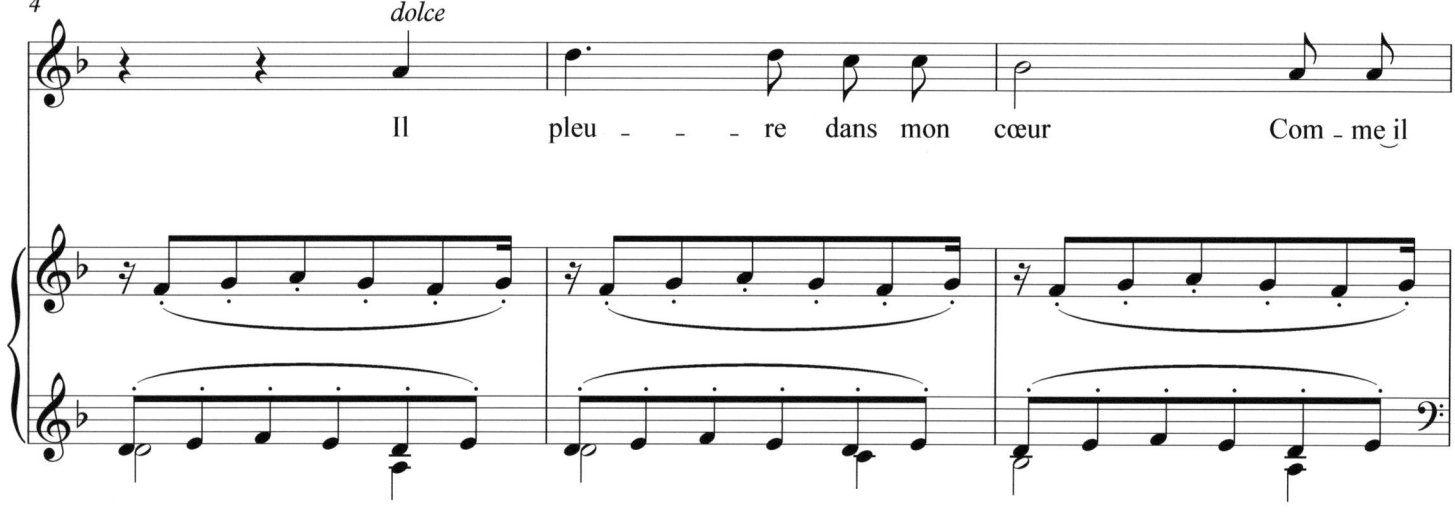

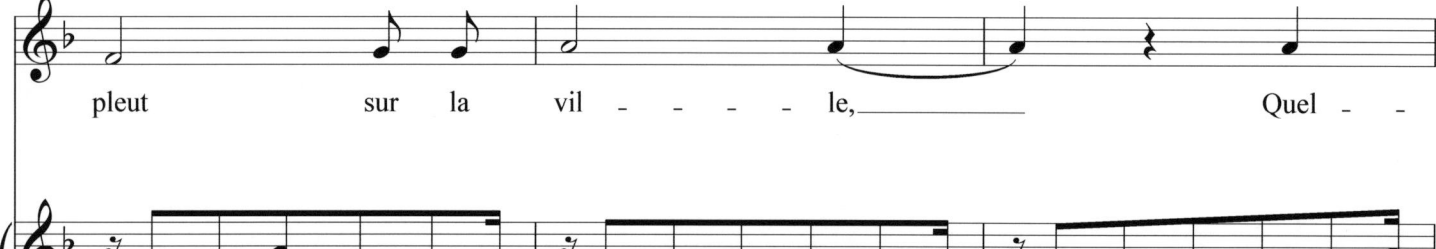

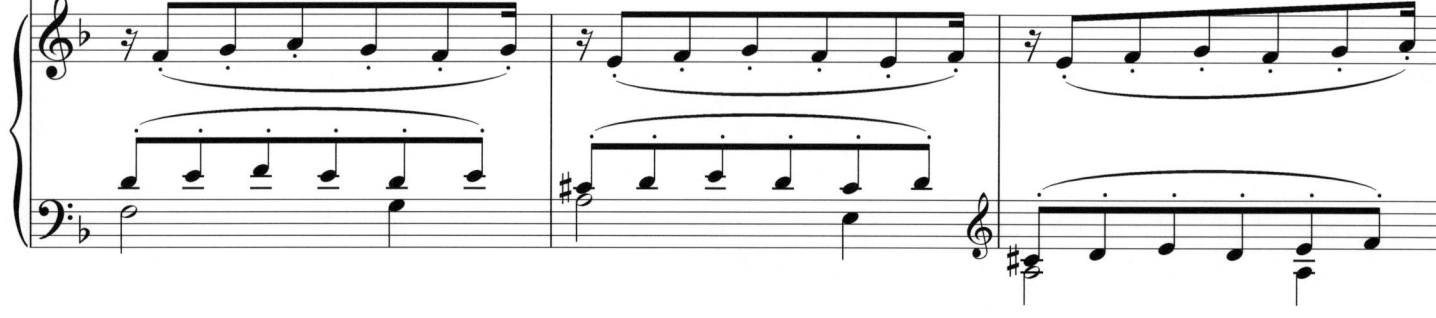

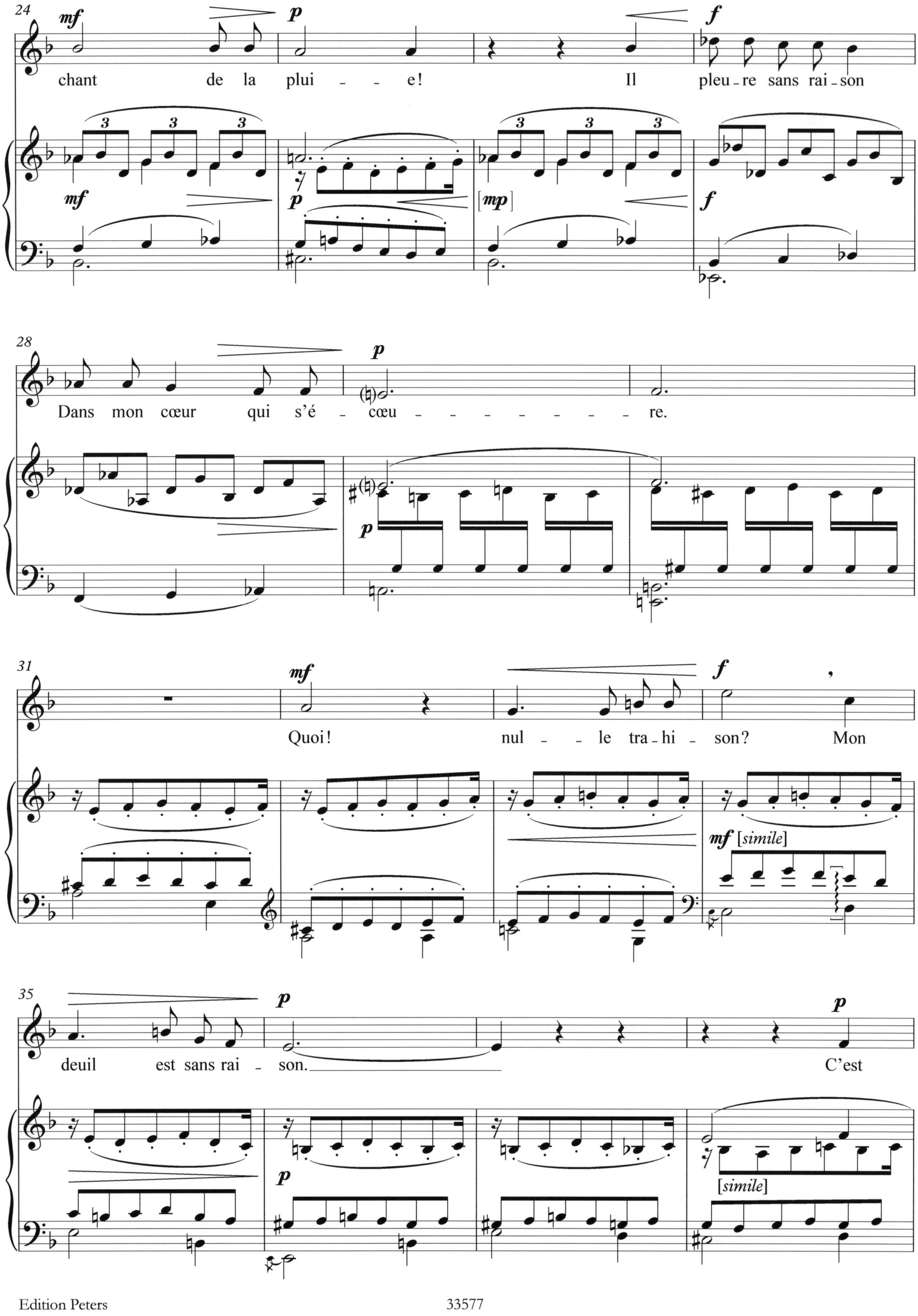
24
mf
p
f
chant de la plui - - - e! Il pleu - re sans rai - son
mf
p
[mp]
f
3
28
p
Dans mon cœur qui s'é - cœu - - - - - - - - - - re.
p
31
mf
f
Quoi! nul - - le tra - hi - son? Mon
mf [simile]
35
p
p
deuil est sans rai - son.
C'est
p
[simile]

44

À Maurice Bagès

11. La Rose (ode anacréontique)

(Leconte de Lisle)

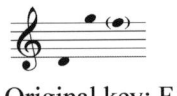
Original key: F

Op. 51 No. 4

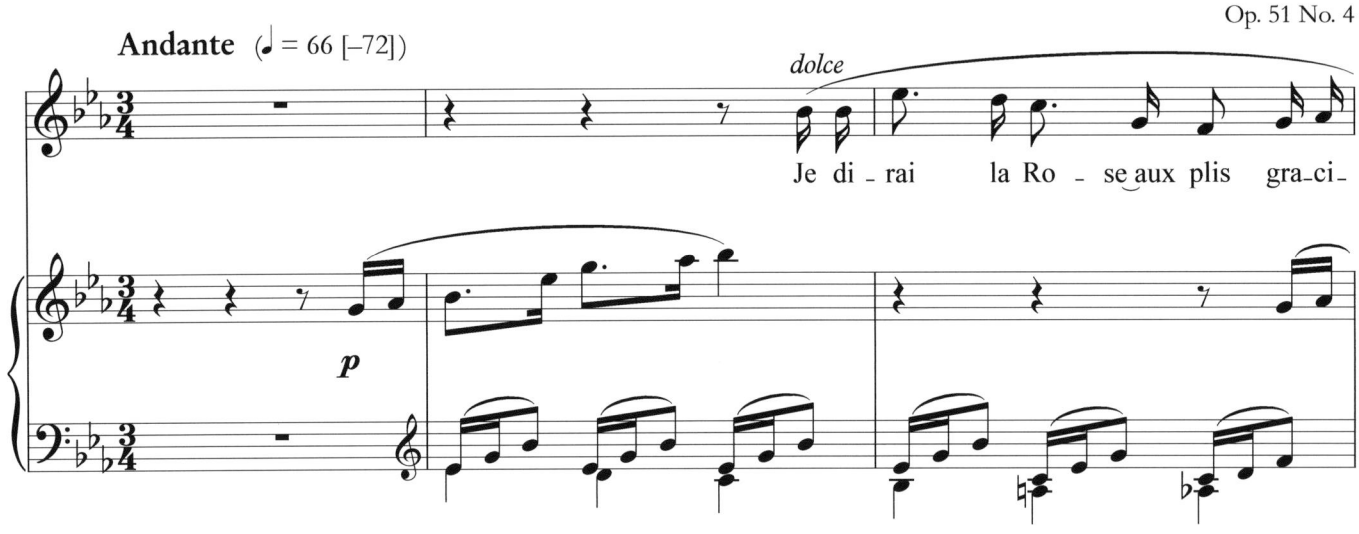

Edition Peters 33577

Version 1 (1890)

Version 2 (1908)

1) See Critical Commentary regarding dynamics / Voir Commentaire critique à propos des dynamiques / Zur Dynamik siehe Kritischen Bericht

(À Paul Porel)

12a. Prélude to "Chanson"[1]
(Shylock)

Original key: B♭

Op. 57 No. 1

1) See Preface / Voir Préface / Siehe Vorwort

12b. Chanson[1]

(*Shylock*)

(Edmond Haraucourt)

Original keys: C (B♭)

Op. 57 No. 1

1) See Appendix 1 for an adjunct version / Voir Appendice 1 pour une version complémentaire / Siehe Anhang 1 für eine entsprechende Fassung
2) Regarding dynamics see Preface / Concernant les dynamiques voir Préface / Zur Dynamik siehe Vorwort

1) **O** places ⟩ a bar later / **O** place ⟩ une mesure plus tard / **O**: ⟩ ein Takt später

14. Sérénade

(*Le Bourgeois Gentilhomme*)

(Molière)

Original key: f

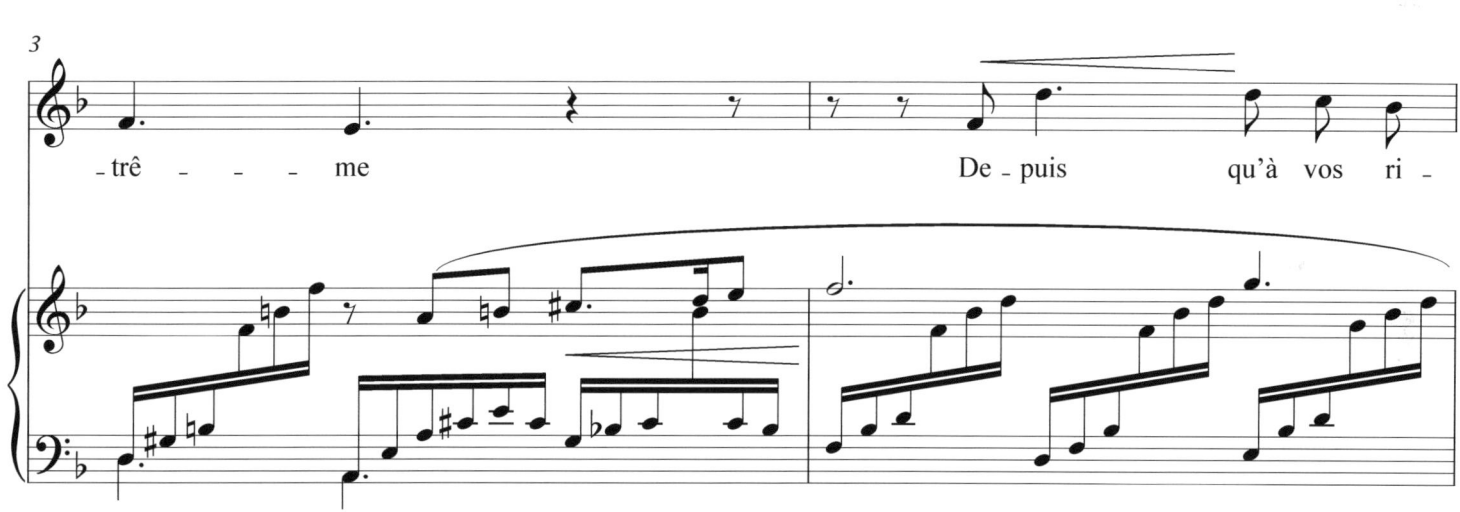

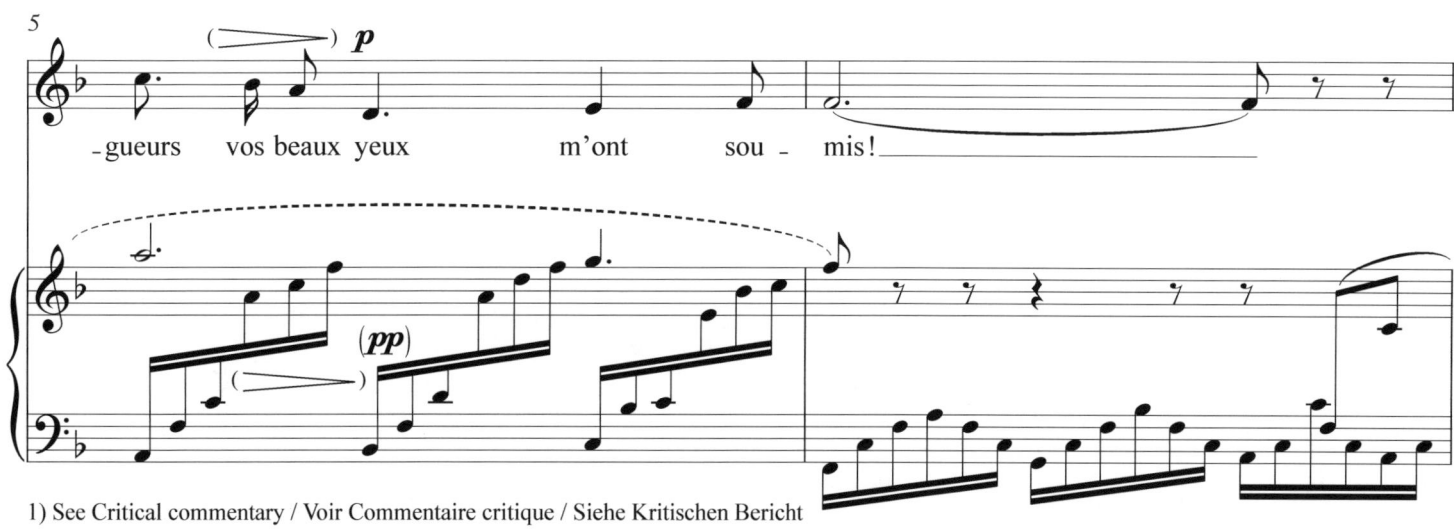

1) See Critical commentary / Voir Commentaire critique / Siehe Kritischen Bericht

15. Prison

(Paul Verlaine)

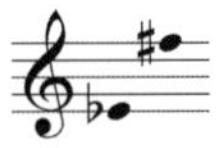

Original key: e♭

Quasi adagio (♩ = 60)

1)Op. 68 no. 1

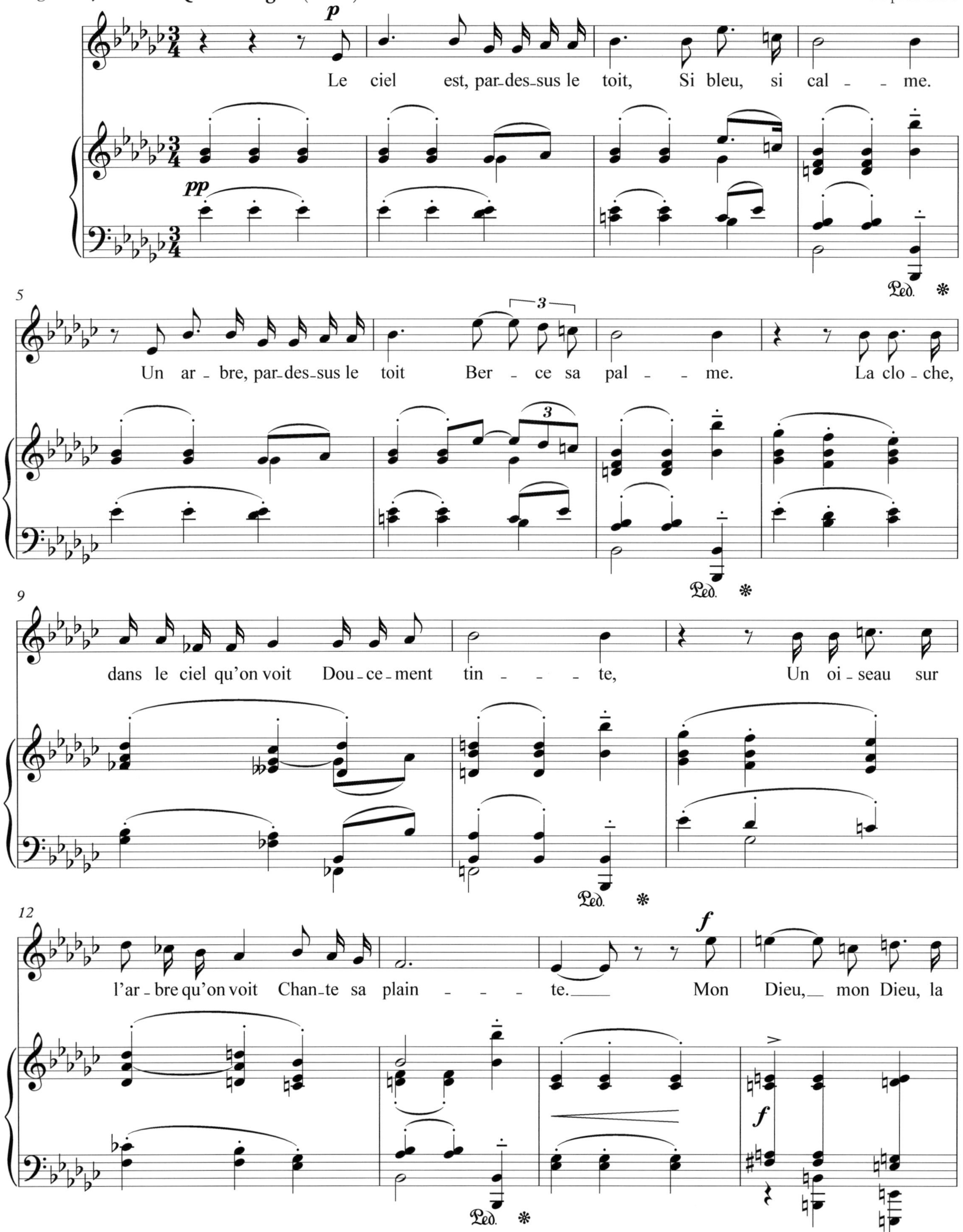
p
Le ciel est, par-des-sus le toit, Si bleu, si cal - - me.
pp
Ped. *
5
Un ar - bre, par-des-sus le toit Ber - ce sa pal - - me. La clo - che,
3
Ped. *
9
dans le ciel qu'on voit Dou-ce-ment tin - - - - te, Un oi-seau sur
Ped. *
12
l'ar - bre qu'on voit Chan-te sa plain - - - - te. Mon Dieu, mon Dieu, la
f
Ped. *

1) See Preface regarding opus number / Voir Préface à propos du numéro d'opus / Zur Opusnummer siehe Vorwort

1) Small note optional; see Critical Commentary / Petite note *ad libitum*; voir commentaire critique / Kleine Note *ad libitum*; siehe Kritischen Bericht

2) **Rc-e₀₈**: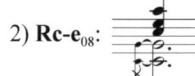

62

16. Soir

(Albert Samain)

Original key: D♭

Op. 68 No. 2

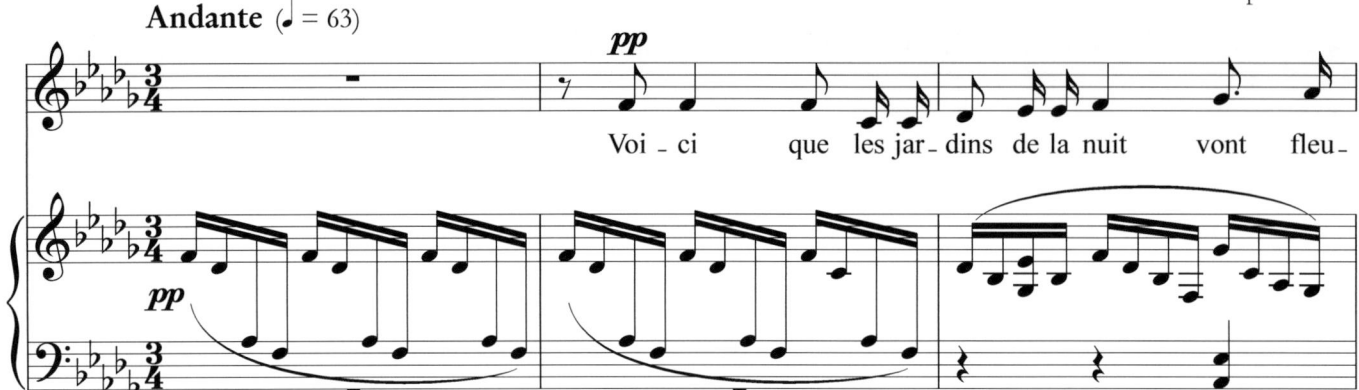

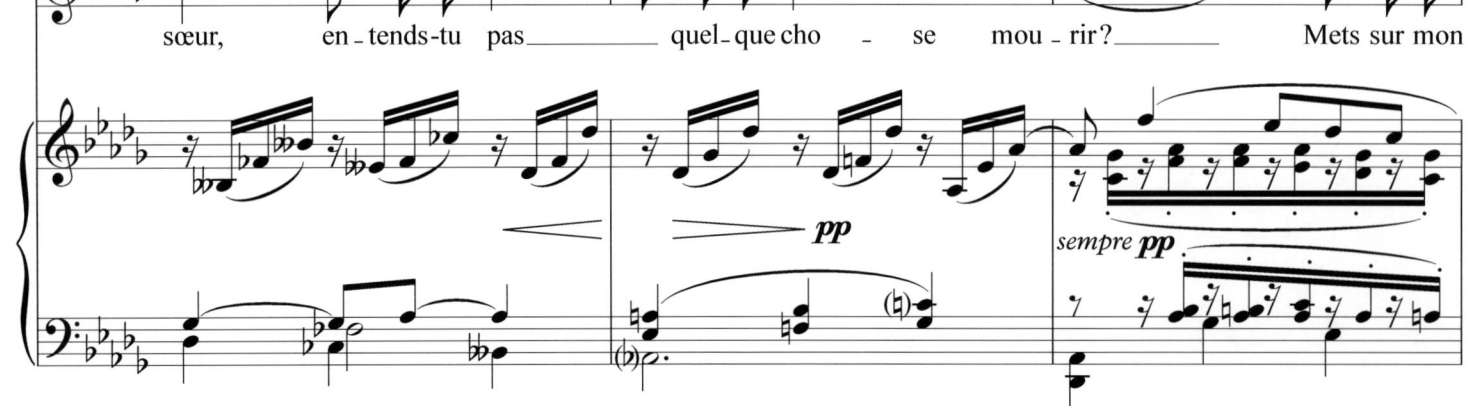

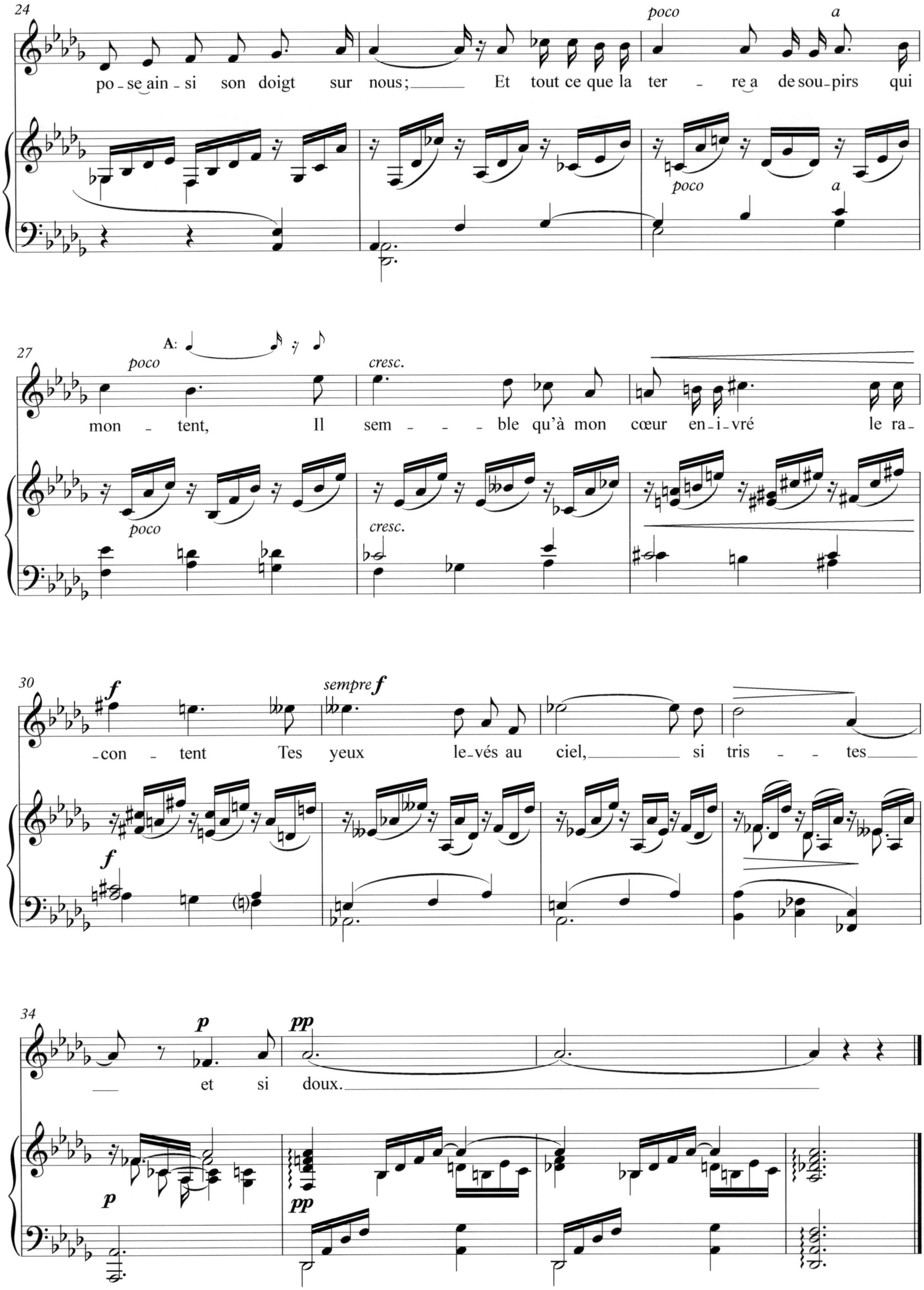
24
poco
a
po_se ain_si son doigt sur nous; Et tout ce que la ter - re a de sou_pirs qui
poco
a
27
A:
poco
cresc.
mon - tent, Il sem - - - ble qu'à mon cœur en_i_vré le ra-
poco
cresc.
30
f
sempre f
-con - tent Tes yeux le_vés au ciel, si tris - - tes
f
34
p
pp
et si doux.
p
pp

1) Tie *ad libitum*: see Critical Commentary / Tenue *ad libitum*: voir Commentaire critique / Bindebogen *ad libitum*: Siehe Kritischen Bericht

À Madame Charles Dettelbach

18. Arpège

(Albert Samain)

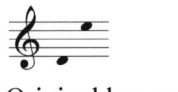
Original key: e

Op. 76 No. 2

Andante quasi allegretto (♩. = 72)

L'â― me d'u―ne flû― te sou―pi― re ― Au fond du parc mé―lo―di―eux; ― Lim―pi―de est l'om―bre où l'on res―pi― re Ton po― è― ― me si―len― ci―eux, Nuit de lan―gueur, nuit de men―

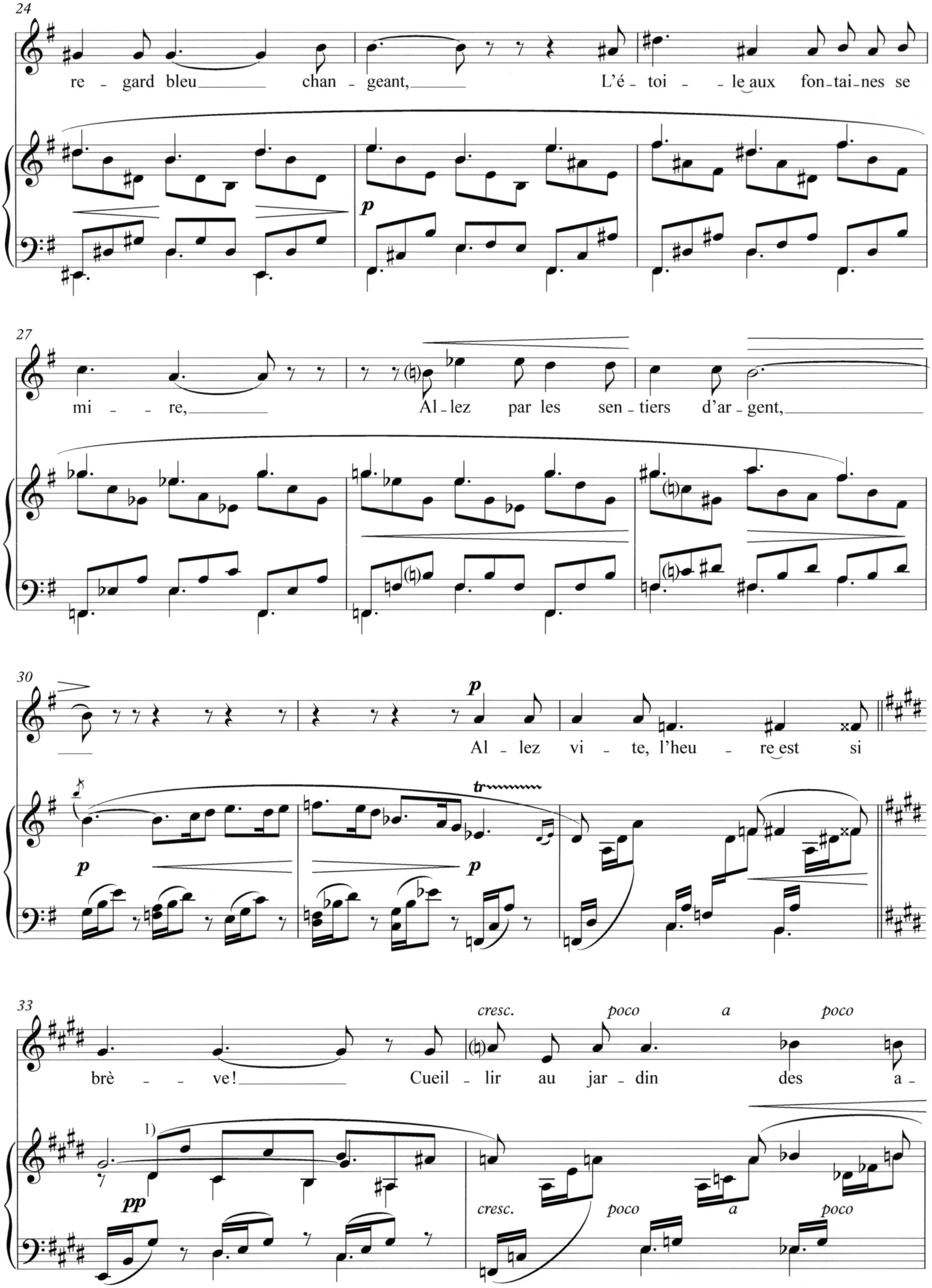

1) See Critical commentary regarding dynamics / Voir Commentaire critique à propos des dynamiques / Zur Dynamik siehe Kritischen Bericht

19. Mélisande's Song

(*Pelléas et Mélisande*)

(Maurice Maeterlinck; English translation by Jack Mackail)

Original key: d

(from Op. 80)

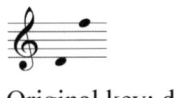

1) Editorial suggestion for more natural declamation of the English
   Proposition des éditeurs pour une meilleure déclamation du texte anglais
   Vorschlag der Herausgeber zur besseren Deklamation des englischen Texts

2)  sis - ters

À Mademoiselle Lydia Eustis

20. Dans la forêt de septembre

(Catulle Mendès)

Original key: G♭

Op. 85 No. 1

Adagio (♩ = 50)

Ra_mu_re aux ru_meurs a_mol_li_es,_ Troncs so_no_res que l'â_ge creu_se, L'an_ti_que fo_rêt_ dou_lou_reu_se S'ac_cor_de à nos mé_lan_co_li_es._ Ô sa_pins a_grif_fés au gouf_fre,_ Nids dé_serts aux bran_ches bri_sé_es, Hal_liers brû_

Edition Peters 33577

1) See Critical Commentary
Voir Commentaire critique
Siehe Kritischen Bericht

À Mademoiselle Pauline Segond

21. La Fleur qui va sur l'eau

(Catulle Mendès)

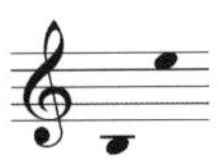

Original key: b

Allegro molto moderato (𝅗𝅥 = 60) Op. 85 No. 2

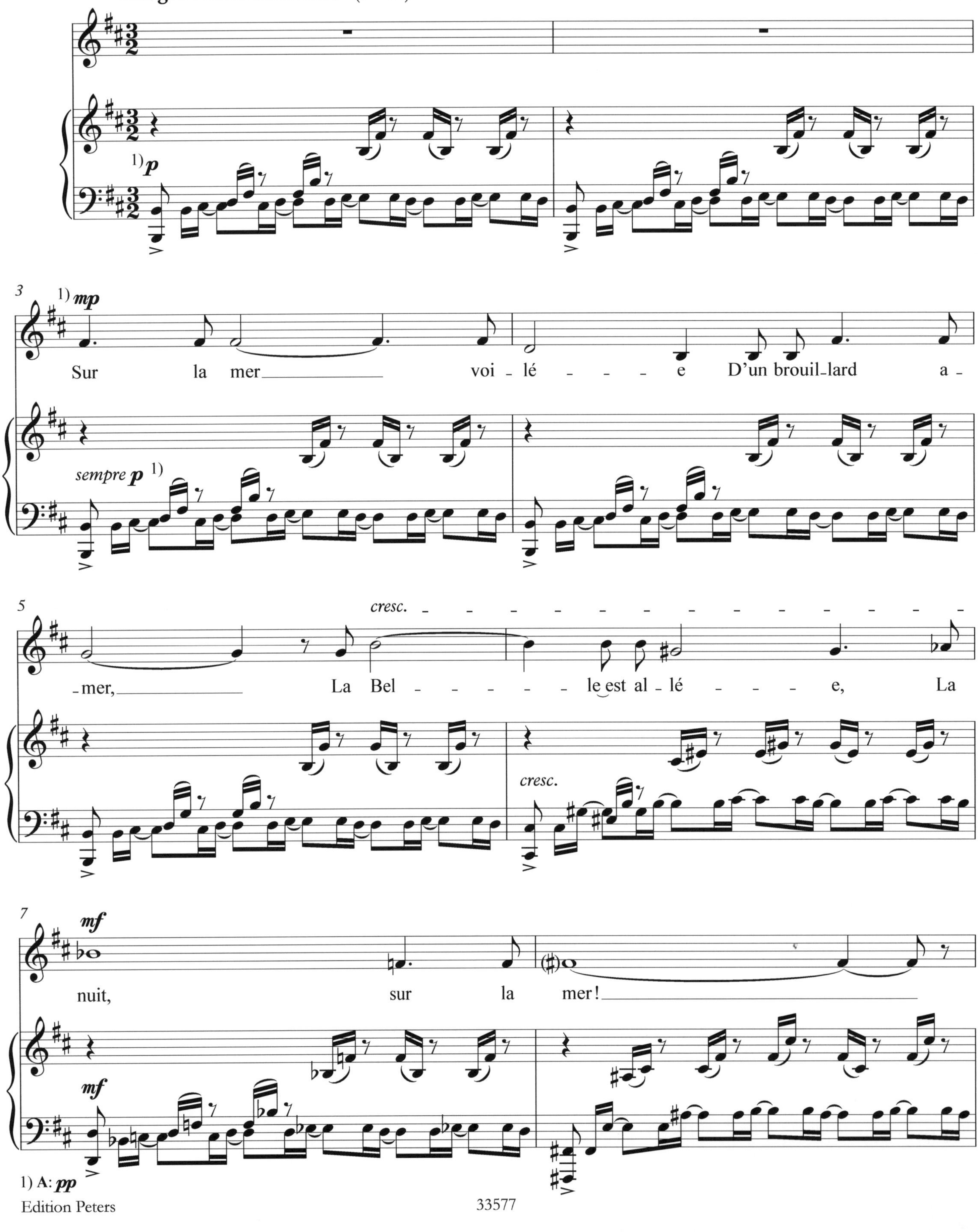
1) p
3 1) mp
Sur la mer voi - lé - - - - e D'un brouil-lard a -
sempre p 1)
5 cresc.
- mer, La Bel - - - - - - le est al - lé - - - - e, La
cresc.
7 mf
nuit, sur la mer!
mf

1) A: *pp*

1) See Critical Commentary regarding dynamics / Voir Commentaire critique à propos des dynamiques / Zur Dynamik siehe Kritischen Bericht

1) Originally **f** *sempre*, no > **p**; see Critical commentary
Primitivement **f** *sempre*, sans > **p**; voir Commentaire critique
Ursprünglich **f** *sempre*, ohne > **p**; siehe Kritischen Bericht

À Mademoiselle Émilie Girette (Madame Édouard Risler)

22. Accompagnement

(Albert Samain)

Original key: G♭

Op. 85 No. 3

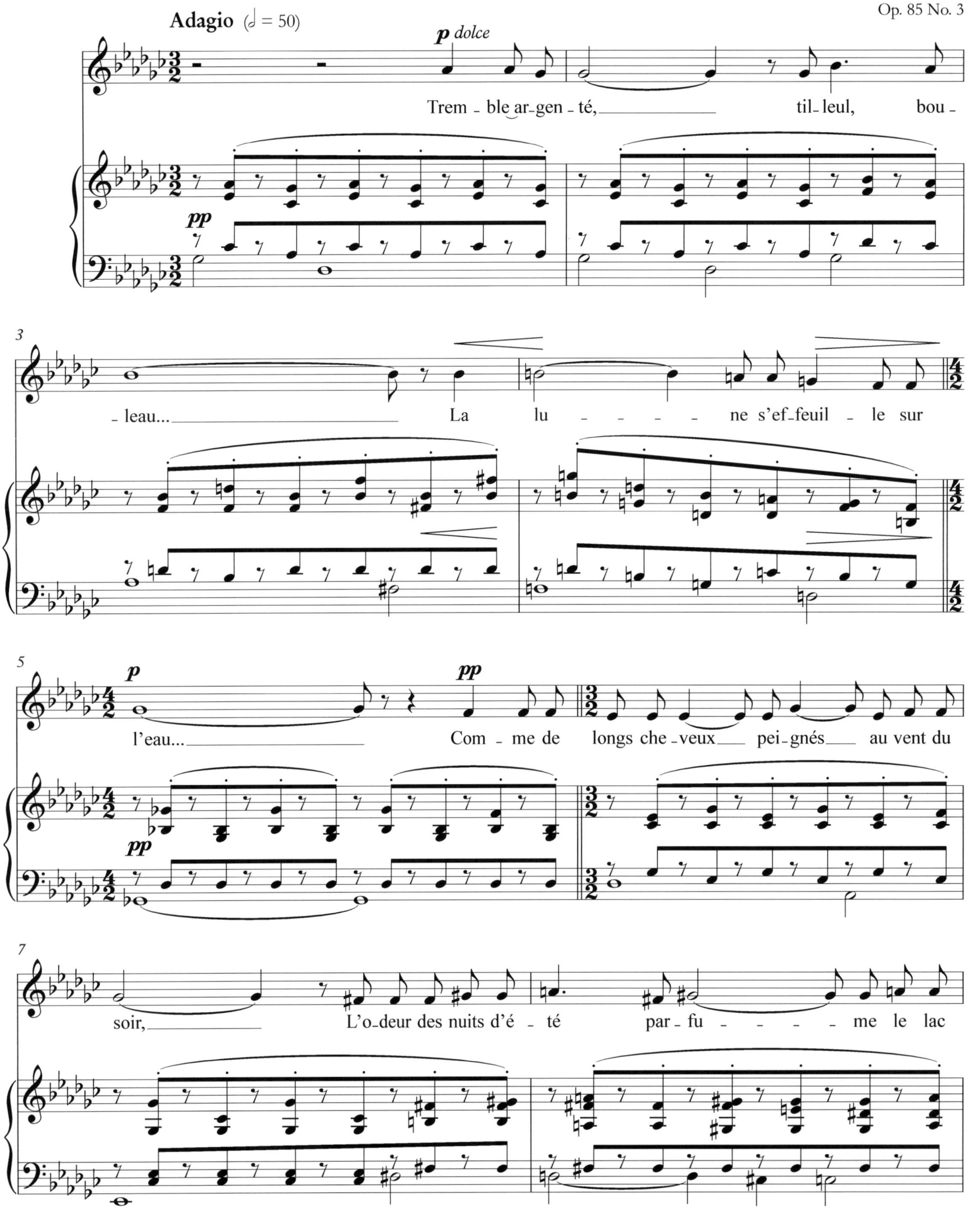

Adagio (♩ = 50)

Trem - ble ar - gen - té, til - leul, bou - leau... La lu - ne s'ef - feuil - le sur l'eau... Com - me de longs che - veux pei - gnés au vent du soir, L'o - deur des nuits d'é - té par - fu - me le lac

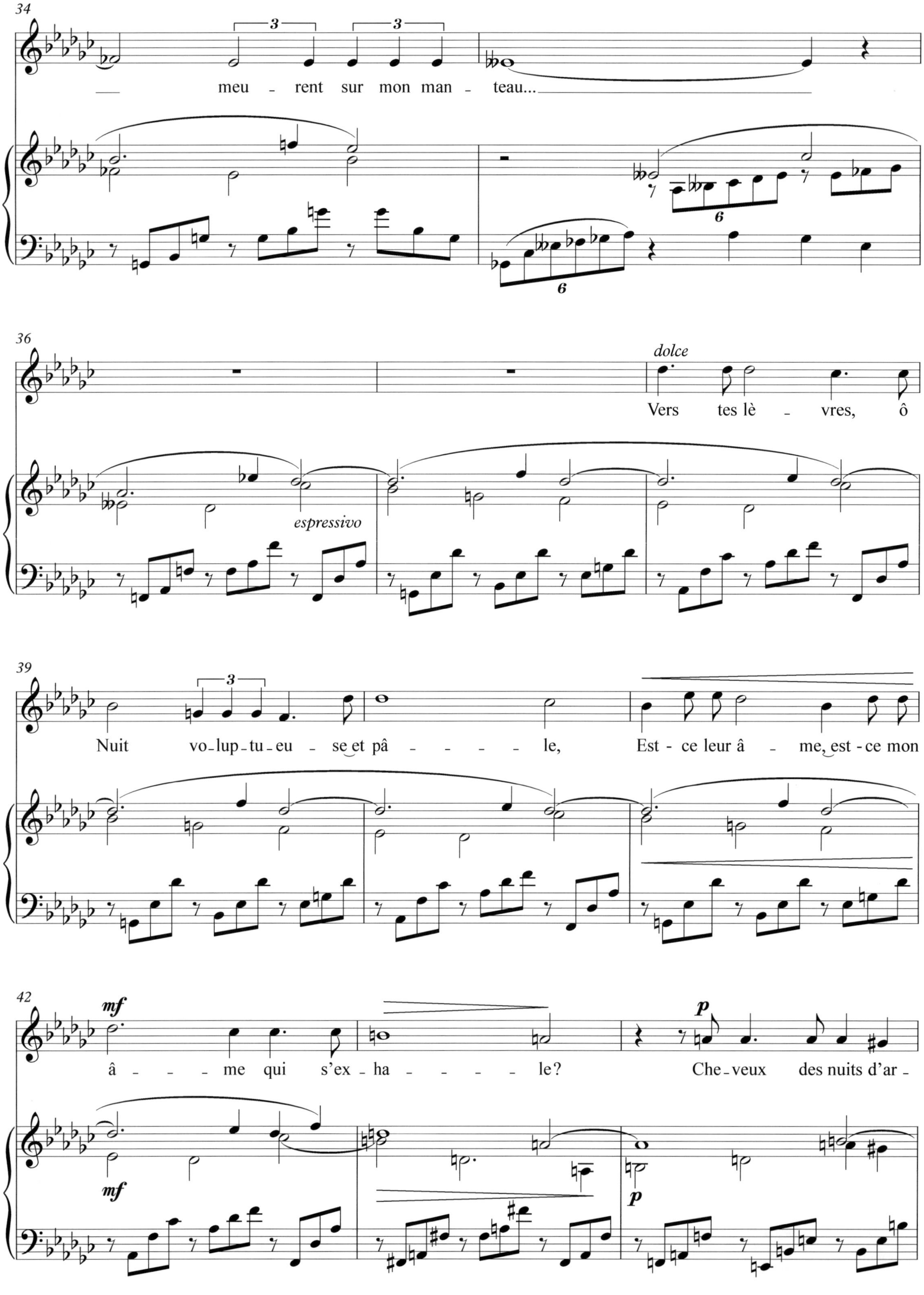
meu - rent sur mon man - teau...
dolce
Vers tes lè - vres, ô
espressivo
Nuit vo-lup-tu-eu - se et pâ - le,
Est - ce leur â - me, est - ce mon
mf
â - me qui s'ex - ha - le?
p
Che-veux des nuits d'ar -

1) See Critical commentary regarding manuscript endings
   Voir Commentaire critique à propos des versions manuscrites de la fin
   Siehe Kritischen Bericht zu den handschriftlichen Schlussvarianten

À Madame Édouard Risler

23. Le plus doux chemin

(Madrigal)

(Armand Silvestre)

Op. 87 No. 1

Original key: f

À Mademoiselle Claudie Segond

24. Le Ramier

(Madrigal)

(Armand Silvestre)

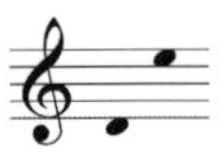

Original key: e

Op. 87 No. 2

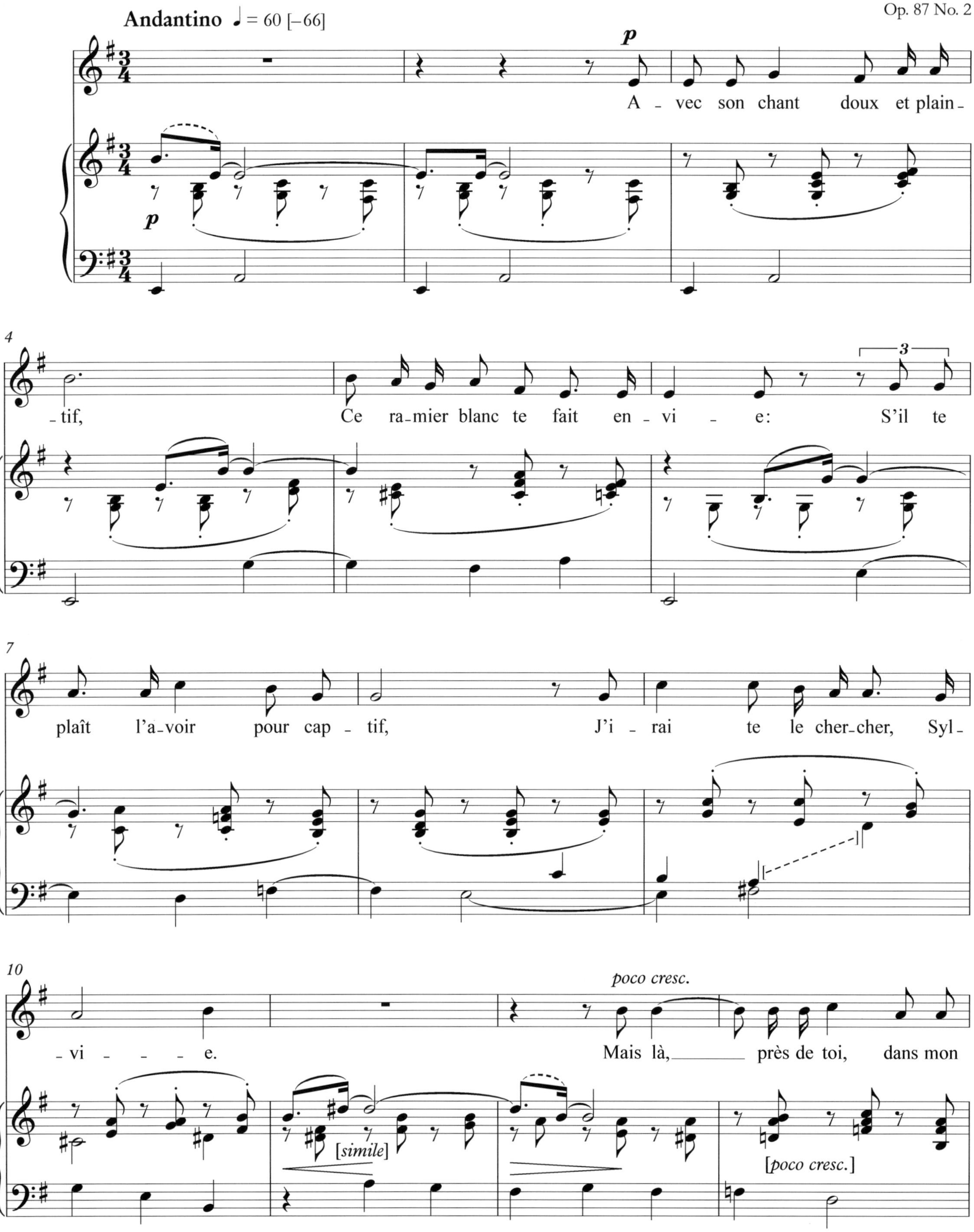
Andantino ♩ = 60 [–66]
p
A - vec son chant doux et plain - tif,
Ce ra-mier blanc te fait en - vi - e:
S'il te plaît l'a-voir pour cap - tif,
J'i - rai te le cher-cher, Syl - vi - e.
Mais là, près de toi, dans mon
[simile]
poco cresc.
[poco cresc.]

À Madame Octave Mans

25. Le Don silencieux

(Jean Dominique)

Original key: E

Op. 92

Andante molto moderato ♩ = 58

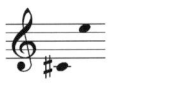

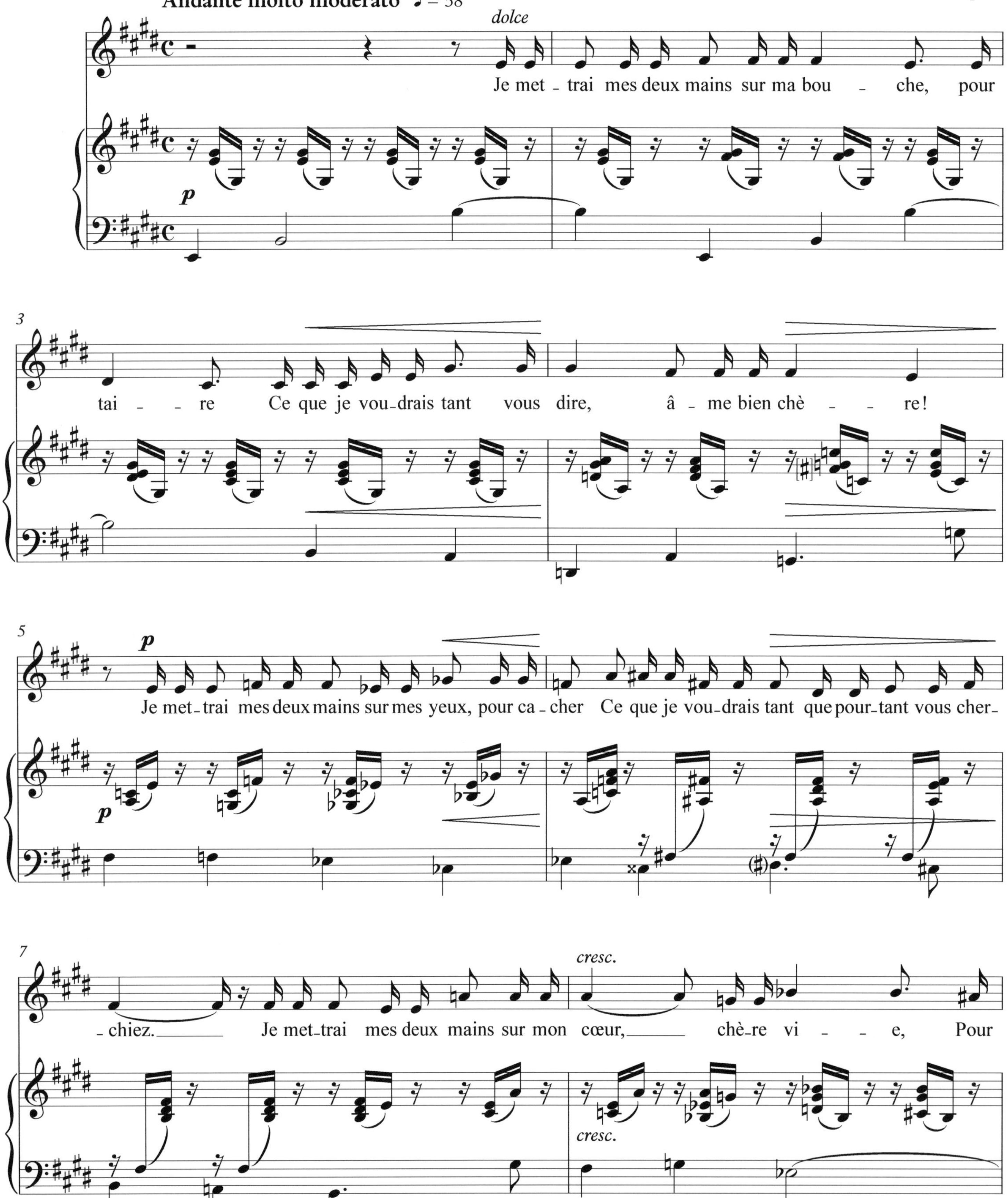

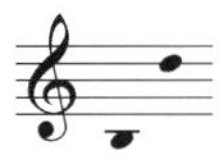

26. Chanson
(Henri de Régnier)

Original key: e

Op. 94

Andante quasi allegretto ♩ = 76

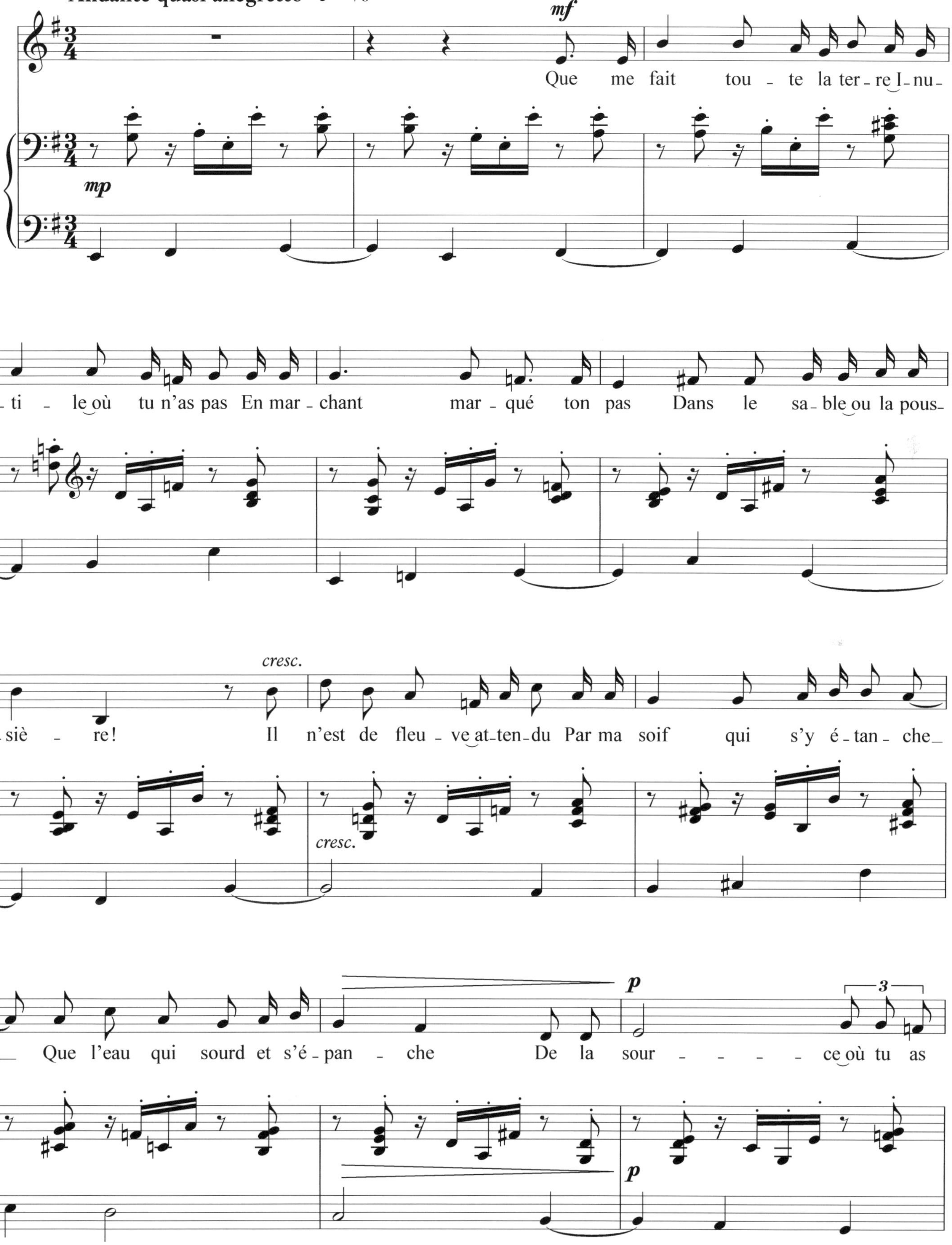

Que me fait toute la terre I-nu-ti-le où tu n'as pas En mar-chant mar-qué ton pas Dans le sa-ble ou la pous-siè-re! Il n'est de fleu-ve at-ten-du Par ma soif qui s'y é-tan-che Que l'eau qui sourd et s'é-pan-che De la sour- - -ce où tu as

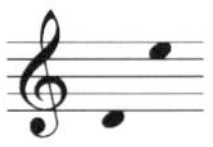

27. C'est la Paix
(Georgette Debladis)

Original key: A

Op. 114

Allegretto giocoso (♩ = 112)

Pen-dant qu'ils é-taient par-tis pour la guer-re, On ne dan-sait plus, on ne par-lait guè-re, On ne chan-tait pas. Mes sœurs, c'est la paix! la guer-re est fi-ni-e, Dans la paix bé-ni-e cou-rons au de-vant De nos chers sol-dats.

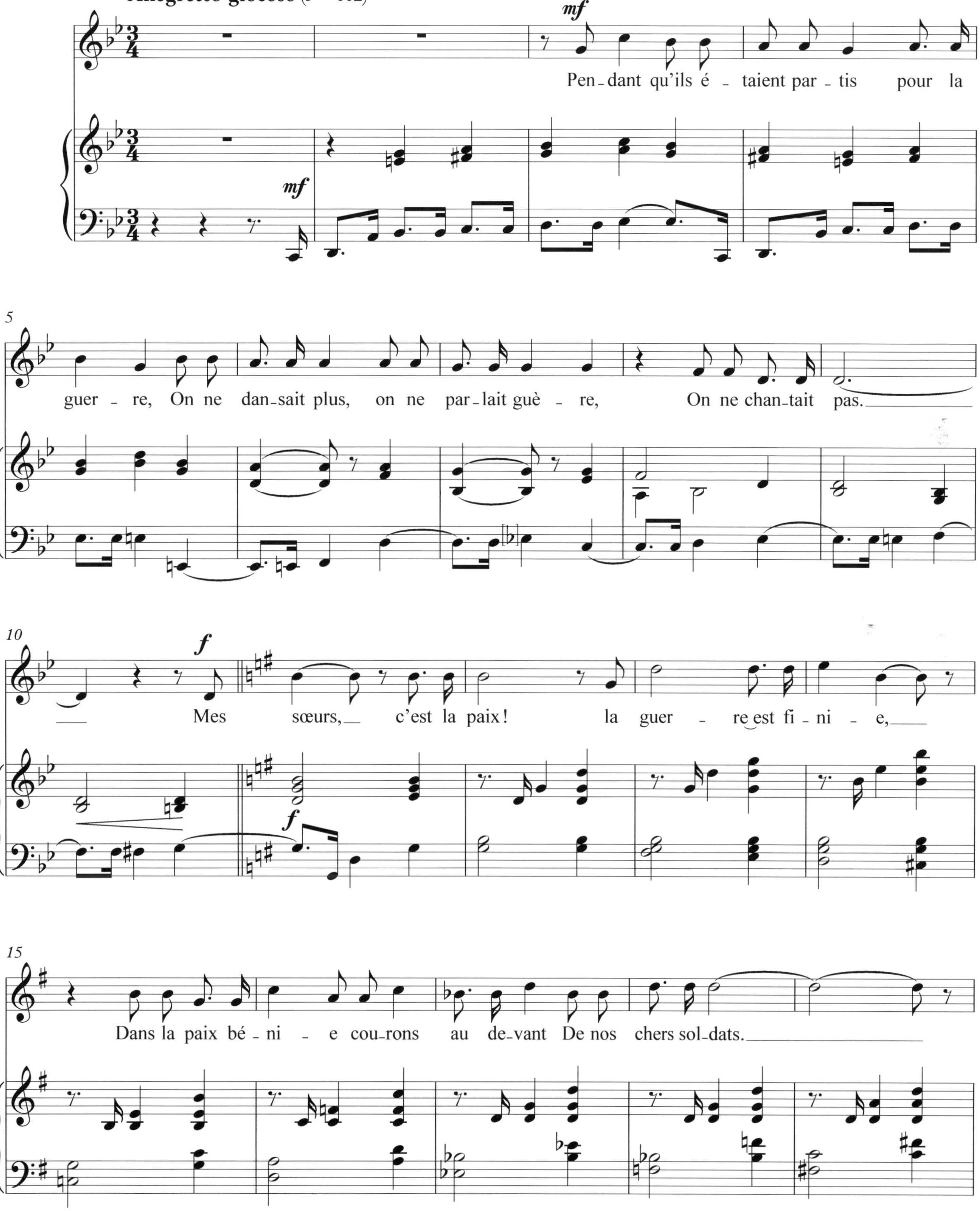

À mon ami A. Talazac

28. Noël

(Victor Wilder)

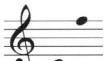

Original key: A♭

Op. 43 No. 1

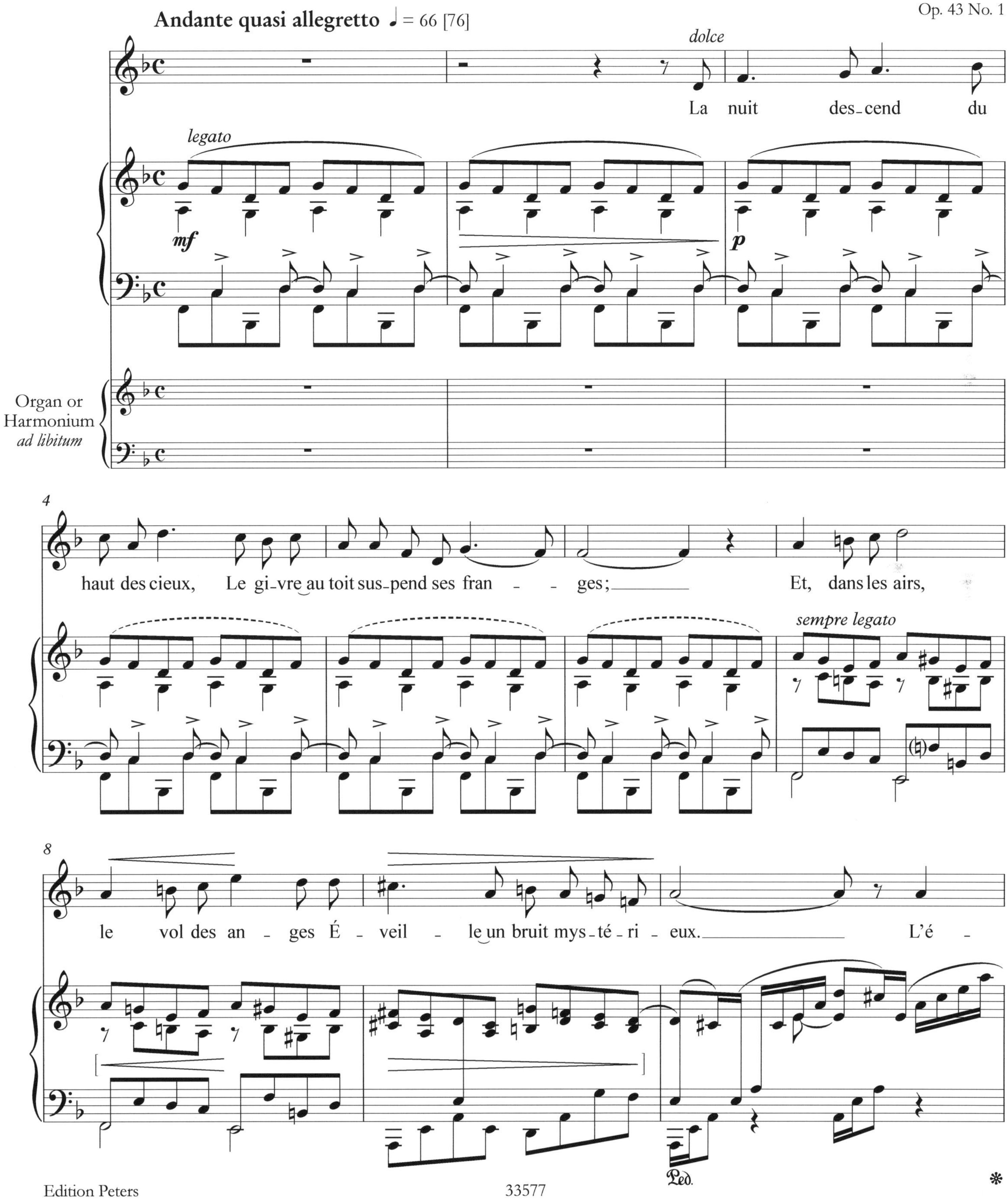

Andante quasi allegretto ♩ = 66 [76]
dolce
La nuit des-cend du
legato
mf
p
Organ or Harmonium ad libitum
4
haut des cieux, Le gi-vre au toit sus-pend ses fran - - ges; Et, dans les airs,
sempre legato
8
le vol des an - ges É - veil - le un bruit mys-té-ri - eux. L'é -
Ped.

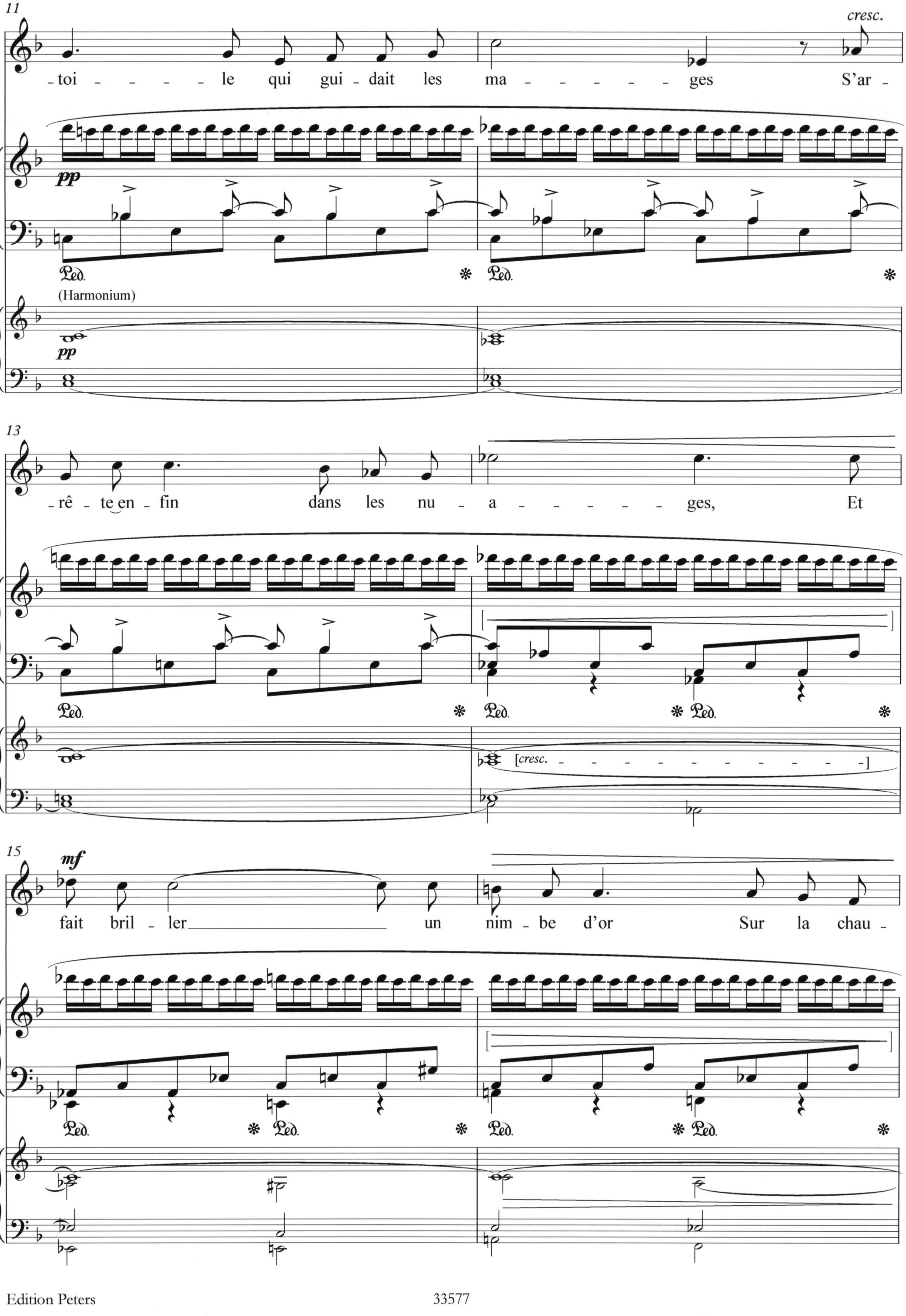
11
cresc.
-toi - - - - - le qui gui - dait les ma - - - - - - - ges S'ar -
pp
Ped.
(Harmonium)
pp
13
-rê - te en - fin dans les nu - a - - - - - - - ges, Et
Ped.
[cresc. - - - - - - - - - - - - -]
15
mf
fait bril - ler un nim - be d'or Sur la chau -
Ped.

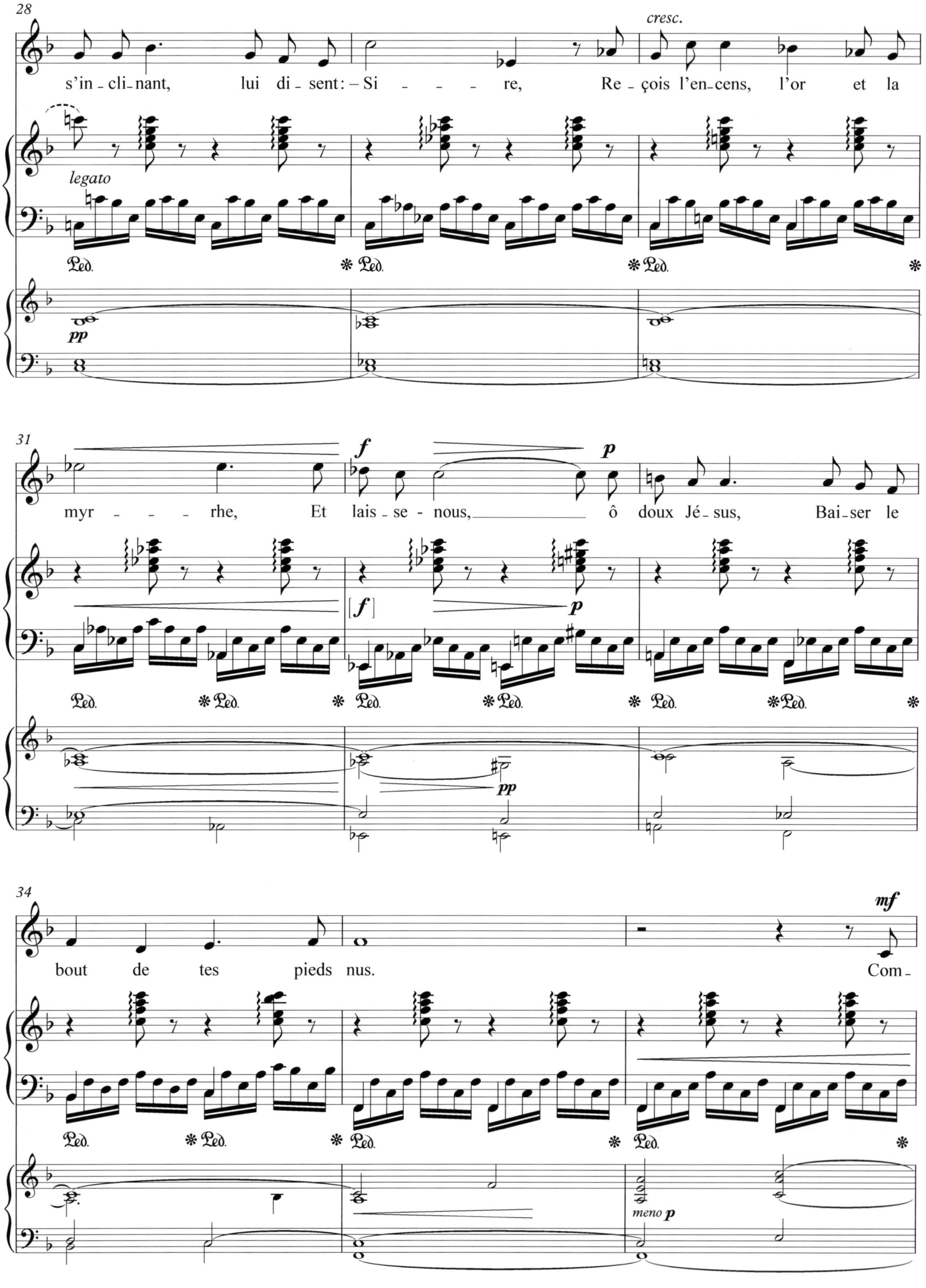
28
cresc.
s'in-cli-nant, lui di-sent: – Si - - - - re, Re-çois l'en-cens, l'or et la
legato
Ped.
31
f
p
myr - - - rhe, Et lais-se-nous, ô doux Jé-sus, Bai-ser le
[f]
pp
34
mf
bout de tes pieds nus. Com-
meno p

Original key: E♭

À Madame Leroux-Ribeyre

29. En prière

(Stéphan Bordèse)

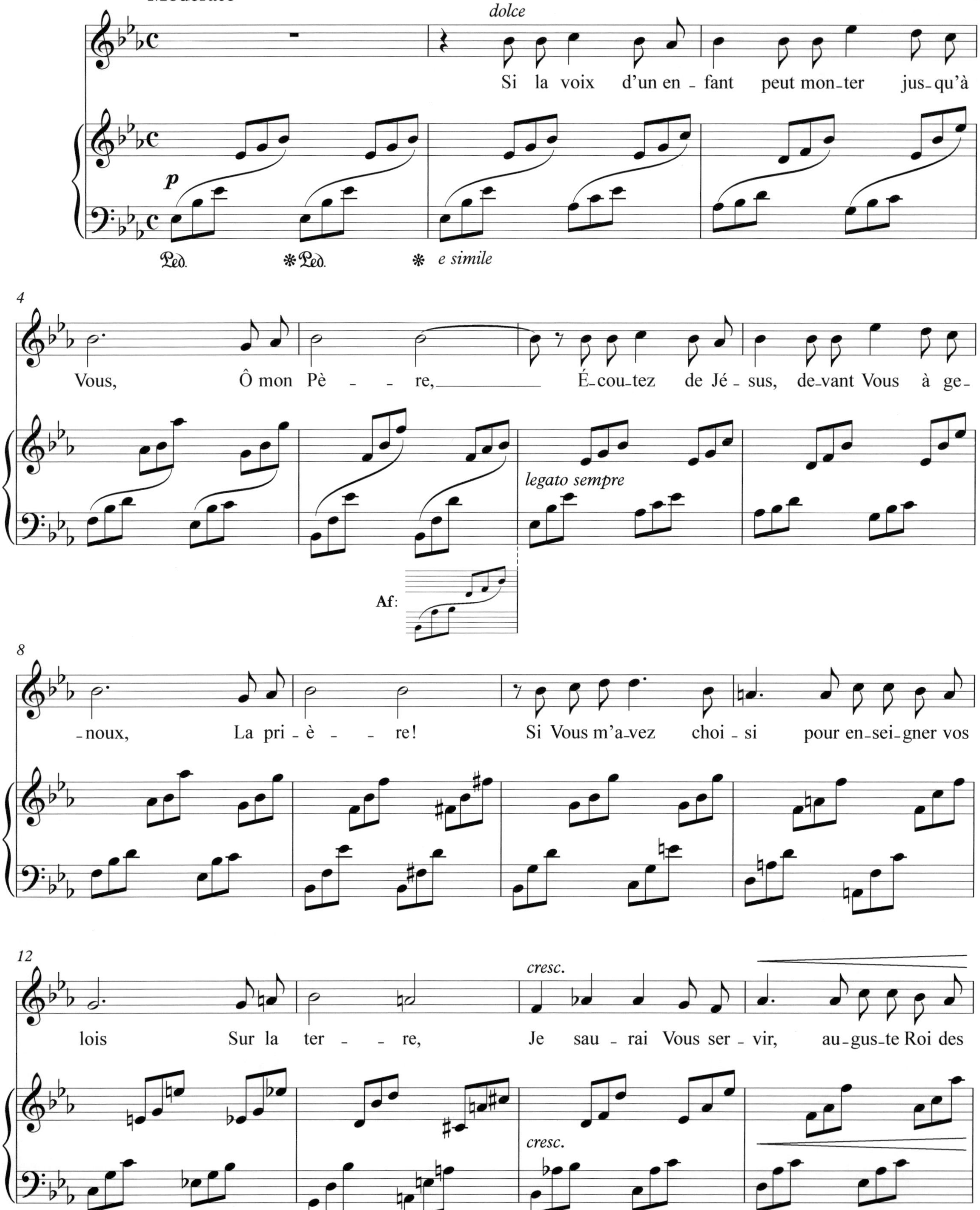

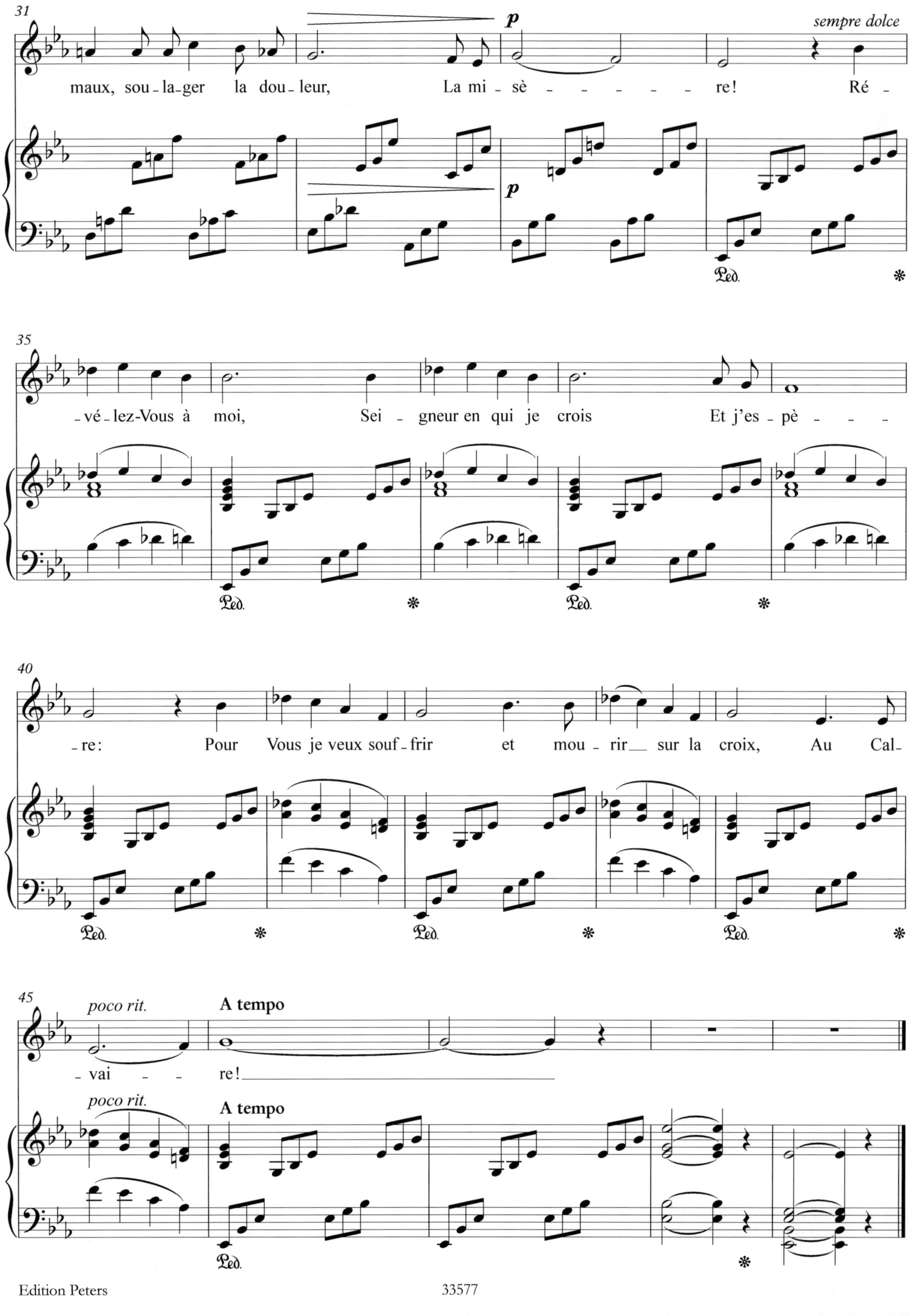
31
sempre dolce
p
maux, sou-la-ger la dou-leur, La mi-sè - - - - - - re! Ré-
p
35
-vé-lez-Vous à moi, Sei-gneur en qui je crois Et j'es-pè - - -
40
-re: Pour Vous je veux souf-frir et mou-rir sur la croix, Au Cal-
45
poco rit.
A tempo
-vai - - re!
poco rit.
A tempo

À Madame Claudie Chamerot et Mademoiselle Marianne Viardot
(Mesdames Georges Chamerot et Alphonse Duvernoy)

30. Puisqu'ici-bas toute âme...
Duo
(Victor Hugo)

Original key: C (for 2 sopranos or soprano and tenor)

[1)] (Op. 10 No. 1)

---

1) See Critical commentary / Voir Commentaire critique / Siehe Kritischen Bericht

(Original key)

À Madame Claudie Chamerot et Mademoiselle Marianne Viardot (Madame Alphonse Duvernoy)

31. Tarentelle

Duo

(Marc Monnier)

(Op. 10 No. 2)

Allegro vivo

1º: Aux cieux la lu_ne mon_te et luit, Il fait_ grand jour en plein mi_nuit! Viens a_vec moi, me di_sait-el _ _ le, Viens sur_ le sa_ble gré_sil_lant

2º: Aux cieux la lu_ne mon_te et luit, Il fait_ grand jour en plein mi_nuit! Viens sur_ le sa_ble gré_sil_lant Où_

1) **O**: beat 2 as in bar 124 / 2ᵉ temps comme mes. 124 / 2. Schlag wie in Takt 124

To Camilla Landi and David Bispham

32. Pleurs d'or

Duo

(Albert Samain)

Original key: E♭ (for mezzo-soprano and baritone)

[1)] Op. 71/72

Andante quasi allegretto

1) See Critical commentary (Publication history) / Voir Commentaire critique (Publication history) / Siehe Kritischen Bericht (Publication history)

1) See Critical Commentary regarding dynamics in bars 26–37
　Voir Commentaire critique à propos des dynamiques aux mes. 26–37
　Zur Dynamik in den Takten 26–37 siehe Kritischen Bericht

1) Pitching dyads in **Es** only / Accords de soutien pour les voix dans **Es** seulement / Diese Stimmakkorde nur in **Es**

À André Messager

33. Madrigal

4 solo voices SATB

(Armand Silvestre)

(Original key)

Op. 35

Edition Peters 33577

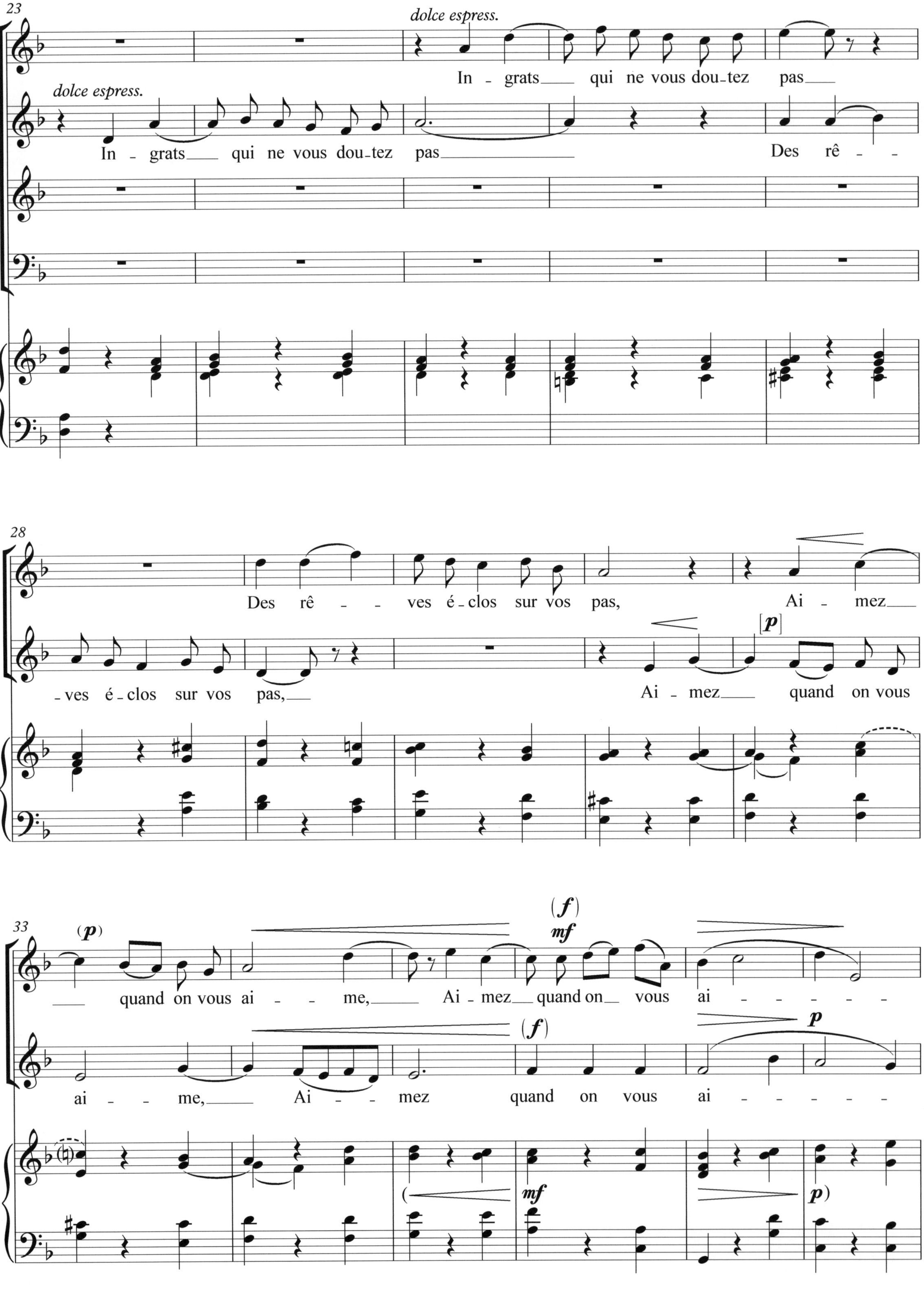
dolce espress.
In - grats qui ne vous dou-tez pas
Des rê - - ves é-clos sur vos pas, Ai - mez
quand on vous ai - - me, Ai-mez quand on vous ai - - - - -
Ai - mez quand on vous
ai - - me, Ai - - mez quand on vous ai - - - - -
S.
A.
T.
B.
Pf.

Chronology and dedicatees
Tableau chronologique ; dédicataires
Chronologie und Widmungsträger

SNM = Société nationale de musique. As far as is known, Fauré was the pianist in each performance listed below with piano.

(s) = soprano   (m) = mezzo-soprano   (t) = tenor   (b) baritone

Title	Composed	First performance	Dedicatee
Aurore	20 May 1884	Marguerite Mauvernay, SNM, 13 Dec. 1884	Mme Henriette Roger-Jourdain: wife of the painter Roger Jourdain, sister-in-law of salon hostess Marguerite de Saint-Marceaux
Fleur jetée	25 May 1884	Marguerite Mauvernay, SNM, 13 Dec. 1884	Marie-Thérèse [Mme Jules] Goüin: an outstanding amateur singer, wife of the inventor and philanthropist
Le Pays des Rêves	30 May 1884	Thérèse Guyon, SNM, 27 Dec. 1884	Mlle Thérèse Guyon: singer
Les Roses d'Ispahan	6 June 1884	Thérèse Guyon, SNM, 27 Dec. 1884	Mlle Louise Collinet: friend of Marguerite de Saint-Marceaux
Nocturne	1886	[not known]	Mme Henriette Roger-Jourdain: see above
Les Présents	1887	[not known]	Robert de Montesquiou-Fezensac: cousin of the Comtesse de Greffulhe, he introduced Fauré to the poetry of Verlaine and Villiers de L'Isle-Adam
Clair de lune	Oct. 1887	Maurice Bagès (t), SNM, 28 Apr. 1888 (version with orchestra)	Emmanuel Jadin: painter and friend of the composer, one of the Baugnies/Saint-Marceaux circle
Larmes	Nov. 1888	[not known]	Mme la Princesse Edmond de Polignac, née Winnaretta Singer:[1] renowned salon hostess and artistic patron
Au Cimetière	Nov. 1888	Maurice Bagès (t), SNM, 2 Feb. 1889	Marguerite [Mme Maurice] Sulzbach: amateur singer and salon hostess; she and her husband, a banker and art-lover, amassed a major collection of paintings and sculptures.
Spleen	Nov. 1888	None traced, though a surviving manuscript copy made for Maurice Bagès suggests that he sang it before publication	Thérèse [Mme Henry] Cochin: Flemish wife of a prominent liberal politician, art historian and musical amateur
La Rose (ode anacréontique)	Aug. 1890	[not known]	Maurice Bagès: outstanding tenor who premiered many of Fauré's songs in the decade 1888–1898
Chanson, Madrigal (*Shylock*)	Sept. 1889	Théâtre de l'Odéon, 17 Dec. 1889, cond. Fauré; M. Leprestre (t), SNM, 17 May 1890, cond Gabriel Marie.	[Paul Porel][2]
Sérénade (*Le Bourgeois Gentilhomme*)	Feb. 1893	-	[none]
Prison	Dec. 1894	Thérèse Roger (s), SNM, 3 Apr. 1897	[none]
Soir	17 Dec. 1894	Thérèse Roger (s), SNM, 3 Apr. 1897	[none]
Le Parfum impérissable	22 Aug. 1897	Émile Engel (t), Paris, 4 Nov. 1897	Paolo Tosti: Italian composer and singing teacher, resident in London from 1880–1912.
Arpège	6 Sept. 1897	Thérèse Roger (s), SNM, 30 Apr. 1898	Doris [Mme Charles] Dettelbach: amateur singer and salon hostess

[1] The autograph and first edition are dedicated to her under her first married name, as the Princesse de Scey-Montbéliard.

[2] Fauré dedicated his complete incidental *Shylock* music to Porel, the director of the Théâtre de l'Odéon.

Mélisande's Song (*Pelléas et Mélisande*)	31 May 1898	Mrs Patrick Campbell, Prince of Wales Theatre, London, 21 June 1898, cond. Fauré	[none]
Dans la forêt de septembre	29 Sept. 1902	[not known]	Mlle Lydia Eustis: amateur singer (pupil of Marie Trélat), salon performer and socialite
La Fleur qui va sur l'eau	13 Sept. 1902	[not known]	Mlle Pauline Segond: amateur singer (pupil of Marie Trélat)
Accompagnement	28 Mar. 1902	First public performance not documented; Émilie Girette (m) gave a private performance of the op. 85 set on 30 Dec. 1902 (shortly after their publication).	Émilie Girette [Mme Édouard Risler]: outstanding amateur mezzo, friend of Fauré, one of his favoured performers in the early 1900s.
Le plus doux chemin	1904	[not known]	Émilie [Mme Édouard] Risler: see above; for her marriage
Le Ramier	1904	[not known]	Mlle Claudie Segond: amateur singer (pupil of Marie Trélat)
Le Don silencieux	20 Aug. 1906	Pauline Segond (m), salon Albert Blondel, 28 Jan. 1907 (private); Jane Bathori (m), La Libre Esthétique (Brussels), 12 Mar. 1907	Madeleine [Mme Octave] Maus: wife of the art critic and writer Octave Maus; organised many avant-garde concerts in Brussels around the turn of the century.
Chanson	1906	[not known]	[none]
C'est la Paix	8 Dec. 1919	[not known]	[none]
Noël	1885	[not known]	[Jean-]Alexandre Talazac: French operatic tenor
En prière	Sept./Oct. 1890	Berthe Auguez de Montalant (m), Théâtre du Châtelet, cond. Édouard Colonne, 29 Dec. 1890.	Rachel-Pascaline Leroux-Ribeyre: soprano (excelling in oratorio); wife of the composer Xavier Leroux
Puisqu'ici-bas toute âme …	c. 1863 / c. 1873	Claudie Chamerot and Marianne Viardot (s), SNM, 10 Apr. 1875	Claudie [Mme Georges] Chamerot and Marianne [Mme Alphonse] Duvernoy: daughters of the legendary mezzo-soprano Pauline Viardot
Tarentelle	1873	Claudie Chamerot and Marianne Viardot (s), SNM, 10 Apr. 1875	Claudie Chamerot and Marianne Viardot: see above
Pleurs d'or	21 April 1896	Camilla Landi (m) and David Bispham (b), St James's Hall, London, 1 May 1896	Camilla Landi and David Bispham: Italian mezzo; American baritone who pursued a distinguished operatic career in England and the USA.
Madrigal (SATB)	1 Dec. 1883	Presumed première at Messager's wedding (1883); Concert premières, SNM, 12 Jan. 1884 (SNM singers) and 30 Apr. 1892 (unnamed soloists and SNM orchestra cond. by Fauré)	André Messager: composer and conductor, first pupil and lifelong friend of Fauré

Critical Commentary

Abbreviations

BnF mus. = Bibliothèque nationale de France, Paris, music department

pf. = piano   LH = left hand   RH = right hand

v. = voice   v1 = voice 1   v2 = voice 2   harm. = harmonium

General editorial procedure is described in the prefatory **Notes on the edition and performance**. The present edition follows the named priority source for each song except as noted in the list of variants. Enharmonic spelling in transpositions follows sources in the same key unless otherwise noted. Omissions of nuances, phrasing, articulation or obvious accidentals and prolongation dots in manuscript or secondary sources are passed over in silence, unless the omission suggests a viable variant. Useful cautionary accidentals are tacitly incorporated from any source that supplies them, including parallel passages; redundant accidentals are tacitly removed. Missing portions of ties (starts or completions across system breaks) are tacitly completed or incorporated from any source when the context allows no ambiguity. Dynamics that sources place above or below the system (usually because of restricted space) are relocated between the staves, as printed sources often do relative to manuscripts, except when musical logic suggests they were intended for just one hand or line. Orthographic variants (mezzo ***p***, ***mp***.***p***.; *dimin.*) are tacitly standardized (***mp***; *dim.*). Apparent duplications such as < *cresc.* are retained when feasible, as the < can sometimes be read as an independent gesture or an intensification. Secondary source readings are listed only when they are of special interest or impinge on a musical or editorial problem. Manuscripts are often revealing for the exact placing of nuances; where no autograph survives the earliest print is paid attention as the closest-to-manuscript source. Useful but non-essential indications from secondary sources are shown in parentheses. Minor variants to vocal lines for the purpose of accommodating English texts (mostly in Metzler editions) are ignored. The present edition tacitly standardizes the text underlay, which can be haphazard in printed sources. Music examples below are shown in their source key; any that quote multiple sources in different keys are given in the present edition's medium-voice key.

Manuscript collections from Fauré's family circle now housed in BnF mus. include those of his own family (donated by his daughter-in-law Blanche Fauré-Fremiet, including his surviving sketchbooks, numbered under Ms 17787), and of his friends Camille and Marie Clerc (donated by their granddaughters Mmes Ceillier & Maspéro) and Édouard and Émilie Risler (donated by their family). An increasing number of these manuscripts can be viewed online at www.gallica.fr.

Publication history

Of the present volume's songs, nos. 1–11, 17–18, 20–23, 28 and 32–33 were first published individually by Julien Hamelle, who also first published nos. 12–13 in the incidental music to *Shylock*, and no. 19 posthumously in 1937. Nos. 30–31 were first published (individually, in 1879) by Antoine de Choudens, before being bought out by Hamelle. Following one of several spats with Hamelle (whose laziness and miserliness were a constant thorn in Fauré's side), Fauré sold nos. 15–16 in June 1895 to Georges Hartmann, acting for the publisher Eugène Fromont under whose imprint the songs appeared as a pair in 1896 (*Soir* indicated as op. 68 no. 2, *Prison* erroneously as op. 51 no. 1).[1] Meanwhile, in January 1896 Fauré signed a contract with the London publisher Metzler, who in 1896–97 issued single editions (with English and French texts) of the present nos. 4, 7, 9, 13, 15–18, 29 and 32 (with *Prison* and *Soir* numbered op. 68 and *Pleurs d'or* op. 71). Metzler was the first to engrave at least *Pleurs d'or*, though by dint of an agreement with Hamelle (in April 1896) his subsequent editions appeared together with or after those of Hamelle (who published *Pleurs d'or* as op. 72).[2] No. 24 was a commission from the Italian branch of The Gramophone Company;[3] after Fauré's final break with Hamelle in 1905 the firm of Heugel published nos. 25–26 (plus a posthumous first edition of no. 14 in 1957), before Durand – who had first published no. 29 in 1890 – became Fauré's exclusive publisher from 1911, issuing no. 27.

After 1905 Fauré necessarily continued dealings with Hamelle over existing contracts. Since 1887 Hamelle had published what is traditionally known as the First Collection (Faure's early songs prior to op. 18, a volume first published by Choudens in 1879 as *Vingt Mélodies*). In 1897 Hamelle issued a Second Collection (*Vingt Cinq Mélodies*), comprising twenty-five songs from op. 18 through to op. 51 along with *En prière*, plus *Prison* and *Soir* by agreement with Fromont. Having meanwhile assigned the opus number 68 to a different item, Hamelle rebranded *Prison* and *Soir* as op. 73, only to be forced to renumber them again shortly after as op. 74, then finally as op. 83.[4]

In 1908 Hamelle issued a Third Collection of Fauré's songs up to 1904 (op. 87). Determined to present this with twenty songs, Hamelle transferred to it the last six songs from his 1897 Second Collection (op. 51 plus *Prison* and *Soir*), moving the early song *Barcarolle* in turn from the First to the Second Collection and republishing the latter with a total of twenty songs. The First Collection he simultaneously reissued, bringing in *Noël* (op. 43 no. 1, which had not appeared in the Second Collection) to fill the gap left by *Barcarolle* and maintain a total of twenty songs there too. Fauré viewed all this redistribution with disgust but was unable to stem it.[5] That said, there is no doubt that the musical retouches introduced in these successive reprints are authorial.

The present songs nos. 1–3, 5, 8–9, 15–16 and 20–24 first appeared in transposition in the Second and Third Collections

---

[1] The misprint doubtless resulted from Fromont using an exemplar of Fauré's op. 51 songs as a style template; the edition's title page lists no opus number. While this was Fromont's first Fauré publication, the firm was effectively run by Georges Hartmann, who in 1871 had issued four of Fauré's early songs under his own imprint.

[2] Hamelle had reserved 71 for Fauré's *Thème et variations* for piano, which Metzler presumably intended to publish as op. 72. In the hope of averting further confusion, Metzler and Hamelle both issued the *Thème et variations* as op. 73, although Hamelle adverts for many years continued to list it as op. 71. Information on Metzler's dealings with Fauré and Hamelle, along with Metzler publication dates, comes from Robert Orledge, "Fauré en Angleterre", *Association des amis de Gabriel Fauré, Bulletin n° 13* (1976), pp. 10–16, and personal communications from Robert Orledge.

[3] This commission was extended to several poets (Graham Johnson, *Gabriel Fauré: The Songs and their Poets*, p. 282), the intention being also to issue recordings, though none appeared of Fauré's song.

[4] This quietly spectacular pileup resulted from Hamelle's appropriation of the opus number 68 for an *Allegro symphonique* for piano duet, arranged by Léon Boëllman from the first movement of Fauré's unpublished Symphony or Suite in F, op. 20. Hamelle's consequent renumbering of *Soir* and *Prison* as op. 73 collided with his hasty renumbering of the *Thème et variations* (see note 2 above). Their subsequent renumbering as op. 74 then clashed with the allotted number for Fauré's Seventh Nocturne. Their final numbering as op. 83 comes from the early 1900s; by 1908 Hamelle had bought out the songs from Fromont. In all versions of Hamelle's Second (then Third) Collection, the varying opus number above these two songs is untidily printed, suggesting amendment at proof, presumably from an original 68.

[5] *Gabriel Fauré: his Life through his Letters*, pp. 274–6, letter of August 1907 to Edgard Hamelle.

(each published for both high and medium voice). Numbers 14, 19, 25–27 and 30–33 were not incorporated in any collection, nor, except for no. 32, published in transposition.[6] Hamelle also issued several songs with obbligato violin or cello parts: devised by fellow-musicians and printed on a separate page (along with a vocal line), these added parts leave the basic text unchanged and are disregarded here.

Text

Punctuation and capitalisation tacitly follow whichever music sources match the printed poems, although several significant variants are noted. Adjustments to punctuation and capitalisation in music sources are respected where they appear consistent, viable and deliberate; see **Preface** (Texts and Poets). Where music sources provide no punctuation, or syntactically unviable alternatives, the original punctuation of poems is restored, as noted in the list of variants. Pages XXXVI–XLVIII present the poems as they appear in the editions most probably used by Fauré (as detailed below under **Poem sources**).

Source sigla

A   Autograph manuscript (**A1**, **A2** etc. as necessary: in such cases **A** is used to refer to them collectively)

C   Non-autograph manuscript

Es Single prints (*éditions séparées*) from various French publishers. High-, medium- and low-voice versions are distinguished as necessary by the suffixes -**e**, -**m** and -**g** (*voix élevées, voix moyennes, voix graves*).

F   Feuilleton (magazine or newspaper) publications

Mz Single prints of nos. 4, 7, 9, 13, 15–18, 29 and 32, in or with English translation: Metzler and Co. L^{td}, London, 1896–1897

Rc Collections (*recueils*):

1) *2e Recueil* / Vingt Cinq / Mélodies / pour / Une Voix / avec accompagnement de Piano / par / Gabriel Fauré.[7] Hamelle [1897], J.4102 H. and J.4103 H. (medium- and high-voice editions); reprinted with minor amendments at least three times [c. 1899, 1902, 1904]. Traditionally known as the Second Collection, this volume introduces metronome indications often absent in the single prints, along with some musical retouches. Originally comprising twenty-five songs, it was reissued in 1908 as *Vingt Mélodies* (see above under **Publication history**), retaining the same plate numbers while removing the word *Cinq* from its title and cover pages, various songs transferred to collection 3 below and some of those remaining showing minor retouches.

2) *Premier Recueil* / 20 / *Mélodies* / pour / *Chant et Piano* / par / Gabriel Fauré. Hamelle [1908], J.3149.H and J.3150.H. (medium- and high-voice editions). This 1908 reissue of what is traditionally known as the First Collection (originally published by Choudens in 1879) incorporates *Noël* (see above under **Publication history**).

3) *3e Recueil* / Vingt / Mélodies / pour / Une Voix / avec accompagnement de Piano / par / Gabriel Fauré. Hamelle [1908], J. 5469 H. and J. 5700 H. (medium- and high-voice editions); traditionally known as the Third Collection, it comprises the songs of op. 51 to op. 87 except for *Sérénade* and *Mélisande's Song*.

High- and medium-voice versions of **Rc** are distinguished as necessary by the suffixes -**e** and -**m**. Successive editions of collection 1) above are distinguished as necessary by publication (or estimated) year in subscript ($_{97}$, $_{[99]}$, $_{[02]}$, $_{[04]}$ or $_{08}$, estimated years in brackets), with arrows indicating chronological concurrence: thus **Rc-m**$_{\rightarrow[02]}$ indicates prints up to and including that of c. 1902, and **Rc-m**$_{[02]\rightarrow}$ that one onwards. Roman and Arabic numerals indicate the location of songs in the collections above, designating respectively volume and song numbers.

VM/VE   Respectively all *voix moyennes* or *voix élevées* printed sources (not manuscripts)

T   Text as in poems (see below and pp. XXXVI–XLVIII)

Poem sources

Unless otherwise noted, Fauré's source is assumed to be the first edition, as listed below.

Armand Silvestre

Le Pays des roses / *Poésies nouvelles* (Paris: Charpentier, 1882): "Matutina" IV [**Aurore**]

Les Ailes d'or / *Poésies nouvelles* (Paris: Charpentier, 1880): "**Fleur jetée**" and "**Le Pays des Rêves**", both in the section *Vers pour être chantés*. Fauré sets just part I of the latter (which is in two parts).

La Chanson des heures / *Poésies d'Armand Silvestre, 1872–1878* (Paris: Charpentier, 1878): [**Le plus doux chemin**], [**Le Ramier**] and [**Madrigal**], all in the section *Vers pour être chantés* / "Madrigaux dans le goût ancien / À P. Lacome", respectively nos. X, III and II. The first two are headed "Pour une voix"; [**Madrigal**] is headed "Pour un chœur alterné". The 1887 Lemerre re-edition of *La Chanson des heures* also incorporates "Fleur jetée" (as "La Fleur jetée"), with some amendments.

Leconte de Lisle

Poèmes et poésies (Paris: Dentu, 1855): "**La Rose**" (*Odes anacréontiques*, IX), reissued in *Poésies complètes* (Paris: Poulet-Malassis et de Broise, 1858).

Poèmes tragiques (Paris: Lemerre, 1884): "**Les Roses d'Ispahan**" and "**Le Parfum impérissable**". The former has six strophes, of which Fauré omits nos. 3 and 5.

> Fauré's source for "La Rose" was *Poésies complètes*. "Le Parfum impérissable" first appeared in *La Revue contemporaine* (30 June 1864, p. 796) and was also included in the multi-author collection *Le Livre des Sonnets* (Paris: Lemerre, 1875); both "Les Roses d'Ispahan" and "Le Parfum impérissable" were published in *La Nouvelle Revue* (15 January 1883, p. 416). *Poèmes tragiques*, published on 25 March 1884, seems to have been Fauré's source for *Les Roses d'Ispahan* (composed just two months later).[8] Several text variants in the music sources of *Le Parfum impérissable* seem to derive from the 1875 *Livre des Sonnets*, notably the substitution of "tient" for "tint" in line 6.

---

[6] Selected songs were also published in American editions between 1912 and 1915, first in an anthology from the publisher Oliver Ditson (c. 1904, ed. Philip Hale), and subsequently Schirmer (supervised by Fauré's friend Charles-Martin Loeffler) and the Boston Music Company (tastelessly overedited by Henry Clough-Leighter). Wholly sourced from French editions, these are disregarded here.

[7] As on the title page; the front cover reads 2e recueil / Vingt Cinq / Mélodies / Chant et Piano / Gabriel Fauré. The covers of the First and Third Collections are worded equivalently.

[8] The poem as printed in *La Nouvelle Revue* gives "Leïlah" rather than the "Leïlah" of the 1884 edition and Fauré's autograph.

Villiers de L'Isle-Adam
Contes cruels (Paris: Lévy, 1883): "Éblouissement" [**Nocturne**] and "**Les Présents**", respectively nos. I and III in the section *Conte d'amour*.

Paul Verlaine
Fêtes galantes (Paris: Lemerre, 1869): "**Clair de lune**". The poem was first published in *La Gazette rime*, 20 February 1867, as "Fêtes galantes", then in *L'Artiste*, 1 January 1868, as "Clair de lune".

Romances sans paroles (Paris: M. L'Hermitte, 1874): *Ariettes oubliées* no. III ("Il pleure dans mon cœur") [**Spleen**].

Sagesse (Paris: Société générale de librairie catholique, 1881): Part III no. VI ("Le ciel est, par-dessus le toit") [**Prison**].

Fauré appears to have used the most recent editions of each collection, all published by the Parisian house Vanier: *Fêtes galantes* (1886), *Romances sans paroles* (1887) and *Sagesse* (1893).

Jean Richepin
La Mer (Paris: Dreyfous, 1886): "**Larmes**" (*Étant de quart*, XVII), "**Au cimetière**" (*Les Gas*, III). "Larmes" has four strophes, of which Fauré omits no. 3.

Edmond Haraucourt
Shylock / Comédie en trois actes et sept tableaux / en vers / d'après SHAKESPEARE / Musique de Gabriel Fauré (Paris: Charpentier, 1890): [**Chanson**] (Act 1 scene 2), [**Madrigal**] (Act 2 scene 1).

Molière
Le Bourgeois Gentilhomme (1670): [**Sérénade**]. The present edition follows the 1862 Testard complete edition (*Œuvres complètes de Molière*), ed. Félix Lemaistre.

Albert Samain
Au jardin de l'Infante (Paris: Édition du *Mercure de France*, 1893): "Élégie' [**Soir**] (9 strophes, of which Fauré set just the last three), "**Arpège**", "**Accompagnement**", "**Larmes**" [**Pleurs d'or**].

Fauré omitted lines 10–11 of "Accompagnement", and the 4th and the final tercets of "Larmes" [**Pleurs d'or**].

Maurice Maeterlinck
Pelléas et Mélisande, trans. John William [Jack] Mackail: [**Mélisande's Song**] (Act 3 scene 1, London 1898)

Catulle Mendès
"Dans la forêt de septembre", "La Belle dans la nuit et **la fleur qui va sur l'eau**": *Le Figaro*, respectively 21 September and 6 April 1902.

Jean Dominique [Marie Closset]
L'Anémone des mers (Paris: Société du *Mercure de France*, 1906): [**Le Don silencieux**] (no. XXVIII).

Henri de Régnier
La Sandale ailée / 1903–1905 (Paris: Société du *Mercure de France*, 1906): "**Chanson**"

Georgette Debladis
"[C'est] **La Paix**": *Le Figaro* Sunday literary supplement, 7 December 1919, the poet's name given anagrammatically as "Gilette de Besgador"; reprinted with a few variants of layout and punctuation in *Le Figaro* Sunday musical supplement, 10 October 1920, p. 8. 5 strophes, of which Fauré omits nos. 3–4 and reworks and compresses no. 2

Victor Wilder
Noël (source untraced)

Stephan Bordèse
Contes mystiques (Paris: Durand, 1890): "**En prière**"

Victor Hugo
Les Voix intérieures (Lausanne: Rouiller, 1837): "[**Puisqu'ici-bas toute âme**]", no. XI (21 May 1837).

12 strophes, of which Fauré omits nos. 4 and 11. The song's many discrepancies and omissions of punctuation leave it impossible to determine which of the poem's many editions served as Fauré's source: for the opening line the present edition adopts the 1858 Hachette edition's added hyphen ("ici-bas"), absent in the 1837 edition and music sources except for the song's printed title.

Marc Monnier
Poésies de Marc-Monnier (Geneva: S. Jolimay-Desrogis, 1872): "**Tarentelle**", in the section *Musiques*, subtitled "(Chanson de Lauzières)". An earlier version of the poem had previously appeared in *Le Courrier Franco-italien*, 9 July 1857. Four strophes, of which Fauré omits no. 3.

Music sources and variants

1. Aurore

Keys: F and G

F   Feuilleton (possibly first) publication, in G: *Album du Gaulois*, 1 February 1885. **F** appears to derive from a manuscript or early proof for **Es**; it shows variant dynamics, with no phrasing or articulation except pf. LH slurs in bars 13–14 and 44–46.

Es   First commercial edition: Hamelle [1885], in G (J. 2287.1 H.)

Rc   II/12, in F and G. A musically identical offprint from the former was later issued: some exemplars show the plate number as just 2287.1 [without letters], others as J. 4102 H. 2287[bis].

Priority source: **Rc-e**

Variants

Text. Bar 4: comma as in **F** and **Rc-m**; other music sources omit punctuation (**T**: full stop). Bar 6: semicolon as in **Rc-m**; **F** has a full stop, other music sources omit punctuation (**T**: comma). Bar 8 beat 3, bar 19: comma in all music sources (not **T**). Bar 27: music sources add a comma

Tempo. F: *Andante molto moderato*, no metronome indication

Bars 3–13, pf. **Es** and **Rc** carry slurs past bar 3 (system break) without continuation or staccato dots from bar 4; editorially completed

Bar 7, pf. **F** omits <

Bar 11, both. **F**: *mf*

Bar 12, v. **F** ends > at the barline

Bar 15, pf. **Es** omits *sempre*. **F**: *sempre dolce*

Bars 19–20, v. < as in **F**; **Es** and **Rc** end it a ♪ earlier

Bars 21–22, both. **F** places > a bar earlier; **Rc-m** omits it for pf.

Bar 23, pf. Pedalling from **F** (which omits *sempre **pp***)

Bar 27, v. **F** rhythm ♩ ♩. ♪

Bars 27–46, both. **F** omits v. *f espress.* at bar 27 in favour of *sempre cresc.* from bar 28, pf. *cresc.* from bar 29 ♩ 3, < across bar 30 (v. only) to *f* at bar 31 (v./pf.), pf. > from bar 31 ♩ 3 to bar 32 ♩ 2, bar 32 v. rhythm ♩ ♪ 𝄾 across beats 1–2 with *mf* at ♩ 3 above pf. ***p***, no dynamics in bars 35–36. **F** then omits bar 39 pf. *cresc.* in favour of < across bars 40–41, with v. < across bar 41, bar 42 v. duration ♪ 𝄾 at beat 1 with *f* at beat 2 above pf. *mf*, then v./pf. > across bar 43 beats 2–4, bar 44 no v. dynamics but pf. ***p*** followed by > across bar 45 to ***pp*** at bar 46. **F** also omits *Poco rit. / A tempo* across bars 42–44. Other sources as present edition except in showing *poco a poco cresc.* (v./pf.) at bar 39 (a relic from the **F** conception) and v. ***p*** at bar 44 (both editorially adjusted here); **Es** also shows a mid-system pf. > across bar 32 ♪s 2–7 (starting under the end of <) and omits dynamics in bars 35–36; these suggest remnants from or interim adjustments to **F**, and are editorially tidied here.

Bar 30, pf. **Rc-m** gives RH ♪ 2 a semitone higher (preceded redundantly by ♭ instead of ♮, obvious misprint)

Bar 35, v. Sources end v. slur a note earlier

Bar 47, both. **F** follows this with an additional silent bar, ▬ surmounted by ⌒

2. Fleur jetée

Keys: d and f

Sources

Es First edition: Hamelle [1885], in f (J. 2288.2 H.)

Rc II/13, in d and f. A musically identical offprint from the former was issued no later than 1908 (J. 4102 H. 2288bis, the double plate number also appearing on **Rc-m**[08]).

Secondary source

C Manuscript copy, in c, along with *Le Pays de Rêves*, unknown hand, undated, using some shorthand: library of the Royal Brussels Conservatoire, shelf mark 63.598 (ex coll. Fernand Leroy). Its interest lies about some variant dynamics (listed below), raising a query about its source (tempo indication as in **Rc-m**, dynamics meticulously entered but pf. part devoid of accents).

Priority source: **Rc-m**

Variants

Text. Bars 8–9: punctuation as in **Rc-m** (none in other music sources; **T** has just a full stop after *rêvant*), the comma in bar 9 retained as a useful breathing suggestion following <. Bar 11: full stop as in **Rc**, no punctuation in **Es** (**T**: !). Bars 19, 27: full stop as in the 1887 Lemerre edition of **T** (no punctuation in 1880 edition); music sources omit punctuation in bar 19 and give a comma in bar 27. Bar 23: full stop as in **Rc-m**; no punctuation in **VE** sources (**T**: !). Bar 36: comma as in music sources (**T**: !)

Tempo. **Es** omits *energico* and metronome indication, **Rc** omits the latter's prolongation dot, **Rc-e** gives the number as 170 [*sic*]

Variant indications in C. Bars 6, 34, pf. <> placed close under LH; bar 14, v. < starts at note 1 (pf. as present edition); bars 16–20, see below; bar 22, v. *espressivo* (from ♪, above present *f*); bar 26, v. > from half bar instead of present *dim.* (beat 1 notated as -*chée* on a single ♩.); pf. *dim.* delayed by a bar. All other dynamics as in present edition.

Bars 3, 17, 21–24, 31, 41–43, pf. Bar 17 LH > in **Rc-m** only, RH > bars 21–24 and 31 in **Rc-m**[02]→ only; **Rc-m** conversely omits bar 3 RH >, bars 22–23 bass >, bars 42–43 1st RH >, and all accents in bar 41 beats 2–3; **Rc-m**[97] omits bars 23–24 LH upper >

Bar 8, v. **VE** sources end < at note 2

Bar 12, pf. All sources: last RH ♪ of each beat repeats preceding chords (doubling LH); lowest note editorially removed (cf. bars 2 and 30)

Bar 15, pf. **Rc-m** omits >

Bars 16–20, both. **C**: v. ***p*** < across bars 17–18, omitting preceding *cresc.* and pf. *sf*, v. > from bar 19 note 1 (pf. dynamics otherwise as present edition)

Bars 19–20, v. **VE** sources place > across bar 19 (from note 1 to barline)

Bars 29–30, pf. **Rc-m** omits <

Bar 34, v. **VE** sources end > at note 2

3. Le Pays des Rêves

Keys: G♭ and A♭

Sources

Es First edition: Hamelle [1885], in A♭ (J. 2289.3 H.: **Es-e**); then [1913] in F (J. 2289ter H.: **Es-g**, titled *AU PAYS DES RÊVES*). Neither has pf. pedalling.

Rc II/14, in G♭ and A♭. A musically identical offprint from **Rc-m**[97] was later issued (2289.3, without letters).

Secondary source

C Manuscript copy, in F (see *Fleur jetée* above), shelf mark 63.597; title as in **Es-e** and **Rc**. Bars 16–26 are indicated by repeat signs across bars 3–13, their text, variant underlay and dynamics marked above the staff. Again its main interest lies in variant dynamics.

Priority source: **Rc-m**

Variants

Text. Bars 4, 12, 45, 55: Lower-case *rêves* as in music sources (which nevertheless give *Rêves* in title as in **T**). Bars 11, 55: Music sources omit comma. Bar 31: comma as in all music sources. Bar 33: ! as in **T** (**Rc-e**: semicolon; **Rc-m** and **Es-e**: comma; no punctuation in **Es-g**). Bar 37: full stop as in all music sources (**T**: colon). Bar 39: breathing comma from **Es-g**, which prints it as a text comma

Tempo. Metronome indication in **Rc** (and **C**) only, omitting the prolongation dot

Bar 1–29, 44–60, pf. LH phrasing misprinted in **Es-g**, which omits it in bars 25–29 and otherwise breaks it across each system change (resulting in single-bar slurs in bars 47, 50 and 53), ending last LH slur at last ♪ of bar 59

Bar 7, v. **VE** sources, beats 2–3: ♩ ♪ ♪

Bars 13–14, pf. $>$ p from **C**

Bars 13, 26, v. Beat 4 enharmonic spelling as in **VE** sources; **Rc-m** spells it in sharps (cf. bar 56 all sources)

Bar 20, v. p from **C** (as reprise of bar 7); cf. note to bar 24

Bar 23, v. **VE** sources, beat 1: ♩·

Bar 24, v. **Es** and **Rc-e** omit mf (present in **Rc-m** and by default in **C**: cf. note to bar 20)

Bar 30, v. **Es-g** omits p, perhaps intending pp (see music footnote)

Bars 32–33, 40–41, pf. **Es-g** omits RH slur completion in bars 33 and 41 (system break in all sources); other sources end slur at bar 32 beat 4 and bar 40 last ♪

Bar 35, v. **VE** sources, beat 3: ♪ 2 ♪ (missing the 2 in **Es-e** but aligned as duplets, possibly a misprint); cf. pf. LH

Bar 37, v. **VE** sources: ♩ –

Bar 40, v. **Rc-m** omits $>$, **Es-g** starts it a full ♪ earlier

Bars 41–42, pf. Sources: $>$ not > at beat 4 (except **Es-g** omits it in bar 41); musical sense suggests >. Cf. also note to bars 32–33 etc.

Bar 44, v. **C** starts $<$ at *beau*

Bars 46–47, pf. RH lower slur from **Es-g**, which omits to complete upper slur in bar 47 (new system); other printed sources end upper slur at last ♪ of bar 47, but with discontinuity in **Es-e** and **Rc-m** which end it at last ♪ of bar 46 (end of system) then carry it over at bar 47. (**C** omits RH phrasing.) See also note to bars 1–29 etc.

Bar 48, v. **C**: p

Bars 53–54, pf. Sources break LH slur across barline, probably a misreading in view of v. entry and bars 10–11. (**C** shows the slur originally continuous across barline (and across bars 50–51), then amended to break as in other sources)

Bar 56, v. **C** places $>$ across bars 57–58 instead (v. only)

4. Les Roses d'Ispahan

Keys: D and E

Sources

A   Autograph, in D, used for engraving **Es-m**, signed and dated "6 juin 1884": collection of Thierry Bodin, Paris

Es   First edition: Hamelle [1885], in D (J. 2290. 4 H.: **Es-m**) and E (J. 2290.4 bis H.: **Es-e1**, plus **Es-e2**, amended reprint [c. 1897]); then [c. 1908] in D♭ (J. 5625 H.: **Es-mg**) and [c. 1913] in B (J. 6752 H.: **Es-g**)

Mz   Metzler [1896], in D (M. 7775), as *Persian Roses*, English and French text (trans. Adela Maddison)

Rc   II/15, in D and E

VM in this song signifies **Es-m**, **Mz** and **Rc-m**

Secondary source

O   Autograph orchestral score, in D [1891]: BnF mus., Ms. 20809 (ex Hamelle archives)

Priority source: **Rc-e**

Variants

Text. Bars 28, 50: Music sources omit comma. Bars 69, 77: punctuation as in **T** (music sources: full stops, except that **OA** has bar 77 !).

Tempo. **A**: *Andantino* ~~moderato~~. Metronome indication in **Rc** and **Es-e2** only

Bars 1, 22, pf. **A** omits mf, instead showing a single p mid-system. **OA**: *espressivo* instead of *marcato* (vc solo); cf. bar 41

Bars 14–15, 33–34, 54, 68–69, pf. **O** indicates $<$ against just the rising line (either solo vc or vns); other sources place it above upper pf. staff in bar 54, elsewhere in mid-system, in bar 14 starting at ♩2 (restricted space; **O** as present edition). Printed sources: additional slur across bar 14 notes 1–2 of rising RH line (cf. bar 33). Bar 68 RH slur start as in **A**; printed sources start it from top of chord.

Bars 20–21, both. Dynamics as in **Es-e** and **Rc**; other sources: $>$ in bar 21, **Es-g** across the whole bar, remaining sources across ♩1

Bar 22, pf. **Es-g**: f not mf; cf. note to bars 1, 22

Bar 29, v. **VE** sources: ' before *Sonne*

Bars 29–31, pf. $<>$ in **VE** sources only

Bars 32, 41, 57, v. **A**: ♩ ♪⌒; cf. notes to bars 68–69 and bar 76

Bars 33–34, pf. RH slurs in **Es** and **Rc-e** only in bar 33, **Rc-e** and **Es-mg/g** only in bar 34. See also note to bars 14–15 etc.

Bar 38, v. f as in **Es-e** and **Rc**; other sources: mf

Bar 39, pf. **A** carries LH slur to barline (end of page)

Bars 39–41, both. $>$ as in **Es-e** and **Rc**; other sources place it across bar 40 (pf.) and for v. from bar 40 ♩2 to bar 41 note 1 (omitting p)

Bar 41, pf. *Espressivo* from **O** (hn solo). See also note to bars 32 etc.

Bar 44, v. ' in **VE** sources only

Bar 47, pf. **Rc-e** omits >

Bars 50–51, pf. **Rc** omits RH tie; **Es-mg/g** omit $<$

Bar 54, see note to bars 14–15 etc.

Bar 57, v. $>$ in **Rc** only. See also note to bars 32 etc.

Bars 57–60, both. Present footnote indicates basic dynamics in **O** (some instruments show other dynamics within these)

Bar 62, pf. **Es-g**: single RH lower-voice slur across both beats

Bar 64, v. **O**: last ♪ a semitone lower

Bars 68–69, v. **A**: ♩♩⌒♪ ⁊ ⁊ ♪. Cf. notes to bars 32 etc. and bar 76

Bars 68–69, pf. All sources except **Es-g** start a new $<$ at bar 69 (new system), in **A** possibly a later addition squashed into restricted space; **Es-g**: single $<$ starting from bar 68 ♩2; editorially adjusted. See also note to bars 14–15 etc.

Bar 74, **Rc-e**[→[99]]: RH chord 1 top note misprinted a 3rd high (corrected in **Rc-e**[[02]→]).

Bars 75–76, both. *Poco rit.* / *a tempo* in **Es-e**, **Rc** only

Bar 76, v. **A**: originally ♪·♪ (cf. bar 50), ♩·♪ then amended to ♩ and $>$ curtailed as in present edition. Cf. notes to bars 32 etc. and 68–69

5. Nocturne

Keys: E♭, F♯ and C

Sources

(A1 *Autograph, in E♭, probably used for engraving **Es**: private collection, presently inaccessible)*

A2 Post-publication autograph, in F♯, signed and dated "4 février 1892": Library of Congress, Washington, shelf mark ML96.F3 Case (Music 1234). Bearing Hamelle's house stamp but no engraver's marks, it appears to have been the source of transposed copies made for **Rc-m**$_{\rightarrow[04]}$ and **Rc-e** (which both replicate a slip it shows at bar 44).

Es First edition: Hamelle [1886], in E♭ (J. 2469 H.). The title page specifies "pour Contralto ou Basse / avec accompagnement / de Piano", with 3 key options listed underneath: "en Mi♭, pour Contralto ou Basse / en Sol pour Mezzo-Soprano ou Baryton / en Si♭ pour Soprano ou Ténor". These last two (G and B♭) were probably never issued (no exemplars are traced); post-1897 reprints amend the listed transposed keys to A♭ and C, in which Hamelle issued unamended offprints from **Rc-m**$_{97}$ and **Rc-e**. Around 1928 Hamelle issued a separate print in G♭ (J. 7471 H.); poorly proofed, it contributes no readings here.

Rc II/17, in A♭ and C (**Rc**$_{\rightarrow[04]}$), then E♭ and C (**Rc**$_{08}$)

Fa Feuilleton publication, in E♭: supplement to *Les Annales politiques et littéraires* 1173 (17 December 1905); mentioned below only where it differs from its source **Es**

Fm Feuilleton publication, in A♭: album of *Musica* 77 (February 1909), pp. 39–40. Derived from **Rc-m**$_{\rightarrow[04]}$ (ironically, given **Rc-m**$_{08}$), it differs only in one phrasing detail, and is otherwise not mentioned below

Version 1 (E♭) sources: **Es, Fa, Rc-m**$_{08}$

Version 2 (F♯) source: **A2**

Version 3 (C) source: **Rc-e**

Version 4 (A♭) sources: **Rc-m**$_{\rightarrow[04]}$, **Fm**

Regarding the present edition's allocation of versions see **Preface**. Versions 3 and 4 displace the piano accompaniment by an octave relative to the voice, and supply the metronome indication plus voice phrasing; they also complete pedalling and pf. LH phrasing (sporadic in **A2**, absent in Version 1 pre-1908). In addition to the LH phrasing, **Rc-m**$_{08}$ carries into Version 1 the bass grace notes at bars 29 and 32 (see below), but not the metronome indication or pedalling; these are carried over here to Version 1 (in parentheses) but not to Version 2. Essential details present in only one source are carried over to other versions as listed below; those missing in just one version are incorporated parenthetically in that version without further comment. A single list of variants is given below (excluding those instantly visible across versions); if necessary comments start with the version or versions affected (**V1, V2, V3, V4**).

Variants

Text. Bar 18: music sources omit comma. Bars 29–30: **A2** has *aux sombres voiles*

V1: bar 5, pf. **Es** omits RH accidental

V1, V3–4: bars 6, 19, pf. ✻ placed as in **Rc-e**; **V4** sources place it just before barline (**E2** shows no pedal here)

V1, V4: bars 7, 9, 22, pf. **V4** sources indicate pedal across each bar, perhaps in error (cf. bar 20 and consistent absence in **Es-e**); editorially omitted

V3–4: bars 8–9, v. Sources with phrasing end slur at last note of bar 8; editorially extended

V3: bar 13, v. Slur end as in **V4** sources; **Rc-e** ends it at last note of bar 12

V1: bar 13, pf. **Rc-m**$_{08}$ misaligns LH cautionary against middle note of chord (inflecting it a semitone upward, as b♮), other printed sources omit it. (Cf. bar 26)

V4: bars 14–15, pf. Pedal change across barline in **V4** sources alone, perhaps specific to this version's low tessitura

V3–4: bar 22, v. Slur end as in **Fm**; **Rc-m**$_{\rightarrow[04]}$ and **Rc-e** end it a note earlier

V2: bar 24, pf. **A2** RH initial triad (same as in bar 20) possibly involves a slip of the pen; cf. bar 11

V2: bar 28, pf. *Cresc.* editorially moved to start of bar; **A2** places it mid-bar because of restricted space

V1: bars 29, 32, pf. LH grace note in **Rc-m**$_{08}$ only; **V3–4** sources also show it, but an 8ve higher relative to the main note

V1–4: bars 30, 33–35, pf. RH stemming and slurs editorially rationalized to match **A2** in bars 30 and 34; printed sources stem bar 34 inversely and single-stem bar 30 ♩3 (ending the slur at top note of chord); all sources single-stem bar 33 ♩3 (again ending slur at top note) and bar 35 (notating its outer 8ve as ♩ ♩)

V1, V4: bars 35–36, pf. ✻ placed as in **V2–3** sources; **V4** sources place it just before barline

V1, V3–4: bars 36–37, pf. RH lowermost tie from **A2**. **Fa** prints bar 36 LH note 1 a tone lower (misprint)

V1: bar 39, v. ***p*** from **V3–4** sources (**A2** has ***mf*** then > across bar 41)

V2: bar 42, pf. **A2**: ♮ not ♯ before RH note 2 *a*''' (obvious slip of the pen)

V3–4: bar 44, pf. **V3–4** sources print RH beat 2 ♩ a semitone lower; **A2** shows the same error later corrected in pencil

V1–4: bar 47, pf. Middle note stemmed as in each relevant source (downwards in **V1**, upwards in **V2–4**)

6. Les Présents

Keys: E♭ and F

Sources

A Autograph, in E♭, signed and dated at end "27 janvier 1892": formerly Bibliothèque musicale François-Lang, Abbaye de Royaumont (where the title page remains, Réserve 24 FAU, the remainder now unlocated; complete microfilm copy at BnF mus., Vm micr. 1058). Bearing Hamelle's house stamp but no engraver's marks, it suggests a companion manuscript to **A2** of *Nocturne*. Although it might be assumed to have been drawn up to serve for **Es-m**, it sometimes clarifies details of layout in the latter.

Es First edition: Hamelle [1888], in F (J. 2853 H.: **Es-e**); then [no later than 1897] E♭ (J. 2853^{bis}H.: **Es-m**)

Rc II/18, in E♭ and F

Priority source: **Rc-m**

Variants

Text. Bars 5–6, 18–19: music sources omit commas. **Bar 21**: *!* as in all music sources except **A** (no punctuation); **T**: full stop. Bar 29: comma as in music sources (**T**: …)

Tempo. *quasi adagio* from **A** (pencilled in later), editorially parenthesized. Metronome indication in **Rc** only

Bars 9–10, pf. LH slur in **Rc-m** only, bar 10 RH slur in **Rc** only, both ending at ♪2

Bar 10, both. > as in **A** and **Es-m** for v., as in **A** for pf.; **Es-e** starts it slightly later and ends it slightly earlier for v. and omits it for pf., **Rc-m** starts it at ♩2, **Rc-e** just after

Bar 16, pf. Slur from **A**

Bars 21–22, pf. **A** ends RH slur at bar 21 ♪4

Bars 27–28, both. **A** starts *cresc.* (v. and pf.) at bar 28 (after a page break), **Rc** at last v. ♪ of bar 27, **Es** from bar 28 ♪2, for v. only. Musical sense suggest present placing

Bar 30, both. **Es-e** omits pf. LH ♩2 lower 8ve. *Poco rit.* as in **A**; **Es** starts it just after ♪1, **Rc** at ♪2

Bars 32, 34, pf. > in **Rc** only

Bars 35–36, pf. Final RH ties in **Rc** only, *pp* in **Rc-m** only

7. Clair de lune

Keys: b♭ and c

Es   J. Hamelle, Paris [1888], in c (J. 2854 H.: **Es-e**), b♭ (J. 2854bis H.: **Es-m**);[9] then [c. 1900s] in g (J. 2854ter H.: **Es-g**)

Mz   Metzler & Co., London [1897], in c (M. 7806.), as *Moonlight*, English and French text (trans. Adela Maddison)

Rc   II/19, in b♭ and c

Secondary sources

AS   Untitled autograph sketches: BnF mus., Ms. 17787 (1). Pages [40–43] present the present bars 1–6 in b♭, followed by 18 bars divergent from the song's final version; p. [44] presents bars 1–4 in g, the vocal line of bars 32–33 written under bars 3–4, followed on pp. [46–48] (after the blank p. [45]) by the present bars 13–16 (still in g, including the vocal anacrusis, with some musical variants), then bars 34 onward in an increasingly divergent form. **AS** shows no performing indications and contributes no readings to the present edition.

C   Scribal copy, in b♭: library of the Royal Brussels Conservatoire, shelf mark 43.928; ex coll. Maurice Bagès. The writing and paper type match an accompanying copy of Fauré's *Au cimetière* (op. 51 no. 2). The opus number and mention "Menuet" are absent; copying errors in bars 3 and 42 are corrected in pencil. The title page bears an annotation by Pierre de Breville stating that the manuscript was used by Bagès for the première at the Société nationale: this must have been the orchestral première on 28 April 1888 (no première is traced with piano), a supposition supported by cue letters matching **O** below, along with traces of erased pencilled instrumental cues apparently in Fauré's hand. This could suggest **C** was copied from autograph and served as a sketchpad for Fauré's orchestration before being passed to Bagès, unless the instrumental cues were entered later for Bagès's benefit. The oddity remains that **C** is not in the key of **O**; although Bagès was normally supplied with transposed copy (**Es** not yet being in print at the above première), he appears to have transposed on this occasion. Presenting no musical variants *per se*, **C** is sometimes the only source faithful to text punctuation as in **T**.

O   Transcription by Fauré for small orchestra, harp and solo string quartet [1888]: 2 scribal copies in c, one with autograph annotations, in different hands from **C** but bearing the same rehearsal cues.[10] Copy 1 (**O1**: Médiathèque Mahler, Paris), shows the subtitle "(Menuet)" on its title page, along with probably autograph pencil annotations "pour ténor ou soprano" and "op 46 N° 2". The music shows revisions in Fauré's hand across bars 1–12 of the harp part. Pencilled conductor markings suggest the score served for the 1888 orchestral première. Copy 2 (**O2**: BnF mus., Rés. Vma Ms 1156), in another hand, has a stencilled cover page specifying "Soprano" and identifying it as Hamelle's hire score (*Partition No. 134 / 497*); some annotations bear witness to its use in the 1919 ballet *Masques et bergamasques*. Fauré's orchestration closely follows the conception and structure of the piano original; dynamics, where present, are closer to **Es** than to **Rc**. In the main theme (throughout), solo vns 1–2 show slurs across each ♪ pair and ♪ pair in addition to the longer phrasing slurs. Although **O** contributes no readings to the present edition, some points of musical interest are noted below.

F   Feuilleton publication, in b♭: *La Musique des annales* 29 (supplement to *Les Annales politiques et littéraires* no. 2019), 6 April 1924, pp. 29–32. Bars 2–9 are absent, as are the metronome indication and dynamics across the present bars 23–37. Above the first system is printed: "Chanté par M. Reynaldo Hahn, sur le grand Canal, lors d'une fête de nuit donnée à Versailles".

Priority source: **Rc-m**₀₈, with input from **Mz**

Variants

Text. Bar 15: 1891 Vanier edition of **T**: *charmants* (possibly a house editor's misreading of the syntax). Bars 20, 34: comma in all music sources. Bars 23, 36, 56: *!* as in music sources but **O** (which has full stops, as in **T**), except that **C** has no punctuation in bar 56. Bars 41, 47: printed music sources add commas after *lune* and *arbres*

Tempo. Metronome indication in **Rc** only; **O**: *Andante*

Bars 1–4, 8–12. O1 (harp), bars 1–2:

poco marcato and downstems in Fauré's hand along with equivalent downstems in bars 3–4 and 8–12; **O2** omits these autograph elements

Bars 2, 4, 10, 12, pf. > from **Mz**; cf. note to bars 58, 60

Bars 7–8, pf. **Es** omits < > ; **O**: < *mf* > across just bar 8 (*mf* at beat 2, solo strings only)

---

[9] Although Hamelle's plate numbering here applies the suffix *bis* (normally signifying transposition, like *ter*) to the version in b♭, **Rc** specifies b♭ as the song's original key, matching source **C** and part of **AS**.

[10] Although no autograph score is traced, the orchestration can be accepted as Fauré's (no source suggests any other attribution); see the discussion in Nectoux, *Gabriel Fauré: A Musical Life*, pp. 258 and 260–1.

Bars 8, 37, pf. RH — from **Mz**

Bar 17, v. **Rc-m** omits beat 3 ♪ flag

Bars 20–21, pf. Sources break phrasing across this barline; editorially joined

Bars 24–25, pf. *mf* from **Mz** (and **O**: **Es-m/g**, like **C** and **F**, omit all pf. dynamics in bars 23–26). ℘. as in **C** and **F**, also **Es-m** and **Rc-m** in bar 24; **Mz** aligns each one a ♪ later, likewise **Rc-e** in bar 24 (omitting it in bar 25) and **Es** and **Rc-m** in bar 25; in bar 24 **Es-e/g** place it ambiguously between the 2 positions. Printed sources place bar 24 ✱ under or just after ♪ (except **C** which omits it); editorially adjusted to match printed sources in bar 25 (except **Es-g** which places it under ♪, and **C** and **Rc-e** which place it just before barline)

Bars 34–37, both. **Es-m/g** (and **O1**) omit dynamics; **C**, **Es-e** and **Mz** show just v. dynamics (added in blue pencil in **C**); **O2** has just bar 37 > (added above Vn1). See also note to bars 8, 37

Bar 39, v. *Espressivo e* in **Rc** only

Bar 48, v. *Meno* ***p*** in **Rc** only; cf. note to bars 52–54

Bar 51, pf. *Sempre* as in **Rc**; **C**, **Es**, **Mz** and **F** place it in bar 50 after ***pp***

Bars 52–54, v. **Es-e**, **Rc-e**, **Rc-m**₍→[04]₎: *poco più* (doubtless superseded by bar 48 *meno* ***p***, noted above). **C**, **Mz**, **Es-g** and **O** omit < > ; **Es-m/e** and **F** place < across bar 54 ♪s 1–3

Bars 54–56, both. **O**: *rall.* from bar 54 ♩ 2, *tempo* at bar 55, in **O2** deleted in blue pencil

Bars 58–59, pf. > from **Es-e**, **Mz**, placed mid-system (editorially relocated to RH). **O**: *rall.* from bar 58, in **O2** deleted in blue pencil then pencilled back in another hand

8. Larmes

Keys: b♭ and c

Sources

A   Autograph, in c, unsigned, undated, used for engraving **Es1**: The Morgan Library and Museum, New York, Robert Owen Lehman Collection, F2655.M528 (ex coll. Alfred Cortot; viewable online via www.themorgan.org). The autograph title page includes the dedication "à Mme la Princesse Wynaretta [*sic*] de Scey-Montbéliard" (as she then was). Title page and music are in black ink except for the pencilled tempo heading and the final v. ***ff*** in violet ink. Dynamics are absent in bars 1–16, phrasing, articulation and pedalling sparse.

Es   **Es1**: First edition: Hamelle [1888], in c (J. 2987 H.). The only articulation and phrasing are as in **A**, plus some additional dynamics. Although the title page lists a medium-voice edition in B♭, only a later unamended offprint from **Rc-m₀₈** is traced in this key. **Es2**: later reprint of **Es1** [?c. 1908], with added dynamics, phrasing and articulation mostly matching **Rc**, but with dynamics reversed across the start of strophes 2 and 3 (bars 16 and 30). It is not impossible that **Es2** postdates **Rc**, though **Rc** shows what appear to be some redundant remnants of **Es2**.

Rc   II/20, then III/1, in b♭ and c

Priority source: **Rc-m**

Variants

Text. Bars 4, 18, 32: Semicolon as in **Rc-e** in bars 4, 18 (other music sources: comma), as in all music sources at bar 32 (**T**: full stop in each instance). Bar 6: full stop as in **T** (**VE** sources: semicolon; **Rc-m**: comma; **A**: no punctuation). Bars 9–10, 35: music sources have *ton*, *tes*, *Puis*. Bars 15, 28, 46: lower-case line start (*en*, *des*, *le*) as in music sources. Bars 16, 47: ! as in music sources (**T**: full stop). Bar 23: full stop as in **T** (**Rc-m**: no punctuation; **VE** sources: !)

Tempo. Metronome indication in **Rc** only

Bars 1–4, both. **Es1** (like **A**) omits dynamics, articulation and phrasing. Bar 3 pf. RH beat 1 > from **Es2**, **Rc-e**

Bars 4, 18, v. **A**, beat 2: ♩

Bars 6, 12, v. **Rc-m**: ♩. ♩ [*sic*]

Bars 6–8, pf. **Es** dynamics: < across beat 3 in bars 6 and 8, > across bar 7 beat 2 (all absent in **A**). The bar 6 < persists in **Rc**, the < across bar 8 beat 3 in **Rc-e** (above the present longer <), undoubtedly by oversight; editorially removed

Bars 9–12, both. Bars 11–12 pf. < > in **Rc** only; **Es1** also omits bar 9 v. > and bar 10 ***p*** (v./pf.). **Es2** inexplicably loses bar 11 v. < (present in **Es1** and **Rc-e** as in present edition; **Rc-m** starts it a note later)

Bars 13–15, both. **Rc-e** omits v. ***f***; **Es1** has ***p*** for both instead, and omits each pf. >

Bars 16–17, both. See music footnote for **Es2** dynamics. **Es1** ends pf. < a ♪ earlier and omits bar 16 bass accents. ***f*** as in **Rc-m**; **Rc-e** places it for v. at bar 17 note 1, other sources have ***mf*** (for v. only in **A**), again placed for v. at bar 17 note 1

Bar 18, pf. **Rc-e**₍→[02]₎ omits beat 3 ♯ for each hand

Bars 20–23, both. Dynamics in **Rc** only. **Rc-m**₍→[04]₎ omits initial pf. LH ♭ in bar 20

Bar 23, pf. **Rc** omits beat 3 ♯. LH ♩ 3 cautionary accidental from **VE** sources; **Rc-m**₍[04]→₎ omits it, **Rc-m**₍→[02]₎ mistakenly inflects the note to match beat 1 RH

Bar 25, both. **Es1** omits <

Bars 28–35, both. **A**, **Es**: dynamics as shown in **Appendix 2** (**Es** curtails the initial > to place ***p*** at bar 29 note 1, and shows a > in bar 32 above pf. RH, doubtless intended for v., as at bar 4). **Rc** retains the accents from **Es2** in bars 31–33 (following a page break), **Rc-m** retains pf. > at end of bar 28, **Rc-e** retains bar 30 < (above pf. upper staff, over the present >), all doubtless by oversight; editorially removed. Bar 34 pf. > in **Rc-e** only

Bar 31, pf. **Rc-m** omits 1st LH ♮

Bar 37, pf. Printed sources add RH ♩ downstem at each beat, not in **A**, doubtless confusion with bar 36

Bars 37–38, both. Dynamics in **Rc** only; dynamics from bar 42 (as marked specifically in **Es2** and **Rc**: see below) suggest the present editorial qualifications in bars 38 and 41

Bar 42, pf. **Rc-e** omits 3rd RH ♩ stem

Bars 42–47, both. **A** and **Es1** omit *molto* (**A** also omits pf. *crescendo*); **Rc**: *molto crescendo* for v. at bar 42 ♩ 3. Bar 46 v. < in **Rc** only (**Es2** instead has *all* [*recte al*]); v. ***f*** and pf. < in **Rc-m** only, ending < for both v. and pf. at ♩ 3

Bar 46, pf. Main reading from **Rc-e** and **Rc-m**$_{08}$ (bar 47 cancelling cautionaries in **Rc-e** only). *Ossia* from **Rc-m**$_{\rightarrow[04]}$, and by default **A** and **Es** (which leave beat 3 ♪ 2 upper note uninflected, on different staff from beat 1). **Es** and **Rc-m**$_{\rightarrow[04]}$ redundantly flat the same dyad's lower note, suggesting a misprinted attempt at proof to establish the present main reading; musical logic, however, suggests the latter itself was miscorrection, the original intent as in the present *ossia* (more logically matching the surrounding enharmonic spelling, and avoiding consecutive 5^{ths} into bar 47)

Bar 49, v. **A**, **Es**: ⌐ (without preceding tie)

9. Au Cimetière

Keys: c and d

Sources

A Autograph, in e, unsigned, undated, used for engraving **Es-e**: location as for *Larmes*. Pedalling in bars 37–55 is added in violet ink, as are some dynamics.

Es First edition: Hamelle [1888], in e (J. 2980 H.: **Es-e1**) and c (J. 2981 H.; **Es-m**); then [1908 or later] b♭ (J. 2981bis H.: **Es-g**). **Es-e2**: reprint of **Es-e1** [1908 or later], incorporating revisions from **Rc**

Mz Metzler [1896], in e (M. 7817), as *The Last Resting Place*, English and French text (trans. "A.S.")

Rc II/21, then III/2, in c and d. (**Rc-e** erroneously lists the latter as "ton original", with a footnote signalling the song's availability in e "pour Ténor".)

Secondary source

C Scribal copy, in e: library of the Royal Brussels Conservatoire, 43.927. The writing matches *Clair de lune* source **C**, without opus number, the title page annotated by Pierre de Breville "C'est sur cette copie que fut chanté pour la première fois 'Au cimetière' à la Société Nationale par Maurice Bagès". Apparently copied from **A**, **C** is musically identical apart from a few minor oversights, with no visible autograph annotations.

Priority source: **Rc-e**

Variants

Text. Capitalisation as in music sources, except for bar 37 (**T** only). Bars 4, 7–8, 12, 27–8, 31–2, 48, 59, 62–3, 67: commas in all music sources. Bar 20: music sources have a comma. Bars 45, 52: *!* as in music sources (**T**: comma after *pauvres*, full stop in bar 52)

Bar 1 onwards, both. Metronome indication and v. phrasing in **Rc**, **Es-e2** only

Bars 3, 37, v. *e sereno* and *Declamato* in **Rc**, **Es-e2** only

Bars 23–25, 31–33, both. Dynamics as in **Rc** and **Es-e2**; other sources have only ⟩ across bar 23, **Es-g** for pf. only

Bar 35, pf. Final > (both hands) in **Rc-e**, **Es-e2** only

Bar 36, pf. ⟨ in **Rc-e** only

Bar 38, pf. **Es-g**: beat 2 LH upper note a 3rd higher (doubtless a misprint)

Bars 46, 50, pf. ✻ as in **A** and **VE** sources (**A** showing relocation to present position); **Es-g** and **VM** sources place it as in surrounding bars

Bars 48–51, pf. LH slurs from **Mz**, **Rc-m**$_{08}$, also in **Es-g** at bar 48

Bars 53–54, v. All sources except **Rc** and **Es-e2** bring off v. a bar earlier, omitting ⟩ (a deleted earlier reading of bars 52–55 in **A** conversely holds v. through to the end of bar 54)

Bars 60–62, v. **Rc-e** ends 1st v. slur a ♪ earlier and starts next one a ♪ later

Bars 65–66, both. ***pp*** *sempre* in **Rc**, **Es-e2** only

Bar 71, v. Slur end as in **Rc-m**$_{08}$; **Rc-m**$_{97}$, **Rc-e** and **Es-e2** continue slur to ♩ 3. This must have been amended on the plates for **Rc-m**$_{08}$, probably to show a preferred breathing point

Bar 72, pf. Articulation in **VE** sources only

10. Spleen

Keys: d and e

A Autograph, in d, unsigned, undated, used for engraving **Es-m**: location as for *Larmes*. The title appears in black ink on the title page, other title details and the music in the same violet ink used for some retouches in *Larmes* and *Au cimetière*. The dedication appears correctly in Hamelle's hand on the title page, then miscopied ("Henri" instead of "Henry") above the first music system, as in printed sources. Dynamics are absent in bars 4–15, pencilled incompletely in bars 21–38.

Es First edition: Hamelle, Paris [1888], in d (J. 2982 H.: **Es-m**) and e (J. 2983 H.: **Es-e**). All known exemplars of **Es-e** appear to be a revised reprint including some dynamics and articulation absent from other sources, sometimes squashed in.

Rc II/22 (1897), then III/3 (1908); in d and e

Secondary source

C Scribal copy, undated, in e; library of Royal Brussels Conservatoire, shelf mark 43.926; ex coll. Maurice Bagès. A cover page shows just the title "Spleen", in Fauré's hand, the only autograph annotation on this source. Opus number, dedication and tempo heading are absent, as are the dynamics that **A** shows in pencil, suggesting that **C** was copied before **A** was completely marked up or the song's title, dedicatee and opus number determined. Dog-eared lower page corners attest to **C** having served for performance.

Priority source: **Rc-e**, with input from **Es-e**

Variants

Text. Capitalisation (haphazard in all music sources) restored as in **T**. Bar 8: music sources omit punctuation. Bars 42, 45: punctuation as in music sources except **C** (which shows no punctuation)

Tempo. Metronome indication in **Es-m**, **Rc** only

Bar 4, v. *Dolce* from **Es-e**

Bars 7–8, 11–14, 31–33, pf. LH articulation from **Es-e**

Bars 11–15, both. *mf* and *p* from **Rc-m**_{[02]→} (pf. only); **Rc-e** also omits >; **Es-e**: bar 15 *p* not *pp* (no dynamics in **A** or **C** across bars 10–15)

Bar 14, pf. **Es-e**: RH ♪ 4 a semitone lower

Bars 22–27, both. Each *mf* and v. *p* from **Es-e**. **Rc-m** omits bar 24 v. >, **A** and **Es-e** omit the matching pf. >, **Rc-e** omits bar 25 pf. <. **A**, **Es-e**: *cresc.* not < at bar 26 ♩ 3, omitting *f* in bar 27. Bars 23 and 25 pf. LH articulation editorial (cf. note to bars 7–8 etc.).

Bar 32, v. **Es-e**: *cresc.* not *mf* (no dynamic in **A**)

Bar 34, both. Pf. *mf* from **Es-e**. **A**: v. *mf* not *f*. Voice ʼ as in **Rc-e**; **A** and **Es-e** omit it, **VM** sources align it above pf. ♪ 2

Bar 36, pf. **Rc-m** omits accidental to LH ♪ 3

Bars 38–39, pf. **Es-e** ends pf. slur at bar 38 ♩, new slur from bar 39 (page break)

Bars 42–43, pf. Dynamics as in **Es-e**; other sources omit < and place *f* at the end of bar 42 (before a system break in **A** and printed sources)

Bar 51, pf. *pp* from **A**, **C**; **Es-e** alone has *pp* at bar 53 instead

11. La Rose

Keys: E♭ and F

A   Autograph, in F, title page signed and dated "La Jonchère, Août 1890", used for engraving **Es-e**. Collection of Nigel Hughes, South Africa (the first music page viewable online through www.sothebys.com, from London sale of 12 April 2007, Lot 39). The title page, bearing Hamelle's house stamp, specifies the published high- and medium-voice keys; Hamelle's annotations above the first music system leave an opus indication uncompleted. The music is in black ink, vocal phrasing and most dynamics and in pencil, the song starting and ending on an outer bifolio surrounding the rest of the song on 2 single folia, each cut from a different original bifolio. The ending is the revised version partly quoted in **AL** and printed in **Es**. No trace appears of the abandoned early ending this replaces; given **A**'s anterior date to **AL**, the early ending might originally have been on the discarded half of one of the inner folios, the replacement ending then copied on the rear half of the outer bifolio.

(**EP**   *Unannotated proof for Es-e, reportedly showing errors or omissions relative to Es-e: location unknown, described in Mimi S. Daitz, "Les manuscrits et les premières éditions des mélodies de Fauré: étude préliminaire", Études fauréennes 20–21 (1983–4), pp. 22 & 26*)

Es   First edition: Hamelle [1890], in F (J. 3193 (1) H.: **Es-e**) and E♭ (J. 3194 (2) H.: **Es-m**)

Rc   II/23, then III/4 (**Rc₀₈**, with revised ending from bar 45), in E♭ and F. Oddly, **Rc-e** (but not **Rc-m**) reverses several revisions in **Es** relative to **A**, suggesting that it was engraved from **EP** above (it is implausible that **A** would have been reused for this); the reversions were probably inadvertent, given **Rc-m**'s retention of the **Es** revisions and addition of some further ones. The revised **Rc₀₈** ending, involving re-engraving of the central 2 systems of the last page, appears never to have been carried over to **Es**.

AL   Autograph letter from Fauré to Bagès, quoting v. bar 46 to bar 49 and pf. LH bar 47 to bar 49: BnF mus., NLA 264; see transcription in present **Preface**

Priority source: **Rc-m** (bar 45 onwards: **Rc-m**_{→[04]} for Version 1, **Rc-m₀₈** for Version 2)

Variants

Text. Bars 3, 5: capitalisation as in music sources (T: *rose*). Bar 14, music sources: *de*. Bar 17: music sources omit comma. Bar 18, music sources: *rose*.

Tempo. **Es-e**: ♩ = 160 [*sic*]; all other sources indicate 66 (pencil in **A**)

Bars 8–9, v. **VE** sources omit > in bar 9 (**A** shows it in pencil); **Rc-e** also omits it in bar 8 (both present in **A**)

Bar 11, v. **A** and **VE** sources add *sempre* after *mf*

Bar 15, both. **Es-e** starts > after note 2 for v., **Es-e** and **VM** sources after note 3 for pf.; **VM** sources omit it for v.

Bar 16, v. **Rc-e** ties the 2 notes

Bar 18, v. **A** and **VE** sources carry slur unbroken through this bar

Bar 18, pf. **VE** sources give beat 2 LH as in bar 17 (cf. v.), probably engraving error (**A** as present edition). **Es-m** starts < a ♪ later, **Es-e** 2 ♪s later, **Rc-m** ends it before last ♪ (restricted space, probably squeezed in at proof though present in **A**)

Bar 20, pf. **Rc-e** misprints penultimate LH note a tone lower

Bar 25, v. All sources except **Rc-m** give beat 1 as ♪ ♫; in **Rc-m** the note spacing and stem lengths show it was amended at proof to present reading

Bars 26–28, v. **A** and **VE** continue slur unbroken over bar 26; **VM** sources start < from bar 27 (inside slur), adding *cresc.* at bar 26 ♩ 2. Bar 28 > as in **VM** sources; **A**, **Rc-e** continue < to bar 28 ♩ 2; **Es-e** prints > inside the slur, extending through most of ♪ 2)

Bar 28, pf. > as in **A** and **VE** sources; **VM** sources start it a ♪ later

Bar 30, pf. *Sempre* from **A**

Bar 31, pf. Reminder *pp* from **A** and **VE** sources; editorially parenthesized

Bars 31–32, 35–36, pf. RH stemming as in **Es**; **A** includes each lower 8ve on initial ♪ stem of each beat, omitting some ♩ stems, notably at bar 31 beat 3 to bar 32 beat 1 and bar 35 beat 3 to bar 36 beat 1 where lower note is on lower staff (upper staff maintaining 𝄞). Printed sources maintain that layout, **Rc** similarly omitting those 4 ♩ stems, **Es** breaking them across the 8ve to make the lower note ♩

Bar 34, pf. **A**, **Rc-e** omit accidental to top voice ♪ 1. *Sempre* from **A** and **VE** sources

Bars 34–37, both. **A**: < across bar 34 beats 2–3 with *al f* written inside it; printed sources render it as < to *f* at bar 35 note 1 (where *f* hardly makes musical or vocal sense). All sources then show pf. < across bar 36 beats 2–3; **A** also shows an erasure above bar 37 v. that started *sempre* (*sempre cresc.*?). Surrounding dynamics prompt the present editorial rephrasing of these dynamics at bars 34 and 36.

Bars 36–37, pf. Pedalling from **A** and **VE** sources. **Es-e** omits pf. LH accidentals at bar 36 ♩ 3

Bar 38, pf. RH textural variant was probably introduced in **VM** sources to ease hand layout in E♭

Bars 38–39, v. **A**, **VE** sources place f a note later, adding *sempre* after it; **VE** sources also start slur a note later

Bar 39, pf. Sources give RH beat 1 lower note as f, followed only in **VM** sources by a corresponding f at beat 2 after an enharmonic change; editorially rationalized here as beat 1 f (high-voice edition) and editorial tie-over to beat 2 (medium-voice edition). **A**, **Rc-e** stem RH beat 3 lower 8ve with upper 8ve as ♪.

Bar 40, v. **VM** sources add *dim.* inside the start of $>$

Bars 40–41, pf. Bar 40 phrasing as in **Rc-m**; other sources break slur across barline

Bar 41, pf. **Rc-e**$_{\rightarrow[04]}$ misplaces LH beat 3 ♮ a ♪ later (cancelling its ♯ in beat 2); **Rc-e**$_{08}$ adds it in the correct position, omitting to remove the erroneous one

Bars 41–42, v. **A**, **VM** sources end slur at bar 41; **VM** sources then tie to bar 42

Bars 41–42, pf. **Es-e** adds *cresc.* under start of $<$, **VM** sources add it at end of bar 41

Version 1 (**Es**, **Rc**$_{\rightarrow[04]}$, the latter abbreviated below to **Rc**):

Bars 45a, 47a, 49a, 51a, pf. Printed sources align ✱ under 𝄾; in bar 45 **A** shows it relocated from there to present position (and placed similarly in bars 47, 49, 51)

Bars 45a–52a, pf. **A**, **Rc-e** omit each bass $>$; **Rc-e** omits LH tie across ♩s 1–2 in bars 48 and 50; **Es-e** omits LH upper slurs in bars 50 and 52. **A** and **VE** sources start $>$ at ♩ 2 in bars 46 and 48, **A** (contrary to **AL**) showing an erased $<$ across each beat 1; **Es-m** omits it in bars 50 and 52. **VM** sources omit bar 50 *mf*

Bars 47a–49a, v. **A** and **Rc-e** omit dynamics. $>$ as in **AL** (see **Preface**); **Es** and **Rc-m** place it a beat later

Bars 47a, 49a, pf. **A**: single slur across LH notes 1–8

Bars 53a–56a, pf. **Es-e** omits *pp*. **A**, **Rc-e** indicate through-pedal from bar 53 ♩ 1 to bar 56 ✱. **Rc-e**$_{\rightarrow[99]}$ prints last RH ♪ of bar 54 a tone lower

Version 2 (**Rc**$_{08}$ only):

Bar 45b pf. **Rc-e**$_{08}$ omits $<$ and bass $>$. Placing of ✱ corrected from **A**; **Rc**$_{08}$ follows Version 1 printed sources in aligning it under 𝄾

Bar 46b, pf. f as in **Rc-m**$_{08}$; **Rc-e**$_{08}$: *mf*

Bars 47b–52b, pf. p, pedalling bass accents and bar 51 LH slurs imported from Version 1 (see note above re pedal), with editorial adjustment of pedalling for texture in bar 52b

Bar 51b, pf. LH slurs from **Rc-e**$_{08}$

Bar 54b, pf. **Rc-e**$_{08}$ omits *pp*

12. Chanson (*Shylock*)

Keys: A♭ and B♭

Sources including Prélude

Es-ep   First edition: Hamelle [1889], in B♭ (J. 3089 H.), no. 1 in the complete *Shylock* vocal score, headed "PRÉLUDE ET CHANSON", the former running directly into the latter as shown in the present 12a; also issued as a separate offprint ("Prélude et Chanson", same title page)

OE   Published orchestral score, no. 1 (headed just "Chanson"), in B♭, voice line labelled "Ténor solo (dans la coulisse)", Hamelle [1897] (J. 4111 H.). The entire number maintains the opening ₵ metre, using triplets as necessary.

Prélude *variants*: metronome indication from **OE** and later reprints of **Es-ep**. Orchestral cues added editorially. Details in parentheses from **OE**, except p at bar 19 comes from separate "Chanson" sources (**OE** has *pp*). Bar 18 *mf* as in **OE**; **Es-ep** prints *sf*

Sources without Prélude

Es   Separate publication of Chanson: in B♭ [1889] (J. 3089 H.: **Es-e**) and A♭ [1898] (J. 3089 H. (3): **Es-m**). From its 2nd page (bar 10) **Es-e** uses the plates of **Es-ep**, musically identical except for the latter's transition at beat 1 of Chanson. All **Es** sources advertise Chanson as available "en Ut, Si♭, La♭, Sol", but no exemplars are traced in C or G; a posthumous edition in F of Chanson (J. 7409 H. [1928], not considered as a source here) lists it as available just in B♭, A♭ and F.

Rc   III/5, in A♭ and B♭

Secondary source

OC   Manuscript orchestral score, in C (without Prélude, which appears not to have featured in the theatre music): scribal copy with autograph annotations: BnF mus., Ms. 17777 (ex Fauré family library), no. 1. Used for theatre performance, **OC** is in ₵ metre, except $\frac{12}{8}$ for harp and v.

Priority source for Chanson: **Rc-m**

Chanson *variants*

Text. Bars 3, 17, 28: ! as in music sources (**T**: comma). Bars 15, 30: music sources omit comma. Bar 41: ! as in music sources (**T**: full stop).

Tempo. **OA**: *Allegretto moderato*; **OE**: no further indication after *Allegro moderato* ♩. = 96 at start of *Prélude*. Metronome indication ♩ = 100 from **Es-ep** (at start of *Chanson*)

Bars 1–4, pf. All pf. sources: *Pédale sur chaque 1er et 3e temps* between staves of bar 1, plus present pedalling underneath, the latter repeated under bars 2–4 (editorially tidied)

Bars 4–18, 30–40, both. **VE** sources omit dynamics

Bar 9, v. **OE**, beats 3–4: ♩. ♪♪♪

Bar 9, pf. **Es-m**: LH ♪ 1 a tone higher

Bars 24–27, both. O dynamics: $<>$ for instruments across bar 24 then $<$ across bar 26 (not bar 25), bar 24 v. $<$ (**OE** only) across just beat 1, omits subsequent f

Bars 37–41, v. Bar 39 main reading as in **Rc-e**, *ossia* as in other sources. **OE**: *dim.* at bar 39 to p at bar 41 (no v. dynamics in **OA**) instead of present dynamics from bar 37

Bars 41–42, pf. Half-bar pedal changes (as in **Es**, **Rc**) editorially parenthesized, as the bass implies half-pedal

Bar 44, pf. **O**: final chord duration 𝅝 (in ₵) with 𝄐

13. Madrigal (*Shylock*)

Keys: E♭ and F

Es No. 3 in the complete *Shylock* vocal score (see Chanson above), in F, also as a separate offprint (J. 3090 H.: **Es-e**). Separate edition in E♭ [1905], as op. 57 no. 3 (J. 3090bis H.: **Es-m**), reused for **Rc-m** (same plates renumbered, otherwise unamended)

Mz Metzler [1897], in F (M. 7813), as *Shylock / Madrigal*, English and French text (trans. "A.S.")

Rc III/6, in E♭ and F

Secondary sources

F Feuilleton publication, in F: album of *Musica* 77 (February 1909), pp. 43–44 (but with the sub-heading "Morceau pour voix de mezzo-soprano")

O Orchestral score. **OA**: autograph, in F: BnF mus., Ms. 17777 (headed by Fauré "no. 3 / Sérénade Madrigal"). **OC**: scribal copy in E♭ with autograph annotations (matching that of *Chanson*), again headed no. 3: part of BnF mus., Ms. 17777. **OE**: no. 3 in published orchestral score (cf. "Chanson" above)

Priority source: **Rc-m**. Dynamics in parentheses come from **O**.

Variants

Text. Bars 32, 47: ! as in music sources (**T**: full stop). Bar 34: 1st comma in piano-vocal sources only. Bar 39: piano-vocal sources add a comma after *écoute*

Tempo. Metronome indication in **Es-m**, **Rc** and later **Es-e** reprints only; musical sense and the irregular number 106 suggest an error for 126

Bar 1, pf. *p* from **Mz** and **O** (**OE** also marks the solo vc. *mf*, despite what follows in bars 3–5)

Bar 9, v. *Con grazia* from **O**

Bar 25, pf. **Rc-m** omits }

Bars 26–32, both. **Mz** and **Es-e** carry pf. RH slur to bar 30, **Es-e** ending it short of the chord, well above the barline (suggesting a manuscript slur left incomplete at a system break)

Bar 33, pf. **Rc-m** omits LH }, other sources show it across just top 2 notes

Bar 37 pf. VM sources omit tie from bass grace note

Bar 49, pf. VE sources omit staccato dot

14. Sérénade (*Le Bourgeois Gentilhomme*)

Keys: d and f

A1 Autograph, in f, notated in 3/4 (71 bars, 3 bars equal to one of the present 9/8), dated "Lundi 27 février [1893]": BnF mus., Ms. 17776 (ex Fauré family library). A title page shows the pencilled non-autograph title "Serenade [*sic*] du Bourgeois Gentilhomme". For clarity of reference, mentions below of **A1** follow bar numbering as in **A2**.

A2 Autograph, in f, unsigned, undated, notated in 9/8: BnF mus., Rés Vma ms. 501. A title page shows the pencilled non-autograph title "Sérénade / Bourgeois Gentilhomme", and "Acte I (Sérénade)" in Fauré's hand above the first music system. **A2** shows some revisions of original readings that matched **A1**. Up to bar 17 performing indications are sparser than in **A1**, then vice versa from bar 19 (for bar 18 both sources show the same indications).

(First publication: Heugel, Paris, 1957 (H. 31580), with English translation by Rollo Myers; based on **A2**)

Priority source: **A2**. Indications in parentheses come from **A1**.

Variants

Text. Bar 2: many editions of **T** (though not that used here) have a comma after *jour*. Bar 6: ! as in **A2** (**A1**: comma; **T**: full stop; other editions of **T** variously have a semicolon or colon). Bars 14, 22: music sources have ! (except that **A2** omits *-mis* altogether in bar 22, following a page turn); the present edition gives ? (as in **T**) at bar 14 but leaves Fauré's ! (as in **A1**) at bar 22, given that the textual repetition is Fauré's, and his consistent usage of ! to reinforce a sustained *f* dynamic.

Bar 1, pf. *Allegretto* from **A1**, which gives present beats 1–2 as

Bar 4, v. **A1–2**: *cresc.* at note 1, followed in **A1** only by < from note 2 (new page, new bar in the 3/4 metre); indications editorially combined

Bar 8, v. **A1** adds *cresc.* above <

Bar 11, both. **A1** places v. > across beat 2 plus one for pf. across beat 2 notes 4–6

Bar 12, both. **A1** gives pf. notes 4 and 6 respectively a 3rd lower and higher, starts pf. > a note earlier leading to *p* at beat 3 (not bar 13), plus v. > across notes 2–3 (as well as present *dim.*)

Bar 15, pf. *Ossia* as in **A1**

Bar 18, v. Last note 𝄽♪ according to **A1** (spelled there 𝄽♪), **A2** originally thus then amended to present ♪

Bar 19, pf. > in **A2** only. RH stemming as in **A1**; **A2** inverts it. Slur end from bar 18 editorially clarified: **A2** ends it above the barline, **A1** just before the barline, pointing towards ♩.

Bar 21, pf. Beat 3 ⌢ and LH stemming as in **A1**; **A2** places ⌢ a 𝄽 later and single-stems the 8ve dyad

15. Prison

Keys: e♭ and e

A Autograph, in e♭, signed and dated "4 décembre 1894": Library of Congress, Washington, shelf mark ML96.F3 Case (Music 1236). The title appears only on a cover page, without opus indication, the music unheaded. Pencilled numbers through the music suggest a pagination cast, doubtless for a scribal engraving manuscript; the musical text is generally close to **Es-m** (missing a tempo indication and most pf. LH articulation, though ⁓ is present in bars 4 and similar).

Es	**Es-m**: first edition, in e♭; no. I of Deux Mélodies (*Prison* and *Soir*, in a single volume): E. Fromont, Paris [late 1896] (E. 1343. F.), as op. 51 [*sic*] no. 1; reprinted by Hamelle without musical amendment from the same plates [c. 1908] as op. 83 no. 1 (J. 5613 H.). **Es-e**: Hamelle [c. 1908], in e, as op. 83 no. 1 (J. 5615 H.)
Mz	Metzler & Co. [1897], in e♭ (M. 7818), as *Prison*, op. 68 no. 1, English and French text (trans. Adela Maddison)
Rc	II/24 (with acknowledgment to Fromont), in e♭ and e, as op. 73 no. 1 (**Rc**$_{97}$), op. 74 no. 1 (**Rc**$_{[99,02]}$), op. 83 no. 1 (**Rc**$_{[04]}$); then III/14 (without mention of Fromont) as op. 83 no. 1. Cf. **Publication history** above regarding the opus confusion.

Priority source: **Rc-e**

Variants

Text. Bars 2, 5: **T** (1881), **A**, **VE** sources: *par dessus* (*dessus* hyphenated across its 2 ♪s in just **A** and **Es-e**); **VM** sources as in present edition (*pardessus* close-spaced in **Rc-m**, syllabicized as *par_des_sus* in **M** and at bar 2 in **Es-m**); **T** (later editions): *par-dessus*. Bars 3, 6: capitalisation as in **T** (music sources lower-case). Bar 4: full stop as in **A** (printed music sources: comma; **T**: *!*). Bar 6: **VE** sources add comma after *toit*. Bar 7: full stop as in **A** and **T** (printed music sources: semicolon). Bars 10, 17: punctuation as in music sources (**T**: full stop). Bar 22, music sources: comma after *voilà*

Tempo. Metronome indication in **Rc** only

Bars 4, 7, 10, 13, pf. $\div$ as in **A** (and **Mz** for LH); printed sources otherwise render it as $\div$

Bar 9, pf. RH tie from **A**, LH slurs and last RH slur in **VE** sources only

Bars 11–12, pf. LH articulation in **VE** sources only, which omit bar 12 tie

Bar 15, pf. Accidental to RH chord 3 lowest note in **VE** sources, **Mz** only

Bars 16–17, both. **VE** sources omit v. dynamics; **Es-e** also omits pf. *p*

Bars 18, 21, pf. Slurs in **VE** sources only. Bar 21 RH chord 3 lowest note from **Rc-e**$_{[02]\rightarrow}$, doubtless omitted in **VM** sources for ease of hand layout (avoiding a thumb stretch to a black key); this would imply the same at bar 18 at **VE** pitch, though all sources include the note there

Bar 20, pf. Articulation in **VE** sources only

Bars 23–24, pf. **A**: pf. $>$ across bar 23, then a separate one across bar 24 (new system) with *dimin.* written inside it, no *p* after it; printed sources: single $>$ from bar 23 ♩2 or ♩3 to bar 24 ♩1 or just after; editorially adjusted. **VE** sources omit middle note of bar 24 RH chord 2.

Bar 25, v. $>$ from **A**

Bars 28–30, pf. Bar 28 RH articulation editorially carried over to LH. **A** omits RH ties across bars 29–30 but shows the same *portato* articulation across bar 29 RH ♩s 2–3 as in bar 28

16. Soir

Keys: D♭ and E♭

A	Autograph, in D♭, signed and dated "Paris 17 décembre 1894": Bibliothèque musicale François-Lang, Abbaye de Royaumont, Réserve 24 FAU. Fauré's signature follows an earlier, undeleted version of the ending; a following sheet contains a revised ending closer to the published version (see **Appendix 2**).[11] The manuscript is of similar presentation to that of *Prison*, without opus indication, the music unheaded with no visible copyist markings.
F	Feuilleton (probably first) publication, in D♭: supplement to *L'Illustration* 2773, 18 April 1896, without opus indication; musically identical with **Es-m1** except for a few minor details, it is mentioned below only when it bears on any editorial issue.
Es	**Es-m**: first commercial edition, in D♭ : no. II of Deux Mélodies (see above), Fromont [1896], as op. 68 no. 2 (E. 1344 F.: **Es-m1**). Reprinted from the same plates by Hamelle [c. 1908], as op. 83 no. 2 (J. 5614 H.: **Es-m2**), with an added accidental in bar 16. **Es-e**: Hamelle[c. 1908], in E♭, as op. 83 no. 2 (J. 5616 H.)
Mz	Metzler [1897], in D♭, as op. 68 no. 2 (M. 7818, number shared with *Prison*),[12] as *Evening*, English and French text (trans. Adela Maddison)
Rc	II/25, in D♭ and E♭ (with acknowledgment to Fromont), as op. 73 no. 2 (**Rc**$_{97}$), op. 74 no. 2 (**Rc**$_{[99,02]}$), op. 83 no. 2 (**Rc**$_{[04]}$); then III/15 as op. 83 no. 1 (without mention of Fromont), re-engraved to remedy cramped spacing and misalignments in **Rc-e**$_{\rightarrow[04]}$. Cf. **Publication history** above regarding the opus confusion. Unusually for such a chromatically complex song, **VE** sources of *Soir* transpose **Rc-m** verbatim without adjusting enharmonics; some overloaded enharmonics that result are addressed in the present high-voice edition (see below regarding bars 16–17 etc.).

Priority source: **Rc-m**$_{08}$

Variants

Text. Bars 7, 21: punctuation as in printed music sources (except that **F** has a comma after *vagues* in bar 7); **A**: commas. Bars 16, 25: music sources have a comma. Bars 28–29: **Rc-m** adds comma after *semble* and *enivré*

Tempo. Metronome indication in **Rc-m** only. **VE** sources add *molto moderato* after *Andante*

Bars 2, 6, v. **VE** sources omit dynamics

Bar 2, pf. **Rc-e**$_{\rightarrow[04]}$: beat 3 as beats 1 and 2

Bars 5–6, pf. RH slurs from **Mz**, **Rc-e** (single slur across bar 6 in **Rc-e**)

Bar 11, both. **Mz** omits v. $>$, **VE** sources omit pf. ***pp***. **A**: v. ***pp*** not ***p***

Bars 12–22, pf. *Portato* articulation editorial in bar 12, associated slurs editorial in bars 21–22 LH, where **VM** sources omit the articulation altogether; **VE** sources print the associated slur at only bar 20 (LH)

Bar 16, pf. ♯ at last RH dyad upper note as in **Es-m2**, **Es-e**, **Rc-m**, **Rc-e**$_{08}$. **Mz**: LH dyad 2 as dyad 1 (lower note a tone higher). *Cresc.* as in **Es-m** and **Mz**; **A** and **VE** sources omit it, **Rc-m** starts it at final ♪

---

[11] For a comparative study see Robert Orledge, "The two endings of Fauré's 'Soir'", *Music & Letters* 60/3 (July 1979), pp. 316–22.

[12] Metzler rear-page adverts list *Prison* and *Soir* together as "Two songs", but all traced exemplars present each song separately.

Bars 16–17, 19, 22, 29–30, both. Present high-voice edition editorially adjusts enharmonic spelling for clarity where **VE** sources uselessly carry over ♯ spelling from **VM** sources; this affects bar 16 beat 2 to bar 17 beat 1, bar 19 beats 2–3, bar 22 beat 3, bar 29 and bar 30 beats 1–2. See also separate note to bar 30

Bar 17, pf. **Rc-e**→[02] omits ♭ at RH penultimate lower voice ♩

Bar 18, pf. *Dolce* as in **Es-m** and **Mz**; **Rc-m** starts it at note 1, **A** and **VE** sources omit it

Bar 19, pf. **Es-e** and **Rc-e**→[04] omit ♮ at LH dyad 2; **Rc-e**→[99] misaligns last bass ♩ a ♪ early

Bars 20–22, both. **A**: *cresc.* < across bar 20 for both v. and pf., omitting subsequent v. *f*; **VE** sources conversely omit *f* for pf. (**Rc-e**₀₈ also omits pf. <). **Rc-e**→[04] misaligns bar 20 pf. RH dyads 1–3 a ♪ early (above LH dyads; spacing cramped). Bar 22 pf. > in **A** only (in addition to mid-system *dim.*)

Bar 23, pf. **VE** sources omit dynamic; **A**, **Es-m**, **Mz**: *pp*, **Rc-m**: *p*. **F** omits 1st ♩ stem

Bars 24–33, pf. RH slurs from **VE** sources, also **Mz** in bars 25–27; bars 31–33 LH slurs from **Mz**. **VE** sources also add slurs across 1st and 2nd RH ♪ groups of bar 24 (new page in **Rc-e**→[04])

Bars 26–30, both. **A** omits *cresc.* and pf. <, starting v. < just after bar 28 last ♪). **Mz** and **VE** sources end pf. < at ♩ 3, **VE** sources also omit pf. *f*

Bars 27 onwards, both. For early endings in **A** see facsimiles and **Appendix 2**, p. 161

Bar 28, pf. ♩ 3 LH stemming as in **Es-e** and **A** 1st version (**A** 2nd version ambiguous: see facsimile); other printed sources single-stem it

Bar 30, pf. Beat 3 enharmonic spelling as in **A** 2nd version (see **Appendix 2** or facsimile, p. VII); printed sources enharmonicize it in ♭s (with ♭♭ to each note), a revision possibly made at proof for **F** (prior to **Es-m**), which shows the ♭♭s squashed in. Flat enharmonics here are also counterproductive for the printed sources' lowered bass note (a semitone down from **A** 2nd version).

Bar 33, pf. LH stemming as in **A**; printed sources give dyads 1–2 separate stems, **F** also in beat 3; cf. bar 27

Bars 34–35, v. **VE** sources omit dynamics

Bar 37, pf. Separate } for each hand as in **A** (final version); printed sources join them across the staves

17. Le Parfum impérissable

Keys: E and G♭

A Autograph, in E, signed and dated "22 Août 1897": Memorial Library of Music, Stanford University, MLM311A. It reads fairly closely to **Es-m** but shows no tempo heading and only sparse pf. articulation; no engraver's or copyist's marks are visible. Revisions include some erased ties that other sources retain. A single performing annotation (illegible) is pencilled in an unknown hand over bar 22.

Es First edition: Hamelle [1897], in E (J. 4118 H.: **Es-m**); then [1899] in G♭ (J. 4429 H.: **Es-e**)

Mz Metzler [late 1897], in E (M. 8002), as *Perfume*, English and French text (trans. Adela Maddison)

Rc III/12

Priority source: **Rc-m**

Variants

Text. Bar 12: **Es-e**, **Rc**, **T** (all sources except 1875 Lemerre edition): *tint*; **A**, **Mz**, **Es-m**, **T** (1875): *tient*. Bar 13: semicolon as in **Mz** and **T** (1875) (other music sources have a comma, other editions of **T** a colon). Bar 23: music sources omit comma

Bars 1–2, pf. **A**: *p*. Bar 1 LH articulation from **A**; bar 2 RH dots from **Mz**

Bars 2, 4, v. **VE** sources omit *dolce* and >

Bar 6, pf. **VE** sources omit RH beat 2 ♩ stem

Bars 7–8, both. **VE** sources start v. < a note later; **Mz** adds *cresc.* above the <; **A** starts v./pf. > a ♩ later. V. dynamic at start of bar 8 *f* in **Rc-e**, *mf* in other sources. **Rc-e** misprints v. ♪ above *sa-* as ♫

Bars 7–8, pf. Sources single-stem RH chord bar 7 ♩ 2 and bar 8 ♩ 1; editorially restemmed for voicing clarity. Slur absent in **VE** sources, in **A** starts slightly right of chord at top staff line, from top of upstem in **VM** sources; cf. bar 23. **Mz** adds *cresc.* above <

Bars 9, 17, pf. Beats 1–2 lowest 3 RH slurs from **Mz**

Bar 11, pf. RH tie from ♩ 2 in **Rc-m** only

Bar 12, both. > as in **A**; printed sources start it at or just after ♩ 1, immediately preceded by *dim.* or *dimin.* (for v. only in **VE** sources). Beat 3 pf. RH as in **Rc-m**; all other sources give middle voice as ⌒♩ instead of 2 ♪s (no tie to bar 13)

Bar 13, v. **VE** sources: beat 2 rhythm ♪ 𝄽♪; **A** shows this amended to the present reading (as in **VM** sources). **Mz** places *p* at note 3

Bars 13–14, pf. **Rc-m** omits RH tie from bar 13 ♩ 2; **Rc-e** omits RH tie from bar 14 beat 2

Bar 15, pf. RH ♩ 1 stemming as in **Rc-m**; other printed sources single-stem it, **A** upstems it all but breaks the stem below the top 2 notes

Bar 16, pf. LH last note accidental confirmed by **VE** sources, missing in **A**, **VM** sources (which spell the note as *a*, omitting to cancel ♭ from beat 1). RH beat 3 slur from **Mz**; **A** and **Rc-e** also omit LH slur

Bars 17–18, pf. Bar 18 *ossia* as in **VE** sources. **A**: bar 17 beats 2–3 RH originally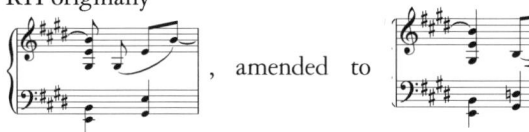

VE sources omit < and bar 18 RH phrasing slurs, **VM** sources omit bar 18 tie, **Mz** omits *f*. See also note to bars 9 etc.

Bars 19, 21, both. > from **A** at bar 19, from **A** and **Mz** at bar 21 pf. (intermediate dynamics present in all sources)

Bars 20–23, pf. **Rc-e** omits first 3 RH ties then prints the last one as a slur from the ♪.; **Mz** omits the 1st and 3rd ties, **Es-e** the 2nd and 3rd; **A** shows the 2nd and 4th erased, the corresponding tie start from bar 22 ♩ 3 missing (preceding a page break) and its completion at bar 23 again erased; the present edition therefore parenthesizes these 3 top-voice ties

Bar 22, pf. **Es-m** and **Rc-m** omit accidentals starting beat 3 RH and to final LH ♪

Bar 23, pf. **A** gives this bar as [music example]; present edition respects this placing of RH slur, which printed sources start from top note or top of ♩ stem

Bar 24, both. > and bass slur as in **A**. **VE** sources omit >, **VM** sources extend it to ♩ 3; printed sources lead bass slur to last ♪

Bar 25, both. **A** and **Mz** omit <. Pf. RH slur from **Mz**

Bars 27–28, pf. LH slurs and < from **Mz**. **A** and **Rc-m** omit *sempre*. Bar 28 ♩ 1 LH stemming as in **VE** sources; other sources include upper note on both stems

Bars 30–32, pf. **VE** sources omit bar 30 RH slur; **Es-e** and **Rc-m** omit bar 31 slur. **Mz** omits bar 32 LH articulation. **A** omits RH tie across bars 32–33, doubtless because of visible emendations (bar 32 beat 1 top note was originally ♩, followed by 3 repetitions of the same chord, the last time as ♩.)

18. Arpège

Keys: e and f♯

A   Autograph, in e, signed and dated "6 Septembre 1897": Library of Congress, Washington, Moldenhauer Archives (viewable online via Library of Congress Digital Collections). The manuscript, unusually clean, shows no signs of having served for engraving; its closeness to **Es** suggests engraving copy was derived from it.

Es   First edition: Hamelle [1897], in e (J. 4119 H.: **Es-m**) and f♯ (J. 4119 (2) H.: **Es-e**). *Arpège* also appeared as the *Supplément musical* to *Le Figaro* on 16 October 1897, musical text identical with **Es-m**, not mentioned separately below.

Mz   Metzler [late 1897], in e (M. 8001), as *In a Garden*; English and French text (trans. Adela Maddison)

Rc   III/13

Priority source: **Rc-m**, with remedial input from **Rc-e**

Variants

Text. Bars 13–14: printed music sources: commas after *poses* and *ondoyant*. Bar 33: *!* as in **T** (**A** and **VM** sources: comma; **VE** sources omit punctuation). Bar 41 *!* as in music sources (**T**: full stop).

Tempo. Metronome indication from **Mz** and **Rc-m**

Bars 1–2, 30–31, both. **Mz** starts < at note 1. **A** omits dynamics, **VE** sources omit bar 31 dynamics

Bars 2–3, 5–8, pf. **VE** sources end RH main slur above 1st or 2nd grace note in bar 2 and at ♩· in bar 6. LH slurs in bar 5 beats 2–3 and bar 6 from **Mz** and **VE** sources. Bar 7 beat 3 RH slur from **A**, **Mz**; **VE** sources instead carry the grace note slur over the barline (as also at several analogous bars along with the present larger slurs)

Bars 2, 11, pf. Beat 2 LH last accidental absent in **A** and **Es**, also in **Mz** at bar 11; **Rc** shows it squeezed in, doubtless at proof. **VE** sources spell beat 3 with B♯ (also for v.), inadvertently altering the trill's auxiliary note; editorially adjusted in present high-voice edition

Bar 6, pf. Sources: additional ♩ downstem on LH note 1, probably an abandoned attempt in **A** at stemming notes 1–2 downwards

Bar 8, pf. **A**: LH ♩ 3 notehead originally a 3rd higher, erased without replacement

Bar 11, pf. > from **VM** sources (**A** also omits preceding <). See also note to bars 2 etc.

Bar 15, v. **VE** sources and **Mz** end < at beat 3

Bar 17, pf. **VE** sources start > 2 notes earlier (**A** omits it). ♮ above trill from **A**

Bar 18, v. **A** ends > above ♩.

Bar 19, pf. *mf* from **VE** sources

Bars 24–25, both. Dynamics from **VE** sources (> placed as in **Es-e**; **Rc-e** starts it at ♪ 5)

Bar 28, both. < as in **Mz**, which precedes it with *cresc.*; other printed sources have only *cresc.* (no dynamics in **A**). ♮ at bar 28 LH note 1 in **Mz** and **VE** sources only

Bars 30–31, see note to bars 1 etc.

Bar 32, both: Enharmonic spelling of last note as in **VM** sources; **VE** sources enharmonicize it as $a'♮$, contradicting the equivalent in bars 34, 36

Bars 32–33, pf. < *pp* from **VE** sources, which place *pp* at note 1, probably in error; alternatively < might be a misprint for >. **VE** sources omit bar 32 LH prolongation dots; **Rc-m** omits 1st RH one in bar 33

Bars 33, 35, 38, pf. **A** gives bar 33 RH beat 3 tie-over as ♪ (instead of ♩.) stemmed to upper note, and omits it in bar 35; in bar 38 the tie-over appears only in **Mz** and **VE** sources, the latter misprinting each of these ties as a slur (cf. note to bars 34–37), except that **Rc-e** omits it in bar 35. In bar 38 **A** omits last 3 RH ♩ downstems

Bar 34, v. **Es-m** omits beat 3 accidentals, **Rc-m** omits the 2nd one

Bars 34–37, pf. **A** carries RH slur past bars 34 and 36 (system breaks) without completing them in bars 35 and 37; printed sources end them at last note of bars 34, 36 (cf. bar 32, with different dynamics, where **A** leads slur clearly to last ♪); **VE** sources slur additionally across bar 37 ♩ ♩ (which they stem down). Bar 37 *f* from **Mz** and **VE** sources

Bar 35, both. Printed sources repeat *cresc.* from bar 34 (after a page turn in **Rc**)

Bar 40, pf. **Rc-m** omits *p*

Bar 41, pf. *Dolce* from **A**, **Mz**

Bars 42–43, pf. **Rc-m** breaks RH slur across barline. **Mz**: bar 43 LH note 6 a 3rd lower

Bar 44, pf. **Es-m** omits ♮ at RH notes 5–6

Bars 45–46, pf. Bar 45 beat 1 ⁀ from **VE** sources. Remaining arpas as in **A**; printed sources join them across the staves, except **Rc-e** omits them at bar 45 beat 3

19. Mélisande's song

Keys: d and e

A   Autograph, in d, signed and dated "31 mai 1898": BnF mus., Ms. 17789 (ex Fauré family library). An otherwise blank title page blank shows the pencil signature "Be[atrice] Campbell" (see volume **Preface**); above the first music system is Fauré's annotation "Acte III Scène I / A terrace before one [of] the castle towers. / Mélisande singing at the window as she combs out her loose hair."

(First publication: Hamelle, Paris, 1937 (J. 7830. H.), based on **A**)

Secondary source

O   Manuscript full score orchestrated by Charles Koechlin; in d: BnF Mus., Ms. 17944 (Nadia Boulanger bequest, ex coll. Alfred Cortot); part of the complete incidental music, in Koechlin's hand. Above the first system is the blue-pencilled cue "pelleas [*sic*]: He is sleepy, he is fighting with sleep, and can hardly keep his eyes open". Bars 17–18, oddly, are deleted in blue pencil, preceding a ⊕ sign (the deletion thus perhaps flagging a reprise cue unconnected with structure); v. dynamics appear only between bars 15 and 20. Occasionally O shows a less refined version of the v. line (bars 11 or 18), occasionally a more refined one (bar 5), suggesting that Koechlin copied from a draft now untraced that Fauré may have revised.

Fauré's 1906 reworking of this song as "Crépuscule" (*La Chanson d'Ève*) maintains the present piano part with only minor differences until bar 18, under a different vocal line. Not treated as a source here, "Crépuscule" is mentioned only where it casts light on any editorial issue.

Variants

Text. Upper-case line starts of **T** restored in bars 8, 10 and 20. Bar 18: **A** omits apostrophe, **O** has *lamp*. Bar 24: **A** has a comma, **O** no punctuation; colon editorial.

Bar 5, v. Beat 3 as in **O**; **A** gives penultimate note a 3rd lower

Bar 8, v. Slur from **O**. Footnote suggestion for bar 8 partly prompted by bar 10 (where **A** shows revision from an original reading closer to bar 8)

Bar 11, v. **O**, beat 1: ♪ 𝄾

Bars 11, 13, pf. **A** single-stems RH dyads 2–3, also bar 11 LH dyad 3. Bar 11 *sempre **pp*** from **O**.

Bar 12, v. Slur from **O**; both sources hyphenate *ho-pe* across the 2 notes

Bar 12, pf. RH beat 2 𝅝 as in **O**; **A** gives it as 𝅗𝅥

Bars 15, 17, pf. Slurs across beats 2–3 from **O**, which also shows LH 𝅗𝅥 2 upper note slurred to present RH beat 2 ♩ 1 (violin 1, *a–d*')

Bars 16, 18, pf. *Ossia* **O** reading also in "Crépuscule"

Bar 17, v. Rhythm for "se-cond" as in **A** (**O** has ♩ ♪ 𝄾), pitches as in **O**: **A** gives these pitches a semitone higher (as *f*', perhaps a momentary misreading of pf. which shows the corresponding *e*'s placed slightly high on their line); while the higher reading is musically possible if doubled by pf., **O** confirms *e*' for both v. and accompaniment. Cf. also bar 15

Bar 18, v. **O**: [musical notation: "Was that the lamp flare"] [*sic*]

Bars 24–26, pf. **A** spells each RH 𝅝 as 𝅗𝅥 𝅗𝅥 (stemmed up in bar 24, down in bar 26, unstemmed in bar 25); spelling editorially rationalized

Bar 29, both. **O**: 𝄐 on last chord and v. rests

20. Dans la forêt de septembre

Keys: G♭ and A♭

A1   Autograph, in G♭, signed and dated (aptly) "29 Septembre 1902": private collection, USA (ex coll. Charles Martin Loeffler, then Louis Krasner). Fauré sent it as a gift to Loeffler in 1921, via John Singer Sargent (*Gabriel Fauré: His Life through his Letters*, pp. 312–313, letter 186). The manuscript is clean apart from some revisions, with no performer's or engraver's markings.

A2   Autograph, in G♭, signed and dated (again) "29 Septembre 1902", used for engraving **Es-m**; former coll. de Penguern, present location unknown, microfilm (dated 28 February 1975) in BnF mus.: Vm. micr. 1064. Its autograph title page includes an annotation absent from **A1**, "– op. [blank] N° 2 [*sic*]". Presentation otherwise is very similar to **A1**, their relative chronology uncertain: **A1** appears to have been started first (with revisions visible that match clean readings in **A2**, plus some clarified layout in **A2**), but then presents cleaner readings later in the song, via several intermediate revisions common to both manuscripts, some of which are shared with or even supersede **Ep**. Besides publisher and engraver annotations, **A2** shows signs of performance, with added voice articulation and dynamics in an unidentified hand (see **Appendix 3**).

Ep   Proof for **Es** corrected by Fauré, date-stamped "18 OCT 02": BnF mus., Rés. Vma 299 (1) (ex coll. Risler). A marginal annotation indicates that a further proof is to follow; the printed opus indication shows a final "2" amended by Fauré to "1". Performing annotations by Émilie Girette (as she then was) are pencilled above the vocal line (see **Appendix 3**). **Ep** is mentioned below only when it affects any editorial issue.

Es   First edition: Hamelle [1902], in G♭ (J. 4876 H.)

Rc   III/18, in G♭ and A♭

Secondary source

AS   Early sketch in one of Fauré's sketchbooks: BnF mus., Ms. 17787 (5), p. [5], musically unrelated to published version: see **Appendix 2**

Priority source: **Rc-m**

Variants

Text. Bar 35: full stop as in music sources (**T**: comma). Bars 36, 39: music sources omit comma; restored from **T** in just bar 36. Bars 45–6: commas from **Es**, **Rc**, not in **Ep** (printed or autograph), suggesting that they were added at a subsequent proof. Bar 52: *!* as in music sources (**T**: full stop)

Bar 2, v. **A**: *mezzo **p***, printed and unamended in **EP**

Bars 5, 8, 21–22, 24, pf. LH stemming editorially rationalized, also RH in bar 24 and at bars 23 and 45 ♩ 3; sources single-stem some of the chords (varying somewhat randomly across **A1** and **A2** and parallel bars)

Bar 5, pf. LH tie from **A1**

Bar 13, both. **A**, **Ep**, **Es**: *cresc.*, absent from **Rc**

Bar 14, pf. **Ep**, **Es**: 𝄽 at LH beat 2; **A** also thus originally, **A2** amended in pencil to printed reading

Bar 19, pf. **A**: additional ♩ downstem starting each beat, deleted in **Ep**

Bar 20, pf. *Dolce* from **A1**

Bar 27, pf. **A1**: RH slur initially from ♩ 1, amended to start from ♩ 2 with *dolce* added above, as in **A2** and printed in **Ep**; amended in **Ep** again to present reading, leaving *dolce* in mid-system at ♩ 2 in all printed sources

Bar 34, both. *Poco cresc.* for pf. from **A**; **Rc-e** starts it 2 notes later for v. **A** omits accidental to pf. RH beat 3; added to **Ep** in red ink, non-autograph

Bar 35, pf. < as in **A1**; other sources end it at last ♪ of beat 2

Bar 36, v. *p* from **Ep** (autograph, not repeated in the margin)

Bars 44–45, v. **A** and **Ep** all show bar 44 last note and bar 45 notes 1–2 originally a 3rd higher, amended to present reading (original reading cleanly erased in **A1**, scored through in **A2** and **Ep**)

Bar 46, v. *Ossia* as in all sources except **A1**, which shows the same original reading amended (neatly in ink) to the present main reading

Bar 46, pf. > as in **A**; printed sources end it at ♩3

Bar 47, v. Staccato dots from **A1** (editorially parenthesized)

Bar 49, both. *f* as in **Rc**: other sources have *mf*

Bars 49–50, pf. RH downstems absent in **A**, added by Fauré in **Ep**

Bars 52–54, pf. **A1**: original reading probably

(not clear exactly when dynamics were entered), then amended as in present *ossia*.

A2:

Ep printed similarly but without *pp*, amended by Fauré to present reading (still without *pp*); published sources follow this but lead LH slur to top note of final chord; **Rc** omits *dimin.*, possibly by intent (cf. v.)

21. La Fleur qui va sur l'eau

Keys: b and d

A Autograph, in b, signed and dated "13 Septembre 1902": McLennan Library, McGill University, Montreal, VZR. F27f. An autograph title page includes the opus number as published, plus a later *envoi* by Marguerite Hasselmans, "Pour ma chère Pauline Donalda / en souvenir / M. Hasselmans / 17 mai / 1927". Bar 28 is tipped into a margin, part of vocal line revision across the present bars 27–29; an added accidental at bar 10, flagged by large crosses, matches one marked on **Ep**, suggesting that Fauré kept **A** for proof checking (the musical text is relatively close to **Ep/Es**). Numbers in margins suggest a pagination cast, doubtless for an intermediate scribal engraving copy.

Ep Proof for **Es** corrected by Fauré, date-stamped "3 NOV 02": BnF mus., Rés. Vma 299 (2), ex coll. Risler. A marginal annotation indicates that a further proof is to follow; on the written opus indication the final "2" replaces an illegible erasure (1 or 3?: cf. *Dans la forêt de septembre* above). The vocal line shows Emile Girette's pencilled performing annotations (see **Appendix 3**). **Ep** is mentioned below only when it affects any editorial issue.

Es First edition: Hamelle [1902], in b (J. 4872 H.)

Rc III/19, in b and d

Secondary source

AS Near-complete autograph sketch, in one of Fauré's sketchbooks: BnF mus., Ms. 17787 (5), pp. [8–17, 20–22], pf. part often in shorthand, no performing indications; contributes no readings to the present edition

Priority source: **Rc-m**

Variants

Text. Bar 11: comma in all music sources. Bars 13, 18: Punctuation as in music sources (**T**: full stops). Bar 36: full stop as in **T**; music sources have a comma.

Tempo. Tempo and metronome indication as in **A** and **VE** sources (in **A** overwriting an erasure, probably of *Andante moderato*); **VM** sources: *Allegretto molto moderato*, same metronome indication

Bars 1, 3, both. **A**: bar 1 *pp*, bar 3 v. *pp*, pf. *sempre pp*

Bars 6–7, pf. *Cresc.* from **A**; **Rc** also omits *mf*

Bar 9, pf. **A** places > across ♩s 1–2, printed sources (including **EP**) across ♩ 3 (bar 10 *p* in all sources); musical sense suggests the present placing (editorially adjusted)

Bar 11, pf. LH ♩ beat 2 last ♪ as in **A** and **Rc-e**; **VM** sources print it a 3rd higher. **Rc** omits beat 3 >

Bar 12, pf. < from **A**

Bars 13–19, both. **A** omits dynamics from bar 13 ♩ 3 except for v. *cresc.*, *f* and *mezzo f*, all initially pencilled then the last of them amended in ink to *mezzo p*; **Ep** shows this amended by Fauré back to *mezzo f*

Bar 20, pf. *p* from **Ep** (autograph)

Bar 22, both. V. ' from **Ep** (autograph). **Rc** (and **A**) omit 1st pf bass >. **A** dynamics: *dimin.* from mid-bar

Bars 27–28, pf. **Ep** shows each LH > added by Fauré then deleted; presumably reinstated at a subsequent proof along with those in bars 25–26 (absent in **A**, **Ep**), likewise the bass lower 8ve note at bar 28 ♩ 1 (again absent in **A**, **Ep**)

Bar 32, v. **A**: *dolce* not *p*

Bars 33–38, pf. Printed sources break phrasing across each barline; **A** carries slurs over end of bars 33 and 35 (system breaks), starting slurs in bars 34 and 36 ambiguously before note 1. Continuous phrasing might also be inferred across bars 37–38, where **A** leads slurs to bar 37 barline (page break) then bar 38 slurs starting from note 1

Bars 39–42, both. **A**: bar 39 *f sempre*, then bar 40 onwards original reading

deleted and replaced as in present edition except without > *p* ; **EP** shows the present > *p* already printed and *sempre* absent after *f*. **Rc** omits bar 40 >

22. Accompagnement

Keys: G♭ and A♭

A1   Autograph, in G♭, undated, used for engraving **Es**: Irving S. Gilmore Music Library, Yale University, on deposit in the Beinecke Rare Book and Manuscript Library, Yale University, Music Deposit 19. Publisher annotations include "6671" on first page and "Voir Livre 'Dépôts'" on last page, along with a pencilled box around the first 2 systems, perhaps attesting to a now untraced facsimile or part-facsimile.

A2   Presentation autograph, in G♭: BnF mus., ms. 19203 (ex coll. Risler). See p. IV for a facsimile of its title page with Fauré's dated dedication to Mimi Girette. Relative chronology of **A1–2** is ambiguous, for each variously shows different minor omissions, emendations matching clean readings in the other, and some revisions common to both, suggesting that both manuscripts were worked on in tandem; up to bar 13 **A2** presents a generally cleaner copy with remedial or advantageous readings, after which **A1** mostly appears cleaner.

Es   First edition: Hamelle [1902], in G♭ (J. 4905 H.); included as a supplement to the *Courrier musical* of 1 April 1903 (same engraving, musical text identical)

F   Feuilleton publication, in G♭: *Le Monde musical*, 30 June 1905 (M.M. 130)

Rc   III/20, in G♭ and A♭

Secondary source

C   Hand copy by Émilie Girette, in G♭: BnF mus., Vma ms. 990. Its cover signed "Mimi Girette" and dated "Aout [*sic*] 1902", **C** follows **A2** with a few minor copying errors, omitting many pf. indications, but showing her pencilled v. performance indications (see **Appendix 3**).

Priority source: **Rc-m**, with remedial input from **A2** notably at bars 11–12

Variants

Text. Bars 9, 19, 35: punctuation as in music sources (except that printed music sources omit bar 19 ellipsis). Bar 11: *La* as in **A2** and **T**, *Ma* as in other music sources. Bar 15: comma as in **A**, **Rc-m** (**Es**, **F**, **Rc-e**: no punctuation; **T**: full stop). Bar 27: music sources omit comma, except possibly **A2** (unclear).

Bar 3, pf. **A1**: 2nd offbeat LH ♪ at same pitch as others

Bar 4, both. **A2**: > across just last 2 ♪s for v., last 3 ♪s for pf.

Bar 5, both. **A**: originally in 3/2 (effectively omitting the present ♩ beat 2), present reading indicated in **A1** by rough pencillings, in **A2** by a neatly recopied loose insert. V. *p* from **A2**. **A2** and **Rc** omit pf. *pp*

Bars 11–12, pf. Lowermost 2 voices as in **A2** (and **C**); other sources start them , possibly a slip for the present reading, or the slur intended as a tie from ♪ 2 (**F** omits the slur in bar 12). Cf. bars 14 and 19

Bar 14, pf. **A2** shows the *ossia* originally ending [music example], the penultimate note then probably amended first to d^1 (matching present main reading) then to c^1 by a ledger line through it

Bars 15–16, pf. Parenthesized accents from **A2**

Bars 17, 19, pf. Bass > in **Rc** only; **A** also omits bar 17 last RH >. **F** prints bar 17 RH ♪ 3 a 3rd lower

Bar 18, pf. **Rc** omits >. **A2** and **C** omit bass downstems; penultimate > conversely from **A2** and **C**, last > from **A2** only

Bar 19, v. **A2**, **C**: beat 2 ♩ not ♪ 𝄾

Bar 20, pf. **A2**: last 2 LH ♪s [music example], doubtless a slip (given the resulting parallel motion with v.)

Bar 21, pf. **F** gives RH ♪ 4 a minor 3rd higher

Bar 29, v. ♩ 2 as in **A2** and **C**; **A1** omits tie, printed sources omit ♪, leaving a gap before aligning 𝄾 ♪♪ (as triplets) above last 3 pf. ♪s of ♩ 2; **F** alone fills the gap with 𝄾

Bar 40, pf. Slur as in **A2**; other sources end it a note earlier

Bars 41, 43, both. Sources add *cresc.* and *dimin.* respectively at start of < and > (editorially removed)

Bar 44, pf. **Rc** and **C** omit *p*, other sources place it at last ♪ of bar 43 (insufficient space in **A** at start of bar 44)

Bar 45, pf. **A2**, **C**: last LH ♪ a minor 3rd lower

Bar 50, v. **Rc** omits *cresc.*

Bars 53–56, both. **A2**: original reading, ending penultimate verso:

deleted and rewritten on final recto first as

then LH offbeat ♪s 3–4 in bars 53–54 amended in pencil as in present edition. **A1** presents bar 53 identically (with the same visible amendment to LH offbeat ♪s 3–4), bar 54 pf. notated as ∕., bars 55–56 as present edition. **C**: as **A2** penultimate reading (shown above), suggesting that the final amendment in **A2** (to LH offbeat ♪s 3–4) was made after **C** was copied

23. Le plus doux chemin

Keys: f and g

Es First edition: Hamelle, in f, as op. 87 no. 1 (J. 5162 H.). Although Fauré submitted the song to Hamelle in 1904, publication was apparently delayed until 1907, perhaps because of fraying relations between Fauré and Hamelle.[13]

F Feuilleton publication, in f, without dedication or opus number: album of *Musica* 74 (November 1908), with a 1907 copyright acknowledgment to Hamelle

Rc III/16, in f and g (the first source to include Silvestre's generic subtitle *Madrigal*). **Rc-m** reuses the plates of **Es**, musically identical except for 4 added slurs; **Rc-e** was later issued as an offprint, music and plate number unchanged.

Secondary source

O Orchestration by Samuel-Rousseau, in g, manuscript c. 1919: BnF mus., Rés. Vm. ms. 1081 (ex Hamelle archives). This was for the ballet *Masques et bergamasques*; it is mentioned below only where it involves any editorial issue.

Priority source: **Rc**

Variants

Text. Bars 15–16: music sources omit comma; *rebelle* from **O** and **T** (*cruelle* in other sources). Bar 31: full stop as in music sources (**T**: *!*)

Bars 17–18, pf. **O**: $<$ (augmenting bar 15 *cresc.*) across bar 17 for violin, viola, cello & harp, extending to bar 18 ♪2 just for violin (none for v.)

Bars 20, 25, pf. **Es** and **F** omit slur; **O** (fl/bsn) slurs from preceding tie start to ♪2, then across ♪s 3–5

Bars 32, 34, pf. **Es** and **F** omit slur; **Rc-e** starts bar 32 slur a ♪ earlier, **Rc** ends it a ♪ earlier; **O** (cl) ends slur as present edition but starts it from preceding tie start

24. Le Ramier

Keys: e and f♯

Es First edition, in e: The Gramophone Company (Italy), Milan, 1904 (G. C. 26 I.), no opus number

Rc III/17, as op. 87 no. 2, in e and f♯ (with footnote acknowledging The Gramophone Company), the first source to include Silvestre's generic subtitle *Madrigal*

Priority source: **Rc**

Variants

Text. Bars 12–13: Music sources omit commas. Bar 14, music sources: *comme*. Bars 16, 21: punctuation as in **T** (music sources: comma, full stop)

---

[13] In a letter of late December 1904 to Édouard Risler, Fauré promises to bring him a proof of "la petite – très petite, je vous préviens ! – mélodie" in early January 1905; this can only be *Le plus doux chemin*, its dedication timed to the Risler marriage a month earlier (Nectoux, "Deux interprètes de Fauré : Émilie et Édouard Risler", p. 21). Whether the proof eventuated is unknown: none figures in the Risler collection. The proof itself was to have been a replacement for the manuscript, which Fauré's letter reports Hamelle as having lost.

Bars 6–7, pf. **Es** omits RH tie across barline

Bar 12, v. Sources start *poco cresc.* from ♪1

Bar 20, pf. Sources place *dolce* at bar 19 ♪3 (ending a page in **Es**)

Bar 22, pf. **Es** omits 1st bass note

Bar 27, v. *Cresc.* from **Es**

Bar 30, pf. **Es** double-stems LH ♪1

Bar 31, both. *A tempo* as in **Es**; **Rc** places it at beat 1

Bars 32–33, v. **Es**: ♩. | 𝄽 ‖

25. Le Don silencieux

Keys: E and F♯

A Autograph, in E, signed and dated "20 Aout [*sic*]": BnF mus., Ms. 17761 (ex Fauré family library). An autograph title page shows the provisional title "Offrande", the published title pencilled above it, and the erroneous opus number 94. At bar 1 the word *Andante* is a later interpolation, the metronome indication left blank without a number.

Es First edition: Heugel (1906), in E, as op. 92 (H. & Cie. 23, 128)

Priority source: **Es**

Variants

Text. Bars 16, 25, 28. Punctuation as in music sources.

Bar 16, v. Beat 4 main reading as in **Es**; **A** has ♪. 𝄾 ♪ [*sic*]

Bars 19–20, both. **A**: $>$ across bar 19 ♪4 not bar 20

Bars 25–26, both. **A** adds *cresc.* at start of $<$ and omits *mf*

Bar 27, pf. **A**: ♩2 RH originally [music example], the *f* lightly deleted in pencil, light pencil mark added just right and below of upper ledger line, possibly readable as a sketched c^1 (probably amended to present reading at proof)

26. Chanson

Keys: e and g

Ep Proof for **Es** corrected by Fauré, date-stamped "14 NOV 1906": BnF mus., Rés Vma 301 (ex coll. Risler). Fauré's annotations (black ink) mostly comprise dynamics; house editor's markings (red ink) involve brackets over triplet groups plus the occasional musical retouch, undoubtedly at Fauré's instigation; all are effected in **Es**. The vocal line shows Émilie Risler's pencilled performing annotations (see **Appendix 3**).

Es First edition: Heugel (1907), in e (H. & Cie. 23,173)

Priority source: **Es**

Variants

Text. Bar 6, music sources: *où* [*sic*]. Bar 11, music sources: comma after *épanche*. Bar 13: full stop as in music sources (**T**: semicolon). Bar 21: music sources omit comma.

Bar 3, pf. Last chord added on **Ep** in red ink

27. C'est la Paix

Keys: G and A

A   Autograph, in A, signed and dated "Monte Carlo / 8 X^{bre} [December] 1919", used for engraving **Es**: Harry Ransom Humanities Research Center, University of Texas at Austin, Carlton Lake Collection (ex Durand archives). The autograph cover page, like **Es**, gives the poet's real name Georgette Debladis.

Es   First edition: Durand & Cie, Paris (August 1920), in A (D. & F. 9859)

F   Feuilleton publication, in A: *Le Figaro* Sunday musical supplement, 10 October 1920, pp. 6–7, the poet identified on the score as "X..." (but cf. **Poem sources** above); musical text as **Es** except for a few trivial misprints, not mentioned separately below

Priority source: **Es**

Variants

Text. Bars 5: comma in music sources (not **T**). Bars 12, 16, 35: **Es** has *La*, *Courons*, *Germaine*; **A** shows these upper cases marked in by a Durand house editor at bars 12 and 16 and written thus by Fauré at bar 35. Bar 18: in **A** "soldats" overwrites a deletion, probably of "poilus". Bars 25, 29: full stops as in **T** (music sources: no punctuation in bar 25, comma in bar 29). Bar 30: music sources add comma after *aimés*. Bars 14, 32, 36: punctuation as in music sources (**T**: semicolons)

Bar 11, pf. RH ♩ 3 lowest note as in **A** (placed slightly low); **Es** prints it a tone lower (repeating previous chord)

Bar 27, v. **A** and **Es** start a tie from ♪ to barline (end of page), probably an unintended remnant after revisions made on **A** at bar 28

28. Noël

Keys: F and A♭

Sources

Es   First edition: Hamelle [1886], in A♭ (J. 2468 H.) and F (2468bis, without letters); includes separate harmonium part (indicated "Orgue ou Harmonium" at bar 1) with v. cue throughout. The title page specifies "pour Ténor ou Soprano / avec accompagnement de Piano / (et d'Harmonium ad libitum)", but lists the mezzo-soprano / baritone option in F. Cf. **Preface** for Fauré's declaration about the harmonium part.

Rc   I/20 (**Rc₀₈** only), in F and A♭, without mention of harmonium

Priority source: **Rc-m**, with harmonium part from **Es**. In the absence of an independent source for **T**, the present edition follows the **Es** harmonium part's vocal line, the most reliable apparent version.

Variants

Text. Bar 6: Semicolon as in **Es** harmonium part; other sources have a full stop. Bar 33, music sources: <u>baiser</u>.

Tempo. Rc-e omits metronome indication

Bar 1–3, pf. RH slurs in **VM** sources only

Bar 2, v. **Rc-e** omits *dolce*

Bars 2–6, pf. **Rc-m** omits 1st > of bar 2, then all sources omit 2nd and 4th of bars 2 and 3, 4th of bars 4–5, and 3rd and 4th of bar 6, undoubtedly by inadvertence; editorially added

Bars 8–9, v. **Rc-e** omits < ; > from **Es-e**

Bar 9, pf. **Rc-e** prints LH ♪ 6 a 3rd lower

Bars 10, 29, 37, 45–46, pf. **Rc-e** omits ✱ and bar 45 ♩ 3 ℘.

Bar 11, pf. **Rc-m** omits *pp*

Bar 13, v. **Es-e** places *cresc.* at bar 13 note 1

Bars 16–17, harm. **Es** single-stems LH except bar 17 beat 3; cf. bars 33–34

Bar 27, pf. 1st slur from **Es-e**

Bar 28, pf. *Legato* from **VE** sources

Bars 30–32, pf. **Es-e** omits LH ♩ stems

Bars 36–37, pf. Dynamics in **Rc-m** only (which adds *Cresc.* over the start of <)

Bar 41, pf. *Suivez* carried over editorially from harmonium part

Bars 42–43, harm. RH tie across barline from **Es-e**

Bar 43, v. **Rc-m** omits upper note option at final ♪

Bar 46, pf. **Es** and **Rc-m** place ✱ just after ♩ chord, **Rc-e** omits it (and preceding ℘); editorially adjusted (harmonium part suggests some latitude or a gentle release)

29. En prière

Keys: E♭ and F

Es   First publication: A. Durand & Fils, 1890, in E♭ (**Es-m**); in *Les Contes mystiques* (a collection of settings of religious poems by Stéphan Bordèse), pp. 31–34 (S. B. 2–4; viewable online via http://archive.org); also published separately with the same plate number, plus a separate edition in F (S.B. 2–4ter: **Es-e**). The plate numbers suggests these were custom editions supervised by Bordèse (a Durand employee). Both editions (E♭ and F) were reprinted by Hamelle in the early 1920s from the same plates, but with Hamelle plate numbers (J. 7193 H. and J. 7193bis H.), music unamended except that the high-voice version loses its final ✱.

Mz   Metzler [1897], in E♭ (M. 7869), as *At Prayer*, English and French text (trans. Elizabeth Bennett)

F   Feuilleton publication, in E♭: *La Musique des Annales* 37 (supplement to *Les Annales politiques et littéraires* 2163), 7 December 1924. The title is printed as "Prière de l'enfant Jésus", musical text identical with **Es-m** except that the last pf. LH note of bar 4 is misprinted a 3rd high; not mentioned separately below

Rc   II/16, in E♭ and F

Secondary sources

O   Orchestration by Fauré [1890], in E♭, surviving in a scribal copy dated 1923 formerly serving as Hamelle's hire score: BnF mus., Vmg. 28962 (ex coll. Hamelle).[14] **O** contributes no readings to the present edition.

P   Non-autograph manuscript score in E♭, for string trio accompaniment (2 vns/vla) plus a viola part, labelled only "Fauré" in blue pencil on the part's outer recto: BnF mus. Ms. 19110 (ex Fauré family library).[15] Unrelated to **O**, **P** comprises *ad libitum* backing for the existing piano part

---

[14] The orchestration appears to have been for the première; see **Chronology and Dedicatees**. All sources specify the keyboard accompaniment as for piano (not organ as listed in some biographies).

[15] Long unidentified, this source was identified in 2013 by Carlo Caballero as belonging with *En prière* (email communication from Carlo Caballero).

Af Autograph album leaf, 1896, bars 1–5, in E♭: present location unknown, facsimile in catalogue 69 (2012) of the Stuttgart music dealer Ulrich Drüner, item 59. Under the music is the autograph *envoi* "À Madame Blanche Marchesi / en souvenir de la plus touchante et poétique / interprétation / Son très reconnaissant / [signed] Gabriel Fauré / Décembre 1896". Devoid of slurs or pedalling and perhaps copied from memory, **Af** shows a variant tempo heading plus a textural variant.

Priority source: **Rc-m**

Variants

Text. Bar 34: *!* as in music sources (**T**: full stop). Bar 44, music sources: *calvaire !*

Tempo. **Af**: *Andante*; **O**: *Moderato quasi allegretto*

Bar 1, pf. **VM** sources: ℞. *sur le 1ᵉʳ et le 3ᵉʳ temps de chaque mesure* (**Mz** adds English translation), absent in **VE** sources; editorially renotated

Bar 2, v. **VE** sources: *p* after *dolce*

Bar 5, pf. The **Af** variant was perhaps aimed at softening the other sources' LH consecutive 5ᵗʰˢ across the barline

Bars 6–12, pf. **VE** sources omit *legato sempre* and continue slurs as in preceding bars until bar 11, then *sempre legato* at bar 12

Bar 14, both. **VE** sources omit *cresc.*

Bar 34, pf. Pedalling from **Mz**

Bars 36, 38, 40, pf. RH chord lowest note from **Rc-m**₍₀₂₎→

Bar 48, pf. **Es-m**, **Rc** and **Mz** place ✳ immediately after beat 3, **Es-e** omits it; editorially adjusted

30. Puisqu'ici-bas toute âme

Keys: B♭ and C

C Manuscript copy, unidentified hand with some autograph corrections, in D♭, undated, untitled: BnF mus., Ms. 20297 (ex coll. Clerc). Written over 2 oblong sheets, with an erroneous 4-flat key signature through the first page, it leaves the pf. part blank in bars 11–14 and 47–53 (repeating earlier passages), with sparse dynamics and articulation and no pedalling or v. accents. **C** may well represent a transposition rather than the original key, given how awkwardly the piano part lies in this key; a repeated pitch misspelling over bars 29–30 and 72–73 also suggests transposition error. Under the last system are pencil sketches by Fauré related to the closing part of *Tarentelle*.

Av2 Autograph v2 part, in C, undated, untitled, accompanying **C** above, same provenance and shelf mark. Written on a more habitual paper type for Fauré, it shows sparse dynamics, no accents and the occasional slip of the pen (*inter alia* it ends a bar short). V1 cues are lightly but fully written in where v2 is silent (thus providing a partial source for v1), the end durations for each voice at such transitions mostly curtailed to avoid voice overlaps at new entries (see below regarding bars 18 etc.).

Es First edition: Choudens [1879], in C (A.C. 2723: **Es1**), "Pour Deux Soprani / ou / Pour Soprano & Tenor"; reprinted by Hamelle from same plates with some amendments [c. 1887] (J. 2712 H.: **Es2**). Post-1896 Hamelle reprints add the opus number 10, a label arbitrarily applied that year to this song and *Tarentelle*.[16] Later Hamelle title pages also list an edition for "voix moyennes (duo ou chœur)", but no exemplar has been traced.

Priority source: **Es2**

Variants

Text. The present edition follow the capitalisation of music sources (1ˢᵗ and 3ʳᵈ lines of each strophe; **T** capitalizes each line). Punctuation of **T** is restored at bars 3, 10, 18, 22, 26, 29, 33, 43–44, 49 (both commas), 51, 65, 69, 72, 76, 80, 84, 88 & 90–91. Bars 26, 28: present edition as music sources which best convey v. phrasing (**T**: comma after *Puisque* not *arrive*). Bar 57: comma as in music sources (**T**: *!*). Bar 65: no punctuation in music sources; comma as in most pre-1869 editions of **T** (later editions mostly have *!* instead). Bar 78: comma as in 1837 first edition of **T** (and others including the the 1869/70 Hetzel edition; various other editions including the 1858 Hachette omit it, as do music sources.

Dynamics. V. dynamics at bars 2, 6–7, 10, 26, 31, 38–45, 51, 56–58, 69–74 and 86 in **Es** only; v2 dynamics at bars 18–24, 29, 33 and 45 and v. dynamics at 49–50, 53, 60–67 and 76 from **Es2**; pf. dynamics at bars 23–24, 41–53, 62–63 and 66–67 from **Es2** (the **Es2** additions often squashed into very restricted space: the present edition tacitly extends or completes hairpins obviously foreshortened through lack of space)

Bar 1, pf. **Av2** omits tempo heading, **C**: *Allᵗᵒ*. **Es**: *Ped.* [*sic*] *à chaque 1ᵉʳ temps* (editorially renotated)

Bar 8, v. > as in **C**: **Es** prints it across beat 2

Bars 14–15, v2. < as in **C**; **Es** starts it a ♪ later (page break)

Bar 16, pf. **C**: last LH ♪ a 3ʳᵈ lower; cf. note to bar 59

Bars 18, 22, 53, 61, 65, v1–2. The curtailed end-of-phrase durations in **Av2** (with no following rests, the bar duration completed by the new v. entry) might simply reflect the alternating voices there on a single staff (cf. source description above); on the other hand **Av2** retains the voice overlap at bar 10, with an independent variant at bar 69, and the basic fact remains that Fauré wrote **Av2** for performance

Bars 22–23, v2. **C**: [music example: *Que la nuit donne aux*]; at bars 18–19 v1 and 61–62 v2 **C** shows the equivalent rhythm and underlay amended to present reading (in what appears to be Fauré's hand in at least bars 61–62)

Bar 22, pf. RH ♪ 2 as in **C**; **Es** prints it a tone higher

Bars 29, 76, v2. **Es2** places > against pf. upper staff (no space above v2); editorially relocated

Bars 29–30, 72–73, pf. **C**: bass dyad at bars 29/72 a 5ᵗʰ lower. **C** notates bars 29/72 RH ♪ 1 and 5 a semitone lower, likewise bars 30/73 ♪ 1 and ♩ dyad upper note (♮ not ♭ before *f / f' / f''*), doubtless a repeated slip of the pen

---

[16] This retrospective opus "ordering" was motivated by Fauré's candidature in 1896 for the Institut de France; the opus numbers 1–8 were analogously pasted, arbitrarily, across the existing First Collection of 20 solo songs.

Bar 31, v1–2. **Es**: >, doubtless error for < (cf. bars 73–74); editorially amended

Bars 33, 76, v2. ♪ 3 accidental from **Av2**; **C** omits it, **Es** inflects it a semitone lower (as in bars 29 and 72)

Bars 34–35, both. Dynamics as in **Es2**; **C**, **Es1**: v. *mf* then < across bar 35 beat 1, no pf. dynamic; **Av2** omits dynamics

Bar 38, v2. **Av2** omits 1st ♪ flag (spacing through bar corroborates present rhythm)

Bars 38, 81, v2. Final cautionary accidental from **C** (the note spelt enharmonically as c'♯ against the 5-flat key signature)

Bar 63, pf. **C**: last RH ♪ a semitone lower (obvious slip of the pen)

Bars 71–72, v1. **C**: additional slurs across bar 71 notes 1–3 and bar 72 ♪s 1–2 (the latter probably confusion with parallel occurrences)

Bars 72, 73, pf. Beat 2 accidental from **C**: **Es** places it a ♪ later in bar 72, omits it at bar 73 beat 2

Bars 77–80, v2.: <> from **Av2**; cf. note to bars 34–35

Bar 80, pf. First 2 LH accidentals from **C**. **Es1**: LH ♪ 6 a tone higher

Bar 81, v2. **Av2**: ♪ not ♪ ♪

Bar 84, pf. **Es1**: LH ♪ 7 a tone lower

Bars 88–91, v1. **C** shows *reste l'amour* later pencilled melismatically (unknown hand) over these bars in place of present word repetition (*reste* to bar 89 note 3, *l'amour* from note 4)

Bar 89, pf. **C**: pf. LH ♪ 1 doubled at upper 8ve, LH ♪ 2 a 3rd higher

Bars 89–92, all. **C** marks *rall.* at bar 90 ♩ 1 for v1, a bar later for pf. with ***pp*** in the middle of bar 92. **Av2**: < across bar 89 beat 1, *poco rall.* from bar 90 (*res-te* originally split across the middle of that bar, matching v1, then amended to break a bar later), > from bar 90 ♪ 2 to just after bar 91 ♪ 1, ⌢ above bar 91 ♪ 3 (**C** shows a break line above v1 after that note). **Es** shows present *poco rall.* only for pf.; **C** and **Av2** omit *p*. **C** and **Av2** place v. *a tempo* just after bar 91 ♪ 4 (but at bar 92 for pf. in **C**); **Es** starts it at bar 92

31. Tarentelle

Key: f

Es   First edition: Choudens [1879], in f (A.C. 3874); reprinted unamended by Hamelle from the same plates [c. 1887] (J. 2713 H.). The opus number 10, retrospectively tagged to the song in 1896 (see note 17), appears never to have been added by Hamelle to the score.

Secondary source

O   Manuscript orchestration by André Messager [c. 1880], in f: BnF mus. Ms. 17783 (ex Fauré family library). This was undoubtedly made in consultation with Fauré: *inter alia* the cover page shows the string disposition pencilled in Fauré's hand.

Priority source: **Es**. Dynamics in parentheses come from **O**.

Variants

Text. Bar 5: comma as in music sources (**T**: full stop). Bars 7, 30–31, 37, 58, 60, 68, 82: ! as in music sources. Bar 50, music sources: *vous, sans*. Bars 96, 98: music sources omit commas, also bar 100 v2. Bars 100 (v1), 102, 105, 107, 119: commas as in music sources. Bars 102–: punctuation missing on repetitions of phrases is tacitly restored. Bars 70–71: **O** has *Sans y penser. !* from **Es** at bar 128, from **O** at bar 148

Bars 1–3, pf. **O** (winds): initial *f* followed immediately by > to *p* at bar 3

Bars 20–23, 104–105, pf. **Es** prints just the upper note of LH dyads with 8 beneath, except bars 22 and 105 omit 8; editorially renotated, with missing 8ves completed (as in **O**)

Bar 24, v. **Es** places *mf* at start of bar (**O** omits it)

Bar 27, v2. **Es**: ♮ before grace note d'', not in **O**; cf. pf.

Bar 28, pf. **Es**: *con Péd. à chaque mesure*; editorially reworded. RH lower slur into bar 29 from **O**

Bars 31–32, v. **O**: bar 31 beat 2 ♪ 𝄾 (v1 only), bar 32 beat 1 conversely 𝄾 ♪ (v1–2)

Bar 49, pf. ♮ at beat 2 d' from **O**

Bar 54, v2, bar 70, v1. Initial ♪ 𝄾 as in **O**; **Es**: ♩ (cf. bars 62–64, 71–72). See also above re text

Bar 71, pf. **Es**: notes 4–6 as in bar 63, doubtless by oversight (cf. surrounding bars); **O** has a slightly different clarinet figuration but keeps the corresponding tessitura consistent across bars 69–72

Bars 103–105, pf. Accidental to bar 103 beat 2 top note, to bar 104 beat 1 middle note and to bar 105 ♪ 2 upper note from **O**

Bars 104, 118, v1. **O**: beat 2 𝄾 ♪

Bars 107, 110, v1: ♮ to bar 107 ♪ 1 and to bar 110 ♪ 6 from **O**

Bar 114, pf. LH note 4 as in **O**; **Es**: a'

Bar 116, pf. LH note 1 as in **O**; **Es** prints it a 3rd lower

Bar 118, v1. **O**: beat 2 𝄾 ♪ (probably a slip; v2 as **Es** and present edition)

Bars 121–127, pf. Slurs from **O** (clarinet)

Bars 128–129, v2. **O** gives this on v1 staff from bar 128 beat 2 (doubtless a copying slip: bar 130 continues on v2 staff after a page break)

Bar 136b, v2. *Ah!* from **O**

Bars 137, 139, 143, pf. **Es** apportions ♭♭ to RH through bar 137 and in beat 1 of bars 139 and 143; editorially reapportioned for consistency (cf. bar 141)

32. Pleurs d'or

Keys: E♭ and F

A   Autograph, in E♭, signed and dated "Paris 21 avril 1896": Bibliotheca Bodmeriana, Cologny, Switzerland (acquired at auction from the Haus der Bücher, Basel, June 1955). A clean copy well marked up by Fauré, it shows no opus number, dedication, or publishing or copyist markings.

Mz   First English edition, in E♭: Metzler [November 1896] (M. 7783), as *Golden Tears*, op. 71, English and French text (trans. Paul England). **Mz** is musically closer to **A** than **Es**, suggesting it was engraved first.

Es   First French edition: Hamelle [late 1896], as op. 72; in E♭ (J. 4014 H.: **Es-m**); then in F (J. 4014 (2) H.: **Es-e**). Despite its matching plate number, **Es-e** shows different fonts and some revised marking up that suggest a later date.

Priority source: **Es-e**, with input from **Mz**

Variants

Text. Bars 7, 11, 17, 23: semicolons as in **T**, also **Mz** at bars 7 and 23 (and on each occurrence in the English text) and **A** at bar 23 (**Es** is inconsistent). Bars 10, 27: capitalisation of **T** restored. Bar 14: "Carmélite" (singular) in music sources. Bar 15: comma as in music sources (**T**: …). Bars 34, 36: *!* as in **A** and **T**, as well as **Mz** at just bar 34 (**Es**: commas)

Dedication. Present only on **Mz** and title page of **Es**, reads *Camille* for *Camilla*

Bar 1, pf. ***p*** from **Mz**. Sources indicate *Ped./pédale sur chaque temps* (editorially rephrased)

Bars 3, 5, pf. **Es-m** omits ♭ at LH ♪ 6 (beat 1 on upper staff, beat 2 on lower staff; **A**, **Mz** and **Es-e** have them on the same staff)

Bars 8–9, all. Dynamics as in **Mz**, *ossia* as in **Es** (absent in **A**)

Bars 9, 17–37, pf. Slurs as in **Mz** and **Es-e** in bars 17, 19 and 34–37, as in **Mz** at bars 32–33 (**Es-e**: single unbroken slur), otherwise as in **Es-e**; **Mz** omits remaining slurs, **A** and **Es-m** omit them all

Bars 11–12, all. **Mz** omits pf. *dolce*, ***p*** not *dolce* for v1–2

Bars 11–16, pf. 1st > of bars 11 and 12 in **Es-e** only; **A** and **Mz** omit them all. Printed sources: 3 separate 2-bar RH slurs (each across a system); **A** slurs somewhat ambiguously, from each system start (bars 11, 13, 15) over to each end-of-system barline (including after bar 16), in a way that would normally be readable as a continuous slur

Bar 14, v. *Sempre dolce* from **Es-e**

Bar 17, v2. **Es-e**: ***p*** (repeated in bar 18)

Bars 18, 20, all. Pf. ***p*** in **Es** only, which omits each pf. < and starts each v. < a ♩. later

Bars 18–20, pf. **A**, **Es-m** omit ♯ to penultimate ♪

Bar 20, v1. **Es-m**: ♮ not ♯ at beat 3 (visibly squashed in at proof)

Bars 21, 23, v. Change to 𝄵 editorially relocated; sources place it at bar 23, using tuplets in bars 21–22

Bars 21–23, all. **Es** omits bar 21 pf. >; ***mf*** and pf. ***p*** in **Es** only

Bar 24, v2, pf. Accidentals to v2 ♪s 3–4 and pf. ♪ 5 in **Es-e** only. Pf. beat 4 ♩· (downstem and dot) from **A**, **Mz**

Bars 26–37, all. Dynamics mostly follow **Mz** (sometimes **A**), any exceptions being noted below, though no single source makes full sense. After the initial *cresc.* (all sources), **Es** has ***mf*** (at bar 26 last ♪ for v., bar 27 note 1 for pf.). Bar 27 v. < as in **A** (**Es** ends it at ♩ 3, **Mz** just after); pf. < editorially extended to match (**Mz** ends it at ♩. 3, other sources omit it). Bar 28 ***f***/***mf*** and bar 29 pf. ***p*** from **Mz**; **Mz** then omits bar 29 pf. < (as does **A**) and has mid-bar pf. ***f*** (***mf*** in **A**, **Es**). Bar 30 > in all sources. Bars 31–32 dynamics as in **A** and **Mz**: **Es-m** gives pf. dynamics as for v., **Es-e** omits pf. dynamics, v2 dynamics bar 31 ***p***, bar 32 ***pp***, perhaps intended for pf. (v1 as present edition). **A** omits dynamics across bars 33–36; bar 34 ***mf*** in **Es-m** only. Bars 35–37 v. dynamics as in **Mz**; **Es** omits bar 35 ***mf***, with *dim.* instead from note 1 (*molto dim.* in **Es-e**), then bar 37 ***p*** (not ***pp***) in **A** and **Es**

Bar 27, v2. **A**: [music example]

Bars 38–39, pf. 𝄻. from **A** and **Mz**, ✻ from **Mz**. Slur editorially adjusted from **Mz**, which leads it to RH chord; **Es-e** ends it a ♪ earlier, **A** and **Es-m** omit it

33. Madrigal

Key: d

Sources

Es First edition: Hamelle [1884], in d (J.2158 H.). Cover and title page specify "pour 4 voix soli" with the added option "ou chœur ad libitum".

Secondary source

O Autograph transcription with orchestra, in d [c. 1892]: BnF mus., Ms 20805 (ex Hamelle archives, formerly their hire score). An autograph cover page includes Fauré's Boulevard Malesherbes address, where he lived from late 1886 until 1911. The score lists each voice in the singular, each string section in the plural. The opening texture is ***pp*** string pizzicato, with light woodwind doubling of voice entries from bar 11, then light staccato woodwind taking over from the pizzicato at bar 23.

Priority source: **Es**. Dynamics in parentheses come from **O**.

Variants

Text. Punctuation of **T** restored at bars 5, 7, 9, 11, 18, 29, 31, 45, 53, 79, 81, 83, 90, 98, 99, 106; capitalisation restored in bars 79, 103, 105, 107, 115. Bar 39: full stops as in **O** (**Es**: no punctuation; **T**: *!*). Bars 42–49: **O** gives tenor the same text as soprano in bars 50–57 (jumping a strophe in **T**), doubtless a copying slip. Bar 51, **Es**: *Amoureux*. Bar 57: *!* as in music sources (**T**: full stop). Bar 65: *!* in **O** and **T** (**Es**: *aime./ Aimez,*). Bar 86 (tenor): comma editorial. Bar 127: full stop as in **Es** (**O**: no punctuation; **T**: *!*).

Tempo heading. **O**: *Allegretto molto moderato*; **Es** starts *allegretto* upper case, suggesting that *Andante quasi* may have been an added afterthought

Bars 16–17, bass. Pitches as in **O**; **Es** gives last 3 notes a major 3rd lower; cf. bars 88–89

Bars 31, 32, 33, pf. **Es** double stems RH ♩ 3; editorially adjusted to match bars 80–82

Bars 37–39, sop/alto. **O**: > across bars 37–38 to ***p*** at bar 39

Bar 42, pf. ♭ to *a*¹ from **O**

Bars 43–45, pf. **Es**: *Ped. à chaque mesure* at bar 43; editorially rephrased

Bars 47, 55, pf. **Es** ends > in mid-bar (restricted space); editorially extended. **O**: > across bar 45 then again across 48 to ***pp*** at bar 49, > across bar 53, *sempre* ***p*** at bar 56 beat 3

Bars 63–64, all voices. < as in **O**, which shows a deleted version of it starting at bar 63 ♩ 3; **Es** has it just for alto, from bar 63 ♩ 3 to bar 64 beat 1

Bars 65–66, pf. **Es** continues < through bar 67; **O** has > for all instruments across bar 67

Bar 102, alto. **Es**: ***pp***, doubtless carried over by error from tenor (**O** has it just for tenor, as in **Es**, **O** at bar 98)

Bar 115, pf. ***pp*** from **O**

Bar 117, pf. **Es** places ✻ under ♪ 2; editorially relocated (cf. bar 121)

Appendix 1. *Shylock* (op. 57), Chanson

Bis version (to stanza 3 of Haraucourt's poem) from original 1889 theatre production; piano part editorially reduced from autograph orchestral score.

Source (**OA**): autograph full score, BnF mus., Ms. 17777, no. 1 *bis* (Act 1 Sc. 2), part of the collective manuscript used for the 1889 theatre production (see source description for songs 12–13). From bar 15 its texture tallies with the score of the main version of *Chanson*. The above piano reduction accordingly follows the latter's piano part from there; bars 1–14 follow the **OA** harp part except for note 2 in bars 1 and 2 which come from viola (harp plays a minor 3rd higher). Pedal indications are carried over from the main version of *Chanson*.

Appendix 2. Extended variants and fragments

I. Larmes

Original dynamics in bars 28–35 (**A**, **Es**):

Pedalling, slurs (except bar 28 RH); and accents in bars 31–33 come from **Es2**. Cf. **Critical commentary**, also footnote to musical text regarding reciprocal dynamics in **Es2** at bar 16.

II. Sérénade (*Le Bourgeois Gentilhomme*)

A1, bars 40–51 (equivalent of main version bars 14–17, equivalent barring shown above systems below):

A2 shows an original reading matching this from its bar 14 (ending a recto side), deleted and replaced on the verso by the final reading.

III. Soir

A, bars 27 onwards, original reading (previous dynamic at bar 23: *p* for v., **pp** for pf.):

Bar 34 was then amended in pencil as shown on right (**pp** doubtles intended to be advanced to beat 2). See facsimile, p. **VI**. In bar 30 beat 1 pf LH *g*♮ appears to overwrite an *e*♭ but could be read as both notes together.

A then shows, added on the following page, bar 27 onwards as published except for the variants in bars 28–30 and 33–36 visible on the present facsimile (p. **VII**), and without *poco a poco cresc.* from bar 26.

IV. Dans la forêt de septembre

Early sketch fragment [1902]: BnF mus., Ms. 17787 (5), p. [6]

V. Dans le ciel clair

Poem by Leconte de Lisle, from *Poèmes tragiques*; incomplete sketches [1902]: intended for Op. 85: BnF mus., Ms 17787 (5) pp. [18–19, 23–32]

[Intermediate line of poem unset: *Ils ne savent plus rien du vol de l'heure brève,*]

Appendix 3

Performing annotations mostly by Émilie Girette Risler, on manuscripts and proofs used in rehearsal or performance with Fauré:

Dans la forêt de septembre (**A2**, unknown hand): bars 5 and 11, tenuto dash on note 2; bar 3, > on notes 1, 3 and 5; bar 13, > on notes 1 and 3, ∧ on note 5; bars 22–23, <> (matching pf., but cf. bars 5–6 and 45–46); bar 24, additional > over end barline (page break); bar 26, < across *pleurant*; bar 29, tenuto dash on notes 2 and 4; bar 30, V after note 2; bar 37, > on note 6; bar 38, tenuto dash on note 6, < across *Ma*; bar 39, tenuto dash on note 1, < from *-ble* to *mon*, > across barline to bar 40 note 1; bars 47 and 48, > on note 1; bar 49, tenuto dash on note 3; bar 50, *sf* at note 1; bar 51, < note 5 to note 6 then > to barline, *p* at bar 52 note 1

Ibid. (**EP**, Émilie Girette Risler): bar 9, *p* at note 4; bar 11, "sombré / chaud"; bar 15 last 2 notes, "fort", bar 16, "*f* puis dim."; bar 19, each syllable underlined, also *pas-sant* in bar 20; bar 21, ∧ on note 1; bar 24, "ouvert"; bar 22 mid-bar, "dim."; bar 24, "très ouvert / expansif"; bar 31, "ouvert"; bar 39, *p* ; bars 43–45, < over note 1, > over note 2 in bars 43–44, over note 3 in bar 45; bar 46, V before last ♪; < and > pencilled respectively above notes 1 and 2 of bars 47–48 and bar 49 notes 1 and 3

La Fleur qui va sur l'eau (**EP**, Émilie Girette Risler): bar 3, "piano" (after printed *mezzo p*); bar 6, V [breath] before last ♪; bar 9, "piano" at v. entry; bar 10, "clair" before last 2 ♪s; bar 11, V before 2nd and last notes; bar 12, slur from *se-* past end-of-page barline (not continued overleaf); bar 22, > above note 1, *p* below it; bars 23 and 25, V before last note; bar 24, slur across last 3 notes (despite the printed text comma); bar 28, slur across last 2 notes, the printed comma underneath repeated in pencil; bar 32, "chant lié / prononcé" at *L'alcyon*, the printed *p* deleted; bar 35, "sombré" from note 3; bar 38, *p* at *Pour*; bar 39, "augmenter" followed by "sans ralentir"

Accompagnement (**C**, Émilie Girette Risler): bar 1, "doux, sombré"; bar 4, "augm[enter]" from note 1, > on *-feuil-* (omitting <>); bar 5, *pp* / "sombré" at beat 4; bar 10, "cresc." at beat 2 (omitting preceding *cresc.* <); bars 12, 13, 14, ∧ on note 1; tenuto dash at beat 3 of bars 13, 15, 17 and beat 1 of bars 14, 16; bar 14, "peu" added before beat 3 *dim.*; bar 27, "sombré, lié / peu prononcé"; bar 38, "chaud", ∧ on note 1; bar 41, "vibrant chaud"; bar 44, "très lié"; bar 47, "mystérieux" (omitting *dolce*).

Chanson (**EP**, Émilie Girette Risler): bar 2, V before v. entry, ∧ on note 1, then "en dehors", notes 1–2 underlined; V after note 1 of bars 5, 6 and 10 and before last note of bar 7; bar 8, "prononcé", initial "P" of *Par* and "s" of ensuing *soif* pencilled against end of preceding word; bar 13, V before last note, then "sombré amiable plus lié"; bar 16, V before note 2, then "chaud"; bar 17, V at beat 3 tie-over; bar 19, "r" pencilled left of *rire*; bar 21, V at beat 3 tie-over; bar 26, "sans voix" above *tes yeux*; bar 27, "bailler" (*sic*).